Clare and its People

A Concise History

Second Edition

Clare and its People

A Concise History

Second Edition

People – Topography – Events

covering an 11,600 year span:

9,585 BC–AD 2015

By

Brian Dinan

Clare and its People

A Concise History

Second Edition

Dedicated to
my mother, Eileen Morgan, and to my father, John Dinan,
and for Michael Morgan,
that most enduring of Irishmen.

Brian Dinan

Dinan, Brian
Clare and its People
ISBN: 978-1-9997455-0-9
Published by Brian Dinan
First printing of this Second Edition on 1 August 2019

CONTENTS

ACKNOWLEDGEMENT

The author wishes to acknowledge the courtesy and services of staff members in both the Clare County Library (Local Studies) and the Limerick County Library without whose help and guidance the compilation of this book would have been a heavy task.

The following organisations were magnanimous in the provision of important material for inclusion in the book: National Library of Ireland, Office of Public Works, Shannon Development (SFADCo), ESB, Clare County Council. Thanks also to Illustrated London News Picture Library, The Lawrence Photograph Collection and the Ulster Museum for the use of their illustrations.

A special word of thanks to Ollie Byrnes who placed his deep knowledge of Clare hurling at my disposal. As one of the county's foremost writers on hurling, Ollie's text has added greatly to the quality of information in the Gaelic games section. In addition he made valuable contributions to various music topics.

Historical descriptions and detailed editing were greatly enhanced by the contributions of Aoife, Edel, Pádraig and Carmel. They played important roles in driving the author to a higher standard.

Hopefully this acknowledgement will be taken as my personal appreciation to each and every contributor.

Brian Dinan.

Ennis.

10-06-2019.

FOREWORD

When I first set out to write a history of County Clare I laid down three main objectives for the initial publication of *Clare and its People*: (1) describe a complete history from first inhabitants right up to modern-day people; (2) produce a readable work rather than a heavy tome; (3) retain the fascinations from other reference works to make interesting reading for the modern Clare man and woman.

If I succeed even to a small degree in doing any of the above I would be fortunate indeed. However, I now dare to better my first effort with this revised and expanded Second Edition. Perhaps in being so bold I will amuse, entertain and inform to an improved degree.

To paraphrase my suggestion in the foreword of the 1987 publication – 'so, dear reader, step away from the gadgetry of the 21st century and return with me through the veil of time. Let's go back to those first tentative steps of ancient people in Clare – back to our beginning in this part of the world. Let us battle through forest, hunger and enemies alike, shoulder to shoulder with our proud forebears. I invite you to live through our historic past – and see then do we return to the present time with the same outlook we held before delving into Clare's history.'

I hope the additional material with the extra illustrations enhances the work and gives more enjoyment to you my much-appreciated reader.

Brian Dinan

Ennis.
1-06-2019.

Text Style

Punctuation: abbreviations, contractions, names, titles, spellings etc are all written in accordance with the University of Oxford Style Guide.

Additionally, where similar-sounding personal and place names are cited, their spellings will be seen to vary throughout the text depending on the spelling in vogue during the period under discussion. It should be appreciated that the spellings of Gaelic words used here are in accordance with the source from which they were drawn.

No attempt was made to set a precedent in the use of Gaelic Surnames vis-à-vis their common and accepted English translations, except to say that whatever style(s) an individual was seen to use then that preference is also followed here.

The apostrophe is not applied to Gaelic surnames. Whether or not it appears in English translations of the same surnames depends on the practice followed by the individual name-bearer.

List of illustrations

Front cover photo: Dromoland Castle taken in 1960 (courtesy of SFADCo)
Back cover illustration: Famine scene from the London Illustrated News of 1848

Chapter 1

Formation and first settlers
(9,585–400 BC)

Having endured a 15,000 year glacial winter the land of Clare emerged from under the polar ice cap as a new landscape, bare, barren and without running water or soil. This event occurred a mere 11,600 years ago when the climate 'suddenly' warmed.

The county is sprinkled with hidden Ice Age erratics scattered from the River Shannon to the Burren limestone plateau. That exposed northern cap of Clare (formed in the seabed some 330 million years ago) was raised above sea level to present 36,00 hectares of stony landscape. Later the melting ice scraped over it during its relentless journey northwards. Some archæologists believe that humans did not live on this newly-formed island of Ireland until after the polar ice cap had receded to present latitudes.

As the 300m thick polar icecap melted it exposed the northern regions of Britain and Ireland. Breakaway ice masses scraped the land as they inched towards the seas, gouging out valleys and fjords and depositing boulders of granite and limestone. Occasionally the loose gravel formed eskers along the melting edges.

Prior to the ice retreating sea levels were much lower than they are today. During that Ice Age of more than 40,000 years ago, 'land bridges' connected Ireland to Scotland and Britain to continental Europe, possibly allowing the migration of animals into sub-Arctic Ireland and Britain.

The great Irish deer (*cervus gigantus*), the woolly mammoth, the brown bear, lemming, Arctic fox and Irish hare all spread onto the tundra-like landscape of the emerging land.

When the ice advanced again some 30,000 years ago the animals were trapped and consequently died off. Ocean levels rose during the ice melting which submerged the land links thereby forming the island of Ireland. In Edenvale (Ennis) and in Aillwee Cave in the Burren some Ice Age bear bones have been found (which supports this theory).

Soon afterwards the land was exposed and soil formed on the barren surface. First vegetation to appear was low-lying juniper scrub; then came birch and patches of grassland. Approximately a thousand years after the ice had fully retreated from the landmass, the island of Ireland grew thick with vegetation to include oak, birch, hazel and ash.

1. The map shows 'land bridges' or possibly coastal mud flats connecting Ireland to Britain, and Britain to France. Ice Age humans and animals may (40,000 years ago) have used these routes to gain access to the Arctic-like lands of Britain and Ireland. When the land bridges became submerged approximately 16,000 years ago Britain was certainly disconnected from the island of Ireland. Land bridges (it seems) played no part in allowing ancestors of the current population onto the land that is now Ireland.

(Brian Dinan)

For 4,000 years (9,600 BC–5,600 BC) after the melting of the ice mass dramatic climatic changes took place. There was an 8° Centigrade rise in temperature, and a rainfall increase of 300 mm over the period. Presently, along the Shannon estuary at low tide, clumps of wood jut out from the mudflats; they are the remains of tree bases once rooted in the dark soil. These have been dated to 6,000 years ago (4,000 BC) giving evidence that sea levels were much lower then than now.

There are Stone Age finds to indicate the presence of hunter-fishers on the shores of Lough Neagh (N Ireland) soon after 8,000 BC. We do not know where those Mesolithic Stone Age (8,000 BC–4,000 BC) inhabitants came from, but we do know that they relied on small tools for everyday work. The tools they used were made from bone, wood, antler and flint.

One of the most sought-after pieces of stone by the Mesolithic Stone Age people was flint. This hard substance was found in large quantities off the north-eastern coast of County Antrim. Flint was such an attraction for Stone Age people that it enticed them into making the perilous sea crossing from Scotland to acquire it. Boats would have been of the most primitive kind with skin and wooden frame constructions offering only minimal opportunities for open sea sailing. Rafts or rough dugouts might also have been used.

The Mesolithic people were nomadic in nature and naturally explored the entire island. They probably sailed in short hops along the coastline to flush out new habitation sites. River inlets such as the Shannon and the Fergus offered easy access to the interior without the need to cut through dense woodland or face the unknown dangers in the depths of mysterious forests.

It is tempting then to envisage small groups of skin-clad crafts making their way up the Shannon and Fergus estuaries. The occupants of those primitive sailing boats could have included men, women and children. Such early nomadic people would have been small in stature and probably of aboriginal European stock.

In time some of the hunter-gatherers abandoned their old way of life and began to rely more on fish traps while they lived at river fords, estuaries, beaches and inlets. As proof of their tenure they left evidence behind on the shores of Fanore. Discarded midden heaps of oysters, mussels, cockles and periwinkles have been unearthed along that coastline – an indication of what those people ate and how they lived. A Riverford Culture has been assigned to one particular Stone Age grouping; perhaps these could have been just such a people.

A second wave of Stone Age people either developed from the indigenous people, or alternatively they migrated onto the island. We refer to them as Neolithic, or New Stone Age people. Archaeologists tell us that they became the first long-term inhabitants of the country as Neolithic farmers. An estimated date for the first permanent settlement of the Neolithic ranges from 4,350–3,200 BC. It was they who selectively cleared elm from the forests, but leaving oak and alder untouched. They introduced crop plants and grazing animals such as cattle, sheep, and red deer; it was the beginning of animal husbandry in Ireland.

The Neolithic Stone Age farmers lived in wooden huts approximately 6 metres x 6 metres in outline. The Roughan Hill settlement in the southeast corner of the Burren was a typical habitation site for the early and late Neolithic. In a 1995 excavation beaker pottery fragments and scrapers were found there. Early Neolithic farmers used plain pottery, polished stone axe heads and leaf arrowheads (from 4,000 BC onwards).

It is likely that the Neolithic people came to where Clarecastle and Ennis now stand. Over the centuries, they and others like them who migrated to this island gradually populated much of the country. They put down permanent roots in the form of land clearance and were also responsible for the construction of megalithic tombs and monuments. All such activities suggests that they had begun to develop a stable and a settled lifestyle.

2. Burren limestone formed beneath the seas some 330 million years ago. In modern times a Karst topography of crevices, underground drainage, sinkholes and caves were eroded through dissolution with rainwater.

(SFADCo)

Ancient chroniclers tell of two groups of people who came to Ireland about this time, namely the Firbolg and the Fomorians.

The Firbolg are one of the oldest group of the legendary people to have inhabited Ireland in early times.

One source claims that their very name describes them as Firbolg in the Gaelic tongue (it could be translated to 'bagmen' in the English language). The story goes that they laboured for a long number of years in Greece, carrying bags of earth to be used during the construction of earthen agricultural works; this theory does seems a bit far-fetched. Also, their name may simply have been descriptive of just their physical appearances alone.

Reputedly, the Fomorians were sea rovers who came from north Africa to settle in the northern and western parts of Ireland. Recent investigations into Irish links with north Africa suggest that a people such as the Fomorians could be ancestors (in part only) to the Irish population. Irish music (present-day traditional) and sean-nós singing bear a remarkable similarity to that of certain tribal music and vocalizations in north Africa. Traditional music is strong in Clare, so it is possible that a small portion of Clare's heritage came from the Fomorian influence. There is no direct evidence for the existence of 'Firbolg' or 'Formorians'; they seem to be more a whimsical notional concept as far as the revisionists are concerned.

3. The striking profile of Poulnabrone portal dolmen is Clare's most iconic megalith. It is located in the Burren standing majestically in public view from the winding R 480 public road which winds its way nearby.

(SFADCo)

Yet one feels there may be more than a grain of truth in the legends.

The Stone Age people of the Neolithic Period are credited with the construction of large stone monuments called megalithic tombs. Based on their type they have been allocated names such as Wedge Tombs, Court Cairns, Portal Tombs, and Wedge-shaped Gallery Graves. Dolmens (megaliths) were found at Ballyhickey, Quin, Caheraphuca, Crusheen, Poulnabrone, Burren, Cappakennedy and Slieve-na-glasha. More than 100

Wedge Tombs have been identified in Clare alone and seem peculiar to this county considering their dense grouping.

There are three megaliths/dolmen (previously called 'cromlechs') in the parish of Noughaval, one in Deerpark and two in Ballyganner. The Ballyganner South example consists of four trilithons capped by a horizontal flagstone measuring 13 feet 4 inches from north to south.

A box-like megalithic tomb with six upright stones supporting two small capstones can be seen at Ballyhickey. This type of construction is common to many other megaliths found in the county, except for one unusual feature – it is almost perfectly square in shape. It is thought that such a feature is simply a quirk of construction at this site.

Easy access can be gained from the main road (R 480) to the wedge-shaped chamber of five standing stones supporting two capstones – the gallery grave at Cahernaphuca. The capstones are more elevated at one end than at the other, probably because the method of construction lent itself to ending with such a feature and for no other reason.

Dolmen usually consisted of two or more upright stones (trilithons) which supported an almost horizontal roof slab. In some cases the trilithons formed part of a larger ensemble of dolmens. Supporting this theory is the fact that there are only three trilithons standing in isolation in the whole of the country and one of these is at Mount Callan in County Clare.

The two remaining types of megaliths left by Stone Age builders are cists and standing stones. Cists are small box-like chambers constructed of stone slabs, normally six in number. In addition there would have been a slab floor and a slab roof. Their purpose was to store the cremated body of a single important person. Many cists contained the precious worldly goods of the dead, including cups, urns and sometimes weapons.

Standing stones are probably the most common artefacts from antiquity to be seen in Clare. They are tall and relatively slender, their average heights ranging from eight to 12 feet, but some do extend to 24 feet above ground level. They have been variously described as grave markers, territory markers or even as ceremonial symbols. They date from the first millennium BC which places them close to the Celtic era.

However, they may also have been contiguous with the previous Bronze and Stone Age periods. Shards of pottery have been excavated from some of them. It is most likely that a standing stone would bear testimony to the burial place of a special person and are perhaps indicative of a sub-culture in their own right. There is a ceremonial standing stone at Magh Adhair, the historic Dalcassian inauguration site.

In the Bronze Age (2,500 BC–500 BC) we are confronted with a more artistic people, namely the mythical race of magic and wizardry – the Tuatha Dé Dannan (people of the goddess Danu). It is thought that the

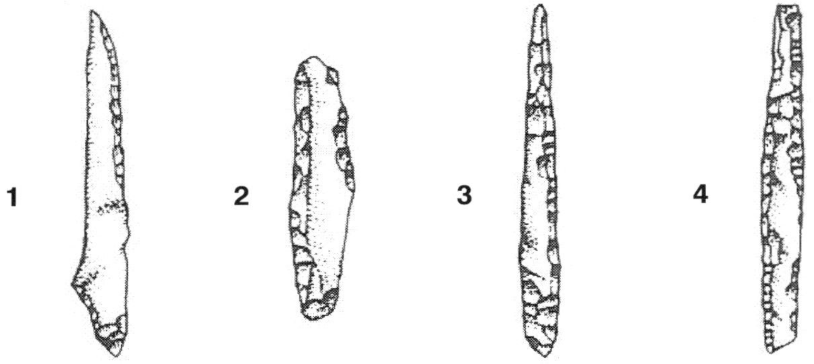

4. Flint microliths from the Mesolithic Stone Age.
1. *Knife or projectile.* **2**. *Scraper.* **3**. *Projectile or spear tip.* **4**. *Projectile or spear tip.*
(Ulster Museum)

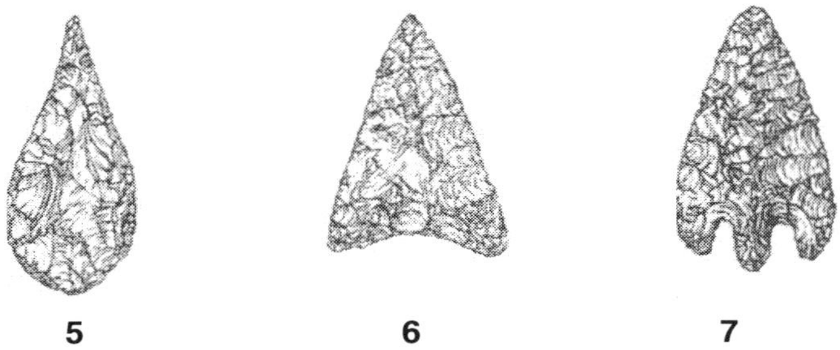

5. Flint arrowheads from the Neolithic Stone Age.
5. Lozenge arrowhead . 6. Leaf arrowhead. 7. Barbed-and-tanged arrowhead.
(Ulster Museum)

6. Gold model of a Celtic boat from the Iron Age in the 1st century B.C.
Part of the Broighter Hoard found by Tom Nicholl and James Morrow near Limavady in Northern Ireland. The model boat measures 7 inches by 3 inches and contains benches, rowlocks, and two rows of nine oars along with a paddle for steering.

(Ulster Museum)

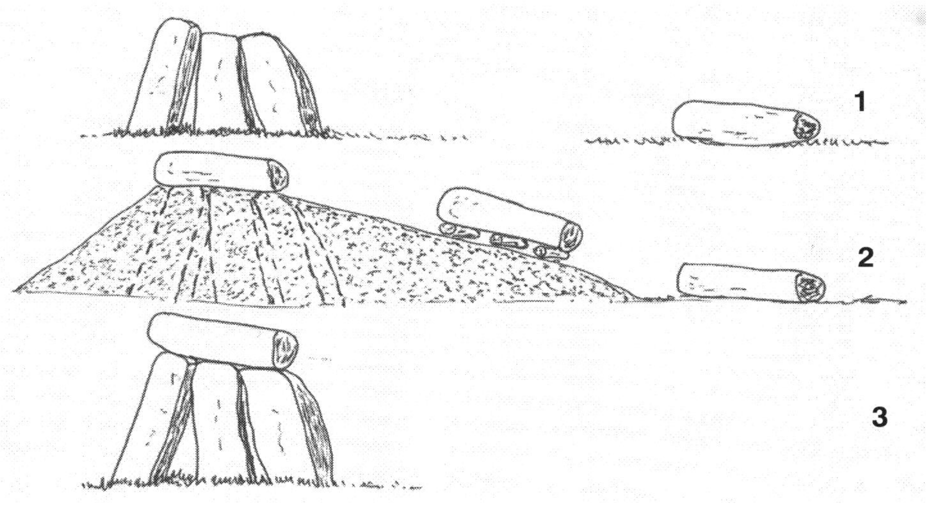

7. The above three sketches show a method for megalith construction:
1. *The trilithons are firmly embedded in the ground.* ***2.*** *They are covered with rubble and earth to form a mound. Then, a large flat capstone is moved up the ramp with the aid of log rollers.* ***3.*** *Finally the rubble is removed.*

(Brian Dinan)

Tuatha Dé Dannan were also referred to as the sword people. With their bronze weaponry they either wrested control from the original Stone Age people or perhaps it was simply a case of the new technology overtaking the previous technology.

Whether they were Tuatha Dé Dannan in myth and legend or Bronze Age people of archæological evidence, they were a unique culture uncommonly skilled in the arts of those times. Even the Celts who later supplanted them regarded Dé Dannan as magicians and sorcerers. At any rate the Bronze Age culture was the dominant culture in the land from 2,500 BC until 500 BC. It was a significant period during which they imprinted their legendary lifestyle in the minds of the people who were to dislodge them.

The Ennis area was at that time surrounded by rich woodlands of hazel, birch, ash and oak – the old primeval forests. The remnants of such forestry can be seen north of Ennis in places like Drumcliff and Dromore. In geometrical terms if a 30 mile radius was described around the Ennis/Clarecastle area it would take in most of the present county of Clare in the circle so described. Twenty miles to the east of the meandering River Fergus at Ennis stand the Ogonnoloe and Broadford Hills. Their rugged summits stand as sentinels over Lough Derg and the majestic River Shannon which forms the eastern and southern boundaries of the county until it reaches the Atlantic Ocean between Loop Head and Kerry Head.

Barren peaty ranges of open land (often lashed by raging storms from the Atlantic) cover the county's western extremity. To the north-west a unique 160 square miles of limestone territory – the Burren – was always a standout landscape as it is in the present day.

With the River Shannon to the east and south, the wild Atlantic Ocean to the west, and the hills of Feakle, Glendree and O'Dea Hills bearing down along the border with the county of Galway the whole landmass forms a unique peninsular tract of territory with ideal natural boundaries. Stone Age, Bronze Age and Iron Age people found it to be a suitable homeland for their smaller and medium size tribal groupings. It was the fate of each in succession to inhabit it as a secure kingdom territory.

The Neolithic people were dominant in Ireland for a period of 1,500 years (4,000 –2,500 BC). Their culture in turn was diminished by the Bronze Age people (2,500–500 BC). At about 500 BC Clare in common with the rest of Ireland was populated by a people relying on stone and bronze tools. They were without the latest development which was then empowering mainland Europe – iron tools and weapons. They were ill-prepared to meet the challenge of a bustling group of people on the move in central Europe – a people who had set their sights on the island of Ireland. The Romans called them Gauls; we call them Celts.

8. *Majestic Cliffs of Moher on the west coast of Clare battling with the Atlantic's furious rage. Land slides are an occasional occurrence from the cliff face.*

(Wikipedia)

Chapter 2

The Celts arrive
(400 BC–AD 400)

From 1000 BC onwards (about the time King Solomon reigned in Israel) a Celtic tribe of people were being jostled about by the Roman, Greek and German races on the mainland of Europe. At 400 BC the Celts found difficulty in settling into a suitable homeland. They had heard that there was gold and great fertility in a newly-discovered land called Hibernia. Believing this to be their true destiny they set forth en masse to the green island that offered such great promise.

Traversing the continent of Europe posed no immediate obstacle for the Celts. Neither it seems did the prospect of sea crossings. In Europe, from Gaul (France) to the Alps and beyond, the Celts were a sophisticated but a widely-feared society. As well as being adept at fashioning iron tools and weapons they were also recognized as miners and agriculturalists. So as a group of people they seemed well poised to make the big move to their promised land of Hibernia.

It is thought that the main expedition (it appears a number of migrations took place over time) was led by Eber and Eremon who were the sons of Mil. Legend tells us that this migration set out from north-west Spain. Although seeming improbable we know today that the people of Galicia have an affiliation with the Gaels of Ireland. Modern-day DNA samplings have shown that the bloods of both the Irish and the Galicians is of similar stock so there is a tenuous connection at least.

These newcomers to Ireland differed physically from the stocky swarthy natives of the island of Hibernia at that time. The Celts who were taller with blue eyes and light-coloured hair were clearly a separate race of people. One description given of the Celts by a Roman historian of the time, Diodorus Siculus, went as follows:

The Gauls (meaning Celtic people who lived in France) are tall in stature and their flesh is very moist and white, while their hair is not only naturally blond, but they do also use artificial means to increase this natural quality of colour. For they continually wash their hair with lime – wash and draw it back from their foreheads to the crown and nape of the neck, with the result that their appearances resembles that of Satyrs or Pans, for the hair is so thickened by this treatment that it differs in no way from a horse's mane. Some shave off the beard; the nobles shave the cheeks but let the moustache grow freely so that it covers their mouth. And so when they are eating, the moustache becomes entangled in the food, and when they are drinking, the drink passes as it were, through a sort of strainer...

The Celts were great talkers and storytellers and somewhat boastful as well. To the Roman observer their appearances were terrifying and their manner gruff with deep and harsh voices. They would use few words in conversation and it seemed to the Romans that they spoke in riddles. Understanding between themselves was so intuitive that they merely hinted at things and seemed to speak in a code which left a great deal to be interpreted or understood. They were prone to frequent exaggerations with the aim of extolling themselves and diminishing the status of others. 'They are boasters and threateners,' said Diodorus Siculus, 'and they are given to bombastic self-dramatisations – and yet they are quick of mind with a good natural ability for learning.'

And so it would appear that those Celtic Milesians who came to Ireland were powerful and warlike in the Celtic tradition. They came to impose their will on the inhabitants of the island they felt destined to possess.

There is some question as to what shape this 'invasion' took – if indeed it was an invasion at all. We must rely on folklore to supply the narrative. It is said that Eremon (one of Mil's sons) and his followers landed at Inver Culpa at the mouth of the river Boyne on the eastern seaboard. Another son, Eber, made landfall at Inver Sceine near Bantry in County Cork. Such stories may have been tales that fitted the legend of their nation. A trickle migration could have followed the main contingent for years until all their tribal groupings were repatriated.

Another variation on how the Celtic people came to Ireland is contained in the following account. After the Celtic tribes were driven from central Europe by Greek, Roman and German tribes, a breakaway group settled in Asia Minor. This territory was at that time called Galatia. [To confuse matters further, a Celtic people were and still are associated with Galicia in northern Spain]. Persevering, we are told that the country of Galatia was named after the Gauls; it is further told in folklore that the Celts came to Ireland originally from Egypt, through Crete and Spain. It would appear that the Galatian contingent were abandoned in that country which is inside modern day Turkey. Ancient folklore also tells of them being named Gaedhal (Gael) because their remote ancestor was called Gaedhal Glas. The story goes that Moses cured the young Gaedhal Glas of a serpent bite. He promised that no serpent would inhabit the happy western isle that destiny would allow his descendants to inhabit (likely to be another empowering legend). Anyway the story links in with the fact that they found no snakes on the island of their destiny.

Niul, Gaedhal Glas's grandson, married a Pharaoh's daughter called Scotia – Ireland in later years would be called Scotia. After some time, Niul and his tribe were driven from Egypt and eventually sojourned in Spain after long wanderings. They heard of a mysterious western isle which was then known as Hibernia. It offered great promise so they took it to be their isle of destiny as foretold by Moses long before. From Spain they sallied forth on a momentous quest to claim their final homeland.

Legend further informs us that their initial attempt to land on Hibernia was thwarted by the wizardry of Dé Dannan who raised up a sea storm against them. Great numbers of the Celts were reputedly lost in the sea. The detail of this episode seems unlikely and may be due to embellishments by their historians. It is of course possible that they encountered some Atlantic storms while attempting to make landfall.

When the Celts eventually came ashore the story goes that they won their first victory over Dé Dannan who were being led by their queen Eire. Their own queen Scotia was lost in the initial foray. The Celts would have encountered resistance throughout the island of Hibernia from Bronze Age people whom some would call Dé Dannan, as well as from the original Stone Age people (Fir Bolg?) who may have been subservient to Dé Dannan. Stone and bronze weapons were no match for the iron weapons of the Celts. So it was that the more sophisticated race came to dominate the less developed tribes on the island. No doubt there would have been some intermingling of cultures but from then on the Celts were to be the predominant people on the island of Ireland.

With their tempered iron implements they cleared land for agricultural use and kept domesticated cattle as their mainstay. This way of life suited them. Slavery was common at the time so it is possible that the previous inhabitants (being a less sophisticated society) were pressed into various roles as servants, builders and for military duty in time of warfare.

The Celts wore simple but colourful clothing made from linen and woollen materials. Tunics and long cloaks were popular and these they fastened at the neck with elaborate pins or brooches. Jewellery was prized amongst the nobles; ornamentation made from gold such as bracelets, torcs, brooches, pins and the gold-braiding of garments would have been widely worn by the nobility.

The various classes of people were identified by the particular colours of their clothing. Kings and queens were honoured with the privilege of having seven colours in their dress. Poets and ollamhs could use six colours; chieftains had five colours; army commanders displayed four colours; agricultural leaders were authorised three colours, while rent payers wore two colours and the lowly serf was allocated a single colour. That might seem somewhat regimented to us in modern times but it was a way of easily distinguishing classes of people at first glance. It is not known how widespread or established the practice was.

The construction of ring forts and stone forts was continued by the Celts; indeed variations were expanded and improved upon right into the Christian era. In the Burren the remnants of stone forts can be seen even today. There is a particularly interesting one at Cahercommaun which is situated at the edge of a steep valley. Its layout resembles the cliff fort of Dun Aengus on Inis More. During the Harvard archæological expedition to Ireland in 1934 it was discovered that the enclosure contained a dozen stone buildings dating from various periods in history. A silver brooch was found in one of the souterrains there; a detailed history could not be linked

9. The stone fort of Cahermacneachtan located in the Burren. A small section of the perimeter wall is shown; the complete enclosure encompasses an area of 100 feet in diameter. Some interesting prehistoric finds have been unearthed there.

(SFADCo)

to the structure because of its deterioration over time.

Not far from Cahercommaun is a fort called Cashlaun Glas. It is difficult to find, being much overgrown and partially concealed on a flat hilltop with a sheer drop on all sides. Inside this fort lie the bare foundations of three or four beehive huts with their outlines now barely discernable.

One of the better known stone forts is Cahermacneachtan which in translation means the stone fort of the son of Neachtan. This is a circular fort of some 100 feet in diameter. Foundations of rectangular buildings can be found within the walls as well as a late medieval two-storied gateway.

This fort was in later times the home of Clare's most respected medieval law school which was run by the O Davorens. Duald Mac Firbis (the famous 17th century genealogist) studied there under the tutelage of Donald O Davoren. Such was the extent of this complex in later centuries that it was described as 'O Davoren's town' in 1657. Obviously it was a development that suited the extended community lifestyle which was in vogue during the Middle Ages.

In contrast to the stone forts of the Burren is the massive late Bronze Age hill fort at Mooghaun near Newmarket-on-Fergus. It is a construction of three concentric stone ramparts ranging from the lower slopes to the hilltop at an elevation of 92 metres (3,090 feet) above the surrounding plain.

In addition to ring forts the development of a different type of defensive settlements took place in both the Bronze Age and in the Iron Age (Celtic

10. This picture shows a modern day construction of a Crannóg (which may not be typical for the period under discussion). It can be viewed at Craggaunowen in south Clare.
(SFADCo)

era). Wooden fortifications in wet areas are called crannóg. Usually they were constructed at lake edges or in areas likely to flood frequently. The construction of a crannóg in water meant that it had to be erected on stilts with perhaps a stone causeway or wooden access way, both of which were made difficult to find and use. If a natural island within a lake was not available the people would construct an artificial one and link it to the land via a causeway (usually cleverly constructed from submerged stones).

Crannógs were typically 100 feet in diameter and surrounded by high stake walls to deter entry. Many of the crannóg contained three large round huts made of wood, straw roofs and wattle walls. An entire community settlement housed at least one extended family unit of approximately 30 people. Parents, children, uncles and aunts lived within the one settlement.

The huts were badly ventilated; they relied on small doorways and permeable thatch roofs (which only sometimes) had an opening to allow the rising smoke from fires to reach the open air. The fires inside the huts were used not only for cooking but allowed burn for long periods to dry animal skins which hung on frames. As can be imagined such cramped structures did not make for healthy living conditions and probably contributed to the relatively short life span of the populous.

As well as having crannógs for family dwellings the people of that time also built forts of stone on firm ground. The ring forts varied in diameter and featured outer perimeter walls of stone. Some earthen ring forts had ditches with a second earthen mound topped by palisades of wooden stakes, all implying the need for strong defences.

Traces of hundreds of such ring forts may be identified throughout the county to this day. The enclosures usually contained three large huts with conical thatched roofs which were supported by wooden beams. Often, a communal fire burned continuously in the centre of the enclosure; it would would have been used for general cooking and to ward off wild animals. The settlement had one entrance gate which would always be closed at night. Domestic animals from outlying fields were brought in before dusk to avoid marauding wolves and others. Some forts contained souterrains – underground passages – often used as hiding places or to store food and precious objects.

The Celts were attracted to Ireland by the lure of gold. Try as they undoubtedly did they found very little. It had been traded by the Bronze Age people for Cornwall tin after it was accidentally discovered that tin alloyed with copper in the smelting process imparted a degree of hardness to the resulting alloy. We refer to that particular alloy as bronze.

However, bronze proved inferior to the Celt's iron tools and weapons; no doubt this helped them in overcoming the indigenous people. Long before 200 BC the Celts had secured and populated the entire country.

Although the Celts were then ruling the land poverty was at its worst since the Campignian colonization (early Neolithic) at the beginning of the Stone Age. The climate improved around 200 BC and thereafter conditions became tolerable enough to allow improvements in social conditions.

Perhaps there was a mingling of cultures but we do not know – whatever happened a new order pertained in the land. The men spent much of their time hunting while women and children would cook food and spin yarn, along with doing other tasks. Women organized the domestic part of life, including control of the family possessions, consequently making them wise in bartering and in the appreciation of goods and family possessions.

In this structured society the women occupied a place of considerable importance within family groupings. The system is called matriarchal where the woman dominated the family lines when males were not available to do so. It was through the women that titles etc were transferred. The son of a king's daughter was quite entitled to assume power when the male line did not produce a qualified heir.

Writing materials (except for stone) and the art of writing was not in use in Ireland at that time. Druids had symbols which they communicated to each other by using hand signals. The Ogham writings or characters which we hear of today are those signals committed to stone. Their origin appears to be in Etruria where they are similar to the early Greek alphabet of that period (c 500 BC).

The Ogham writing probably came into use in Ireland around AD 300. The name is derived from Ogmios who was the Celtic god of writing. Its alphabet is made up of sets of five strokes on either side of a central line; the central line in some cases could be the edge of a stone. Inscriptions began at the bottom, climbed to the top and continued down the other side.

All knowledge deemed important to the tribes was passed on in the vernacular. This practice pertained right into the Christian era and maybe even beyond. Consequently some errors crept in over time, dates varied, and sometimes prominent individuals were transformed into super heroes. No doubt exaggeration and embellishments played their parts in the heat of tribal storytelling.

The druids of the time were priests and soothsayers. They would have enjoyed the respect of ruler and ruled alike. They knew 'science' and poetry, and were obliged to commit to memory long tracts of verse and folklore to be passed on to their successors for posterity. Their religion demanded that a human sacrifice was required in time of war. In the first century AD, Strabo the historian wrote of them: 'They used to stab a human being to death (one to whom they were devoted) in the back with a dagger and foretold the future from his convulsions'.

The Celts were what we now call pagan people, which is to say they worshipped a supreme being who was represented to them in the sun, in fire, and in sacrifice. As far as is known their important religious days were Samhain which was celebrated on 1 November; Imbolg was celebrated on 1 February; Bealtaine was celebrated on 1 May; Lughnasa was celebrated on 1 August. Notably those same days are traditional feast days of religious celebrations right down to modern times.

Ardsolus or Ath Solus, a Place of Light (near Newmarket-on-Fergus) as a place name shows the esteem the early Celts had for sun. Another district to derive its name from a place of sun worship was Tuamgraney, or Tuaim Greine, which means 'Altar of the Sun'. Names with 'greine' in their composition could mean that the place in question was an important venue for worship – place names had become common by then.

Savagery was not unusual; men were slain in petty squabbles. Battles were fought for reasons that would seen avoidable in present society under similar circumstances. Cattle, land and slaves were the main reasons behind all their conflicts. Women took their place in battle alongside the men.

A common intoxicating drink of the time was mead which was a strong rich wine made from honey. Drunkenness was common and it was not regarded as being shameful. It was believed that the person in such a state was in communication with and under the influence of the gods!

Stemming from the Celtic (sometimes called Goidelic) settlement of the country was the dividing of the island into five kingdoms: Ulster, Munster, Connaught, Leinster, Midland (part of present-day Leinster). At the time Connaught was the most powerful kingdom. This national division into five fifths would have been implemented c 50 BC.

The leaders of the Goidelic or Celtic settlement of Ireland had been the brothers Eber and Eremon. Many of the most important people of Ireland and Clare are said to be their descendents. The tribes of Eremon were most prominent in the northern half of the island, while those of Eber populated the southern half, principally present-day Munster. If indeed this Goidelic invader did exist, as legend tells us that he did, then it would be from him that the prominent families of Clare can claim descent.

In the second century AD, Conn of the Hundred Battles was generally regarded as the most powerful ruler in the country. He was a descendent of Eremon whose desire it was to rule much more than the northern half of Ireland. Conn had great difficulty in containing Mogha of the Silver Hand who was the Munster king and a descendent of Eber. Mogha was very warlike and is credited with defeating Conn in ten battles before he was slain in Moylea in the midlands by Conn's warriors.

The kingship of Munster needed to be settled. Conn was most anxious that an amicable solution should be reached. He therefore gave his daughter, Sabia (Sadhbh), to the only son and heir of Mogha, Oilioll Oluim. He further installed him as ruler of all Munster – which made him the first king of the whole province as a complete entity.

Conn's arrangements soon paid off for we note that eight sons were born of the union. Oilioll Oluim willed that the descendents of his two sons, Eoghan Mór and Cormac Cas, should alternate the crown of Munster between them. It is from Cormac Cas that the famous O'Briens (Uí Briain) of Clare and Thomond are descended. This Cormac Cas married a daughter of Oisin (one of the most famous men of the Fianna). Oisin was a son of the legendary and most noble of all ancient Irish warriors, Fionn Mac Cumhaill himself. Also a son-in-law of Conn, Conaire II, is the famed father of the three Carbris one of whose descendants, Carbri Baiscin, populated Corcobaiscinn in west Clare.

Fourth in descent from the marriage of Cormac Cas and the daughter of Oisin was Luighaidh Meann. This man came to Clare to claim it for his own. Until then, the Clare area was one of the few places largely inhabited by the older settlers (Firbolg?). In many skirmishes he drove those original occupants out of An Clár (Clare or later called County Clare). It is said they went to Galway where they were overthrown in a last great battle at Moytura. From Galway they fled the country and set sail in crude boats to the Hebrides where they were attacked by the Picts.

The Firbolg returned to Meath during the reign of Cairbre Nia-Fear shortly before the Christian era took hold. Even though they made some pacts with the local chieftains they failed to form a lasting relationship. In a clandestine movement they crossed the Shannon at Killaloe into An Clár. They were led by their chief, Umor, one of whose sons, Cutra, settled in the place now known as Lough Cutra (which is near Gort at the border of the present-day counties of Clare and Galway).

Another son of Umor led many of the Firbolg to the Burren area where they remained. A third son, Aengus, with many of his followers made his way to the largest of the Aran Islands, Inismore. There they established themselves permanently and erected the large fort still known as Dún Aengus. They thrived and prospered there without interference.

Luighaidh Meann (a Milesian of the Celtic race of people) had secured the An Clár territory for posterity. This kingdom remained in possession of a member of his lineage down through the years. From him is derived the name Tuadh Mhumhann or Thomond (North Munster). The name was Anglicized to the well-known version of Thomond by the English administration in the 17th century.

This beginning by Luighaidh Meann was to be the start of an historic attachment to the same land by the same people down through the centuries to the present day. No other European people save the Greeks and Romans can lay claim to such antiquity. Even though there would be many invasions suffered by the Dal gCais (as the people of An Clár came to be known) the intrinsic families remained intact, Celtic Irish and a race apart. To this day their descendants are still in possession of those ancient lands acquired by their forebears.

Conal of the Fleet Steeds had a son called Cas – the man from whom all the An Clár tribal families can be traced. His clan became known as Muintir Dalgais, or Dalcassian in translation. The most renowned Dalcassian family names which are traced from Cas, include: O'Brien, O'Dea, MacNamara, MacMahon, O'Grady, O'Mahony, as well as the MacClancy, MacInerney, O'Quin, O'Hehir, O'Liddy clans and indeed many more.

The eldest son of Cas, who was named Blod, was ancestor to the O'Briens. The O'Briens who by right of birth as well as by force of their strong arm (lamh laidir in uachter) were most powerful in Clare. Second only to the O'Briens came the MacNamaras, descended from Caisin.

Before Christianity came into prominence around AD 432 social order had improved considerably in the country. Prior to the arrival of Patrick (the saint credited with introducing Christianity to Ireland) 27 high kings had already reigned at Tara in County Meath. The country was also well advanced in culture and music. Story tellers and musicians were supplementing the druids as men of respect and were much sought after by chiefs and kings.

In AD 365, Eighy Moyfeon, the High King of Ireland, died and was succeeded by Crimthan, King of Munster. Crimthan was head of the house of Eber and as such a Dalcassian. The seat he vacated in Munster was first occupied by Corc (who was of the race of Eoghan More) until AD 366. Corc was then succeeded by Conal Eachluaith who was also a Dalcassian. The strength of the clan can be seen from the fact that two of their numbers were ruling Munster and Ireland at the same time.

Crimthan's sister was embittered by the appointment because she wanted her own son, Brian, to take over. To dispose of Crimthan she prepared a poisoned drink which she first sipped. By so doing she hoped that Crimthan would not become suspicious. Apparently he did not for we are told that he died in AD 379 near Cratloe on a mountain called after him, Slieve-Oighe-an-Righ (the hill of the king's death). Ironically the kingship fell to Niall, who was a son of the old king's second wife. With the death of Crimthan the connection between the Dalcassians and the High Kingship ceased for the next 600 years.

At this time the Irish high kings were notorious for their military expeditions to Britain and Gaul. They frequently plundered the coastal settlements and returned with many slaves to be sold to Irish rulers. Niall of the Nine Hostages brought back a horde of young captives around AD 405, one of whom was to change the course of Irish history. The slave's name was Patrick. His teachings would send men not on military expeditions for human bodies but on missions of peace in the name of Christianity. They went out to preach Christianity in the very lands their ancestors had previously plundered.

Thomond territorial place names which have come down from ancient times (see map next page): *Boirenn* (Burren); *Corcomruadh* (Corcomroe); *Ui Bracain* (Ibrickan); *Corcobaiscinn - West* (Moyarta); *Corcobaiscinn* - East (Clonderlaw); *Trioca Ced na n-Oilean* (Islands); *Cineal Fearmaic* (Inchiquin); *Ui Caisin* (Bunratty Upper); *Tradraige* (Bunratty Lower). *Ui Ainmire, Ui Cearnaig, Ui Floinn, Gleann Omra, Ui Toirdealbhaigh* - (all in Tulla Lower). *Tuath Ectghe, Ui Donghaile, Ui Congaile, Ui Rongaile* - (all in Tulla Upper).

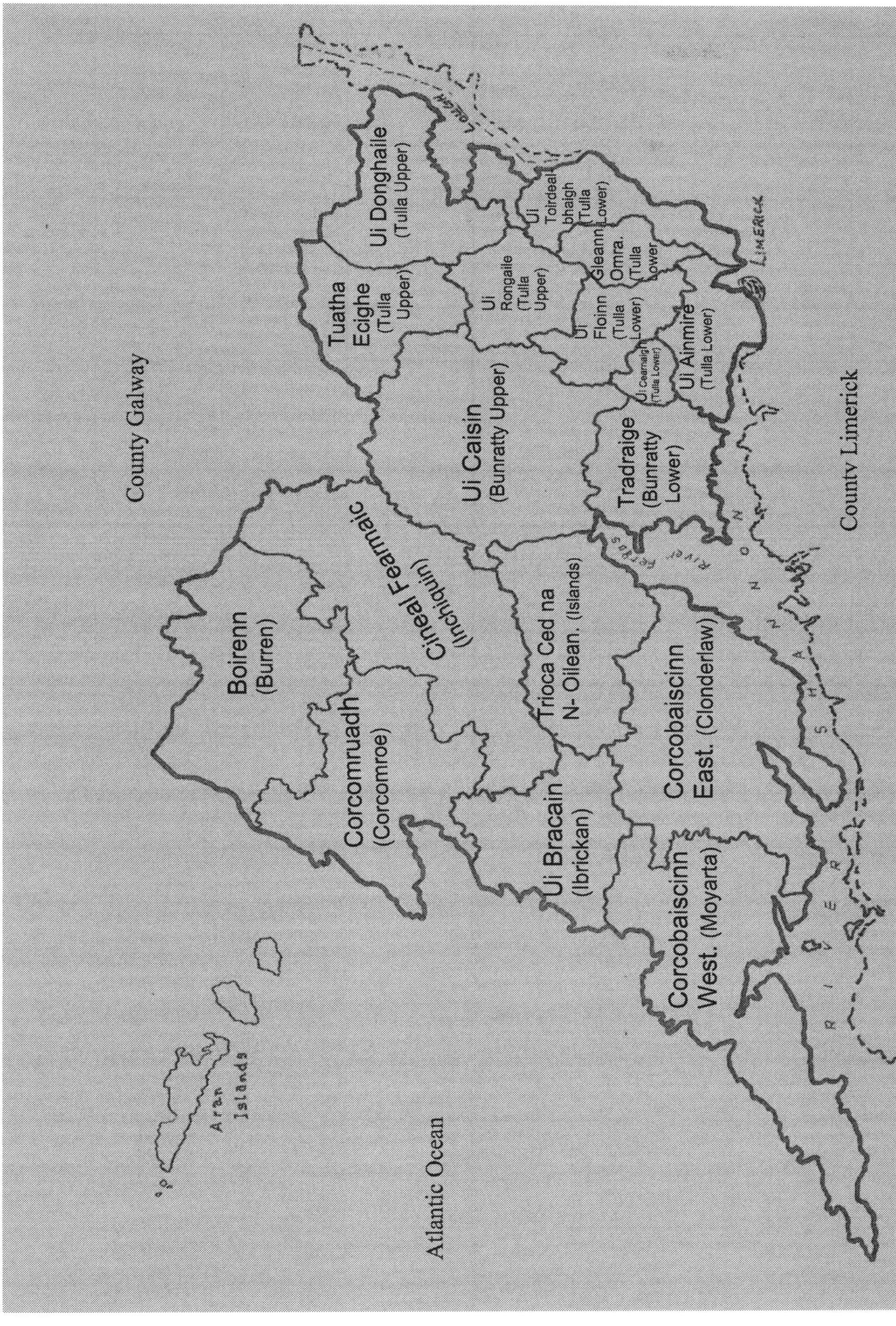

11. *Thomond (now County Clare) – ancient clan territorial divisions.*

(On the authority of John O'Donovan)

(Brian Dinan)

Chapter 3

Christian and Norse
(AD 400–1014)

Early in the 5th century a boy called Patrick was detained as a slave on the slopes of Slieve Mish in County Antrim. After six long years in captivity he escaped his masters and boarded a ship setting sail from Wicklow. It was bound for France although Wales was his homeland. In France he studied for the priesthood. He made it his life's ambition to return to Ireland to convert the heathens who had enslaved him.

After being consecrated a bishop Patrick returned to Ireland in AD 432. He landed on the east coast of the country and immediately proceeded to the Irish High King at Tara. He sought permission from King Laoghaire to preach Christianity to his subjects. The king consented to this request even though he did not take to the new religion himself. His example set a precedent for many of the local kings about the country; in spite of this we do note that there was not a Christian king in Cashel until AD 490, perhaps an indication of the authority and independence of the regional kings.

The impoverished classes embraced the new religion with considerable zeal simply because it offered hope and salvation to them. The greatest opposition to Patrick and his Christian teaching came from the powerful druids. They were quick to realise that their positions of authority were put in jeopardy. Cleverly, Patrick ensured that the pagan beliefs of the people were not entirely supplanted. Some of their customs were absorbed into the new religion: some have remained on in the form of phiseogs and other misguided beliefs in supernatural powers.

Religious celebration days which have transcended from ancient times right down to the present day include St. Brigid's day, which is celebrated on 1 February each year. In ancient times it was known as the feast of Imbolg, or the new Fertility Feast. The Celtic Samhain was traditionally celebrated on 2 November as a barrier to superstition; it is now known as All Saints Day. Halloween reaches back to our pre-Christian ancestors; for them it was the turning of the year – a time when the spirits of the other world attempted to escape back into the material world.

During the period when Patrick and his followers set out to establish the Christian church the country was without towns or villages. The Roman Empire (which played a major role in establishing infrastructure in other lands) never reached Ireland. Consequently, a non-centralised church evolved in Ireland. The church buildings of this period were small in size and were used for localized veneration rather than congregational use. Effectively what developed was a monastic church. The monks did travel quite a bit to spread the Christian word throughout their communities.

Patrick, as head of the Irish church, traversed much of Ireland preaching the new religion directly to the people and establishing churches in their localities. Bishops were appointed during his circuit of the country. It seems he found it expedient to appoint men who came from distinguished local families mainly because they would have been better educated and their family names carried status and power within their communities.

Although he came as far as Patrickswell in the present County Limerick, Patrick never crossed the Shannon into An Clár. From an elevated position in County Limerick he viewed the land of Thomond and gave it his blessing. He is credited with stating that a native son of the kingdom would rise up to administer the new religion to its people. Forty years later a man from Molougha near Kilrush became one of the district's holiest of men. AD 488 is St Senan's birth date and he spent his early life outside of the kingdom but returned to establish many churches.

Senan had monasteries built on Inislunga and on Inisluaidhe at the junction of the Fergus and Shannon estuaries. Also constructed under his guidance was a house of holy retreat on Mutton Island. The place most associated with Senan was to be Inis Cathaigh (Scattery Island) where he had a church and round tower constructed. He lived on the island during AD 540–4 and he was buried there when he died. His monastery was ravaged by Vikings in AD 816 and again in AD 835; indeed it may have been occupied by Vikings until Brian Boru finally routed them in the early part of the 11th century.

Additions were made to the Scattery settlement in the 13th and 14th centuries – the ruins of seven churches may now be seen there. In AD 1359 Pope Innocent V1 at Avignon appointed a bishop to the island but he was not recognized by the local clergy. It is still a place of pilgrimage to this day; St Senan's bed of stone on the island is reputed to be the final resting place of the saint. Legend has it that he allowed no women on Scattery during his lifetime [a curious notion perhaps without substance].

Another monastic church of note is the one currently in use at Tuamgraney – the oldest of its type in the country. A monastic settlement was founded on the site in AD 550. The western part of the church is reputed to have been rebuilt by the abbot Cormac O Killeen in AD 969. It is thought that Brian Boru carried out some repair work there c AD 1000.

Except in local isolated kingdoms the majority of the population adopted the Christian religion within the span of 100 years. Many monasteries were founded to become seats of learning for literary, scientific [sic] and religious disciplines. Foreign students attended from all over Europe to live simple lives of austerity in the monasteries with their tutors. It was from such centres of religious zeal that Irish monks went as missionaries to all parts of Europe. They were enthused with a burning desire to impart their new-found faith to the unbelieving of Britain, France, Germany, Switzerland and even Italy itself.

12. Ornamental Romanesque doorway of Dysert O'Dea Church. There has been a church on this site at Dysert O'Dea since the 8th century. It is believed to have been founded by Saint Tola. (SFADCo)

It was from the ruling district of Killaloe (Clare and North Tipperary ie Thomond) that the Diocese of Killaloe derives its name as well as its ruling structure. Killaloe was the seat of the first bishops and/or abbots who administered to the structure of the monastic-styled church. It is no surprise therefore that the seat of power of the church coincided exactly with that of the ruling princes in Thomond and likewise in all other kingdoms.

13. Partial round tower and ruined church at Drumcliff located three miles north of Ennis. It was once the parish church of Drumcliff and is an early Irish monastic settlement which dates back to the 10th century or possibly before.

(Brian Dinan)

Surprisingly not much is known about St Flannan's life or when he lived. It is recorded sketchily that a holy man named Flannan did exist in the middle of the 8th century. He was a sixth generation ancestor to the great high king, Brian Boru who it seems was proud to have the holy man in his family tree; subsequently he did much to keep alive the saint's heritage. This ensured that St Flannan became the most important cleric in the Kingdom of Thomond (who would argue with the mighty Brian Boru). As a result the principal church in the Kingdom of Thomond (equates with the Diocese of Killaloe) was always dedicated to St Flannan during the era of monastic administration.

The present-day 10th century Gothic church of St Cronan located at Tuamgraney is the oldest church building in continuous use in Ireland. It was one of the most important ecclesiastical sites in the country and is mentioned no less than 32 times between AD 735–1582 in the *Annals of the Kingdom of Ireland.* Brian Boru also effected many improvements to the structure and visitors can still walk in his footsteps there.

Away from the churches and monastic buildings the habitations of the general populous were both crude and uncomfortable. Standards of living remained poor amongst the vast majority and this gave rise to unsanitary living conditions. Social order was at a low ebb and we are not surprised to learn of yellow plague striking the country in AD 666; it was one of the most frightening diseases to ravage any land. There were numerous unrecorded deaths, so it would be foolhardy to estimate numbers.

After AD 700 it is noted that a bishop was equal in standing and privileges to the king of a tuath (local district). The lowest ruling rank of Aire Desa was required to possess a substantial land division of 14 cumals (grazing for 42 cows) as well as a grinding mill, a kiln to dry grain and a barn to store his corn in. A person not being noble by birth needed double the property of his counterpart in nobility in order to be be judged equal to him in dignity. He was obliged to keep an open house for visitors and could refuse no man hospitality no matter how many times he called – perhaps an explanation (in part) of the present-day famous Irish hospitality.

The skilled people were seen as inferior to the nobility but were privileged freemen. Belonging to this class were the carpenters, masons, goldsmiths, coppersmiths and blacksmiths. Those skilled in arts and crafts such as physicians and lawyers were also placed in this category. Education in itself was seen as an entitlement to be a freeman. The lawyers referred to above only served in the lower courts and were of modest standing. Others such as musicians, public entertainers and minor craftsmen held no affiliations or positions of privilege. The above qualified people could be regarded generally as commoners of good standing.

Below the commoners or skilled people came two classes of vassals. The first type were nobles of an inferior grade who were entitled to receive livestock from the local king. In return they provided him with an annual gratuity and military service when required. A second type of vassal had less rights but had greater obligations with regard to payment for stock taken over from their supporters. Normally their rent consisted of various types of food given to their king when he visited them twice a year.

A look at the dress of the early Irish shows the uniqueness of these island people as a separate race. The Cota was a thin long skirt made from wool and plaited with strips of linen, which were dyed yellow and attached to it by sewing. It was a long garment which could be wrapped around the body and made fast by a girdle folded round the loins. Some of the styles had short sleeves, while others showed a preference for sleeves which came right down to the waist.

The Truis or Straith Bracca was a lower body garment of various colours. It covered the ankles, legs and thighs and fitted high on the loins so close that the movement of every muscle was clearly displayed.

A Cochal, essentially an upper body garment, was something like the long cloak but with a large hanging collar or hood. It came in many different colours and hung as low as the middle of the thighs. The Cochal was fringed with a border of shagged hair. Because it was worn slung over the shoulder it was fastened on the breast with a clasp or buckle.

Another distinctive item of clothing of the emerging Irish dress was the Channabhas. It was large and loose – indeed not unlike the Cochal and was probably worn as a substitute for it. The Channabhas covered the shoulders and spread over the whole body. When the hood of the Channabhas was drawn over the head it served to completely disguise the wearer.

On the head it was usual to wear the Barrad which was a conical cap. This was not unlike the cap later worn by the grenadiers. It had one distinct difference, the cone of the Barrad was allowed to hang behind.

Let us not pass without mentioning the dress of the druids. They wore uniformly and universally white robes which were emblematic of the purity of their minds. In order to render their appearances more venerable they allowed their beards grow to great lengths.

Three classes of labourers who had no political rights of any kind worked on the land of their overlords. Many of them were descended from original inhabitants who had been living in the districts prior to the arrival of the Celts. A system of settling on land was permitted which facilitated the hiring of labourers for menial tasks. The lowest ranking of those people was the mug (a male slave) and the cumal (female slave). Interestingly, the Christian religion worked to alleviate their hardship. It is not surprising therefore to find that the number of slaves in the country diminished quite considerably in the early Christian period. Unfortunately the lowly practice of trafficking in human beings was to be re-introduced in later times when the Norse raiders came on the scene.

It is recorded that the king of Cashel (a Munster king) was entitled to receive from the territory of Corcobaskin the following – 1,000 oxen and 1,000 cows. He could also claim from the Burren district 1,000 cows, 1,000 oxen and 1,000 rams and a 1,000 cloaks. Although it is difficult to imagine the production of such wealth being credible, it can be taken that large amounts of tribute were paid annually (even if in name only) in this system. The cost of not meeting one's obligations could mean being dispossessed entirely. Tributes also passed the other way; we note that the king of Corcobaiscinn was entitled to receive a drinking horn, two steeds, and a king's apparel each year from the king at Cashel.

The Munster kings at that time relied heavily on the loyalty of the Dalcassians to supply a supporting armed force in times of major conflict. Their bravery was acknowledged by the phrase 'the first into battle and the last out of it'. The Thomond clans were often out-voted during the provincial election of kings. Because of the lopsided nature of the arrangement it was the Thomond dynasties which suffered and the southern Eoghanacht clans usually won out in the election of Munster kings. As a result Thomond did fall from prominence due to Eoghanacht power within the Munster Kingdom. Commencing about the middle of the 8th century

Cashel was ruled by a race of Eoghanacht priest-kings. Although it must be said one of them, Cormac MacCullenan, was a renowned scholar and a man of remarkable character.

The 9th century opened on a disastrous note for the Thomond Kingdom. In AD 801 on the eve of Saint Patrick's Day, a raging storm howled along the west coast of Clare and brought with it much thunder, lightening and raging seas. The land between Baltard and Hags Head collapsed and plunged into the sea. Earth tremors occurred in some villages and either killed or injured hundreds of people. With collapsing rock and a subsiding coastline the whole area became extremely dangerous resulting in many inhabitants losing their settlements.

The battle against nature was often hard for the ordinary inhabitants but never as consistently tyrannical as the foe who was at that time making inroads into the country. The highly navigable rivers provided the springboard for this latest invasion. The Norse who were until then busying themselves raiding throughout Europe, now turned their attention to Ireland and in particular to the wealth of isolated churches.

When the Norse sailed their long galleys into the wide estuary of the Shannon and Fergus the local inhabitants were taken completely by surprise. The holy islands in the Shannon and Fergus estuaries like Scattery Island and Canon Island, and even the Holy Island in Lough Derg were raided and laid waste. The heavily-armed Norse with axe and sword easily overcame the defenceless communities along the waterways. In addition to the ravaging of monasteries and churches they slaughtered cattle and carried off hostages.

Regretfully the reintroduction of this unwholesome practice was soon copied by the native princes. Feidhlim, a son of Crimthan King of Munster in AD 831–2, burned and sacked the monastic settlement at the renowned Clonmacnoise site. Flann as the monarch of all Ireland was outraged at the renewed atrocities. In AD 877 he marched on Munster and attacked the kingdom from Killaloe to Cork. The then king at Cashel, Cormac, retaliated by rounding up his own clans to include the Eoghanacht's and the Dalcassians; they inflicted a crushing defeat on old adversaries.

It would appear that Cormac, in appreciation for services rendered, declared Lorcan a prince of the proud Dalcassians. It was further confirmed to him that he was in direct line of descent from their common ancestor, Oilioll Oluim. It was a significant acknowledgement.

By the early part of the 10th century the Norse had become firmly entrenched in the country, bolstered mainly by their strong fortresses in Dublin, Cork, Wexford and Waterford. When they finally occupied Limerick in AD 920 they had put in place a chain of Viking colonies and harbour fortresses which held the country in a vice-like grip.

In the middle of the 10th century the Dalcassians were ruled by a man called Cennédig (Kennedy). This chief who was descended from the royal line of Oilioll Oluim was father to Eoghan Mór (of the Eoghanachts) and Cormac Cas (of the Dalcassians). Cennédig had two sons, Mahon who was the eldest and would rule first, and Brian who was born in Thomond in either AD 940 or 941. Some sources have put his birth date at AD 926. [It seems unlikely since this would make him an incredible 88 year of age at the Battle of Clontarf]!

Mahon and Brian spear-headed a monumental campaign against the Norse. While many of their battles were fought in the Munster area Brian did receive sterling support from a deposed high king, Malachy of Meath. Malachy had attained the high kingship by defeating a Norse contingent at Tara in AD 980, and from that action we can judge how important it was to repulse Viking invaders. However, the Norse had the country fairly well subdued except for the strongholds held by Malachy in Meath and Brian in the Kingdom of Thomond.

Malachy did score some notable victories over the Norse but because he lacked collective support from the country as a whole he seemed to be fighting a losing battle. In Thomond the Dalcassians continued to strongly oppose the Norse (mostly Danes) who had recently taken control in Limerick city. They were happy to keep the Dalcassians away from Limerick and bottled up in what was effectively the peninsula of An Clár. Because the River Shannon formed a natural boundary between Clare and Limerick it somewhat thwarted the Norse advances. Brian was obliged to use guerrilla tactics when his forces became depleted due to long drawn out battles and skirmishes. A low point came when he could muster barely 15 fighting men to accompany him on daring raids.

Such was the standing of the brothers Mahon and Brian that in AD 963 on the death of Donnchad, Mahon felt he could lay claim to the throne of Cashel (ie Munster). To consolidate his position he felt it was necessary to crush the Norse in Limerick because their leader Ivor had allied himself to the Eoghanacht. Matters came to a head when the respective forces met at Sulcoit near Tipperary town. It resulted in a raging hand-to-hand battle which lasted from sunrise to midday at which point the Norse under Ivor were forced to retreat in haste to Limerick. However, many were captured and killed without mercy; those who survived were put into slavery. The date for this notable victory is recorded at AD 968 in *The Annals of the Four Masters*. Ivor, together with his two Eoghanacht allies, Donovan and Molloy, escaped overseas. Mahon then ruled as king of Munster but much of his reign was troubled by the warring efforts of the remaining Danes.

Once again matters did not settle for we note that Ivor was soon back in the country and conspiring again with his old allies Donovan and Molloy. Mahon was enticed on some false pretext to go into Molloy's country in the heart of the Munster Kingdom. When he reached a point near the present Cork/Limerick border he was attacked and treacherously slain. This foul act not only enraged Brian but made it possible for him to take over the Munster seat at Cashel. The great leader soon made it plain that it would be a foolish man who would provoke him. He immediately set about revenging the dastardly murder of his brother. As we shall see blood flowed freely throughout the land until he had gained his satisfaction.

Brian routed the Norse from the islands in the Shannon estuary and he subsequently drove some more from the south-west Clare territory of Corcobaiscinn in AD 975. He slew Ivor (his old Norse protagonist) on Coney Island in AD 977 before heading into Limerick to dispatch Donovan who had conspired in the death of his brother. While on this campaign his forces harried Maelmuidh who was another conspirator in the murder of Mahon. It was Brian's young son, Morogh, who had the honour of slaying Maelmuidh of the Eoghanacht after which the victorious Dalcassians returned home with the spoils of war.

Now that they had firmly installed themselves on the Munster throne much rejoicing followed at their headquarters – the palace of Kincora near Killaloe. It was a momentous occasion for the Dalcassians to be re-instated on the throne of Munster after such a long and unlawful absence. For many years before this event the Eoghanacht clan had consistently refused to employ the alternate change of rule plan as laid down in Brehon Law.

Thereafter Brian turned his attention to Ireland as a whole. When he overran Ossory, Malachy the king of that district, made retaliatory incursions into Thomond. Malachy attacked the very heart of the kingdom at Magh Adhair (the inauguration place of the Dalcassian chiefs). The site was marked by a great oak tree with a mound and ceremonial enclosure. Part of the inaugural ceremony consisted of the chief of the second most powerful clan in Thomond, the MacNamaras, handing over the wand of power to the incoming chief. [Remnants of this ancient site can still be seen adjacent to the present village of Quin]. After Malachy's attack on Magh Adhair, Brian made a scathing attack into the country of Westmeath, the home territory of Malachy.

A period of peace followed during which Brian devoted much time to the restoration of old Celtic values and customs. He built or had rebuilt numerous churches, including those located at Killaloe, Iniscaltra and Tuamgraney. Original monasteries and old seats of learning were restored. Copies of hereditary books which had been destroyed or lost were acquired from foreign libraries. It was the Norse, who had established a number of commercial seaports in Ireland, who quickly moved to expand trade with foreign lands. In some instances the Norse became part of Gaelic culture to such an extent that King Brian Boru could count on them in time of war.

14. The only medieval convent for nuns in the diocese of Killaloe is Killone Abbey. Founded by Donal More O'Brien in the 12th century for the sisters of St Augustine. The ruins are located near the isolated Killone Lake three miles west of Ennis.

(Brian Dinan)

He also constructed roads and bridges as well as fortifying and expanding his own palace at Kincora near the fording place of Killaloe.

By AD 993, Brian was in a position to command his Norse allies to sail their long galleys up the River Shannon to Lough Ree from where he was in a position to dominate Connaught and Meath. He had learned a valuable tactic from his onetime Norse enemies – warfare from the waterways. In AD 995 we find Brian waging war deep in Malachy's territory of Westmeath. This constituted an attack on the High Kingship itself, but Malachy (being the astute leader he was) settled with Brian to divide the country between them. It was agreed in AD 998 that Malachy should rule the northern half of Ireland while Brian would reign as supreme monarch of the southern half to include the vassalages of Dublin city as well as some other Norse towns.

There was much unrest throughout the province of Leinster when Sitric and Maelmora (the Norse and Leinster allies) set about recovering the kingdom of Leinster from Brian. In order to quell the unrest Brian marched his Dalcassian allies from Kincora to Dublin to engage and defeat the Norse and Leinster allies at Glenmama (a site west of Dublin) in AD 999.

By this time Brian of the Tributes was about 59 years of age and was in the process of handing over the reins of leadership to his two sons, Morogh and Taigh. However, he was not beyond falling for a cleverly devious woman named Gormflath (she was previously married to Malachy). Gormflath was also responsible for prompting Sitric and Maelmora to rebel against Brian. He married her and she bore him a son called Donnchad. At Gormflath's influence Brian restored Sitric to his old command of Dublin and to Maelmora he gave the kingship of Leinster.

Brian was still aching to hold sway over all of Ireland. To achieve this long-held ambition he engaged Malachy in a military foray at Tara. Supporting Brian were all of the Munster and many of the Leinster clans, along with some of the Norse warriors and chieftains who lived under his rule and paid him homage. Malachy called on O'Neill from the north to support him. The O'Neills failed to respond to his call which forced him to concede Brian's claim on the kingship. Thus it was they avoided the disastrous but common practice of slaughtering each other for power.

15. *Clare Abbey; an abbey of the Canons Regular of St Augustine. Founded by King Donal More O'Brien around AD 1194. It is located a short distance from Clarecastle.*
(Brian Dinan)

The year of Brian's accession was 1002. Since the death of Crimthan about 600 years before no Dalcassian chief had served as high king of Ireland. This was Brian's opportunity to firmly establish himself as High King with the Dalcassian clans supporting him in his bid for the throne.

After Brian had installed himself as High King he immediately went on the all-Ireland circuit of the High King with a pomp and splendour that was never seen before, or indeed thereafter. From Kincora he marched through Connaught and from there he went to Armagh in Ulster. Having attended mass in the cathedral of Armagh he laid 20 ounces of gold on the altar as a gift to the religious community. He marched to Tara; this was very important symbolically because of Tara's association with the highest powers in the land. After Tara he marched to Dublin and then back through Leinster and Ossory until finally and triumphantly to a tumultuous reception at the seat of the Munster Kingdom – Cashel itself.

It was the most emphatic and dominant claim over the whole Gaelic race ever made by a high king. The good work of rebuilding which he had begun in the Kingdom of Munster he then expanded to the whole of the country. In 1007 he revived the great Fair of Tailtean – an event which had not been celebrated for some 800 years previously. Brian's magnificent Celtic revival signalled an end to the Norse tyranny and influence. It is noteworthy that every corner of Ireland acknowledged him as the supreme ruler. Such was his authority that he was able to claim previously unknown quantities of tributes. His famous epithet of Brian Borama (Brian of the cattle tributes) or Brian Boraime (Brian from Bel Boraime) was confirmed and has been famously anglicised to 'Brian Boru'.

In any case Brian's many tributes entitled him to hundreds of cows, hogs, cloaks, and mantles from Connaught, Tirconnel, Tirowen and Leinster. The Norse of Dublin were equally obliged to fulfil their obligations to him. It was a fact that he annually received 365 pipes of red wine from the Danes in Limerick.

But in those turbulent times nothing could remain certain or be taken for granted. Brian had ten years as high king in which to build up the country to a new level of sophistication. He went on to make great strides in this noble task. He reinforced the authority of the Christian Church with its principal seat of rule being firmly fixed at Armagh; it is a situation which pertains to this day in the Catholic Church.

Gormflath, the woman cast aside by Brian and Malachy, was again stirring up rebellion in the hearts of Sitric and Maelmora in the province of Leinster. For Malachy, keeping order in the northern half of the country was proving difficult. When things got out of hand he summoned Brian to his aid in 1013. Brian besieged Dublin from September until Christmas of that year only to be forced to withdraw due to a lack of provisions.

Early in the year 1014 further unrest erupted in the east of the country. Gathering up all his Dalcassian fighting men as well as supporting clans from Munster and south Connaught, Brian once again marched on Dublin. On this occasion he resolved to eliminate every last usurper forever – in particular the Norse who were at the root of most insurrections.

Brian's army arrived on the high ground between Dublin and the River Tolka where the opposing forces took sight of each other on the eve of Good Friday. Malachy was standing by with a large contingent of his own troops; meanwhile bands of true Gaels were simultaneously arriving from Scotland to join in the fray when needed. Brian would have been about 74 years of age at that time, therefore somewhat old and frail for the strenuous hand-to-hand fighting where battle axe and sword were the standard weapons. Of course he could not be prevented from being at the battlefield but he was persuaded to inspire the troops from behind the battle lines. His son Morogh and grandson Turloch led the Dalcassians forces into combat.

Facing Brian's armies were 2,000 of the best fighting men the Norse had mustered from most of Ireland, parts of Scotland and from the Isle of Man. They were further assisted by the Leinster clans, namely the O Byrnes and the O Tooles who were well noted for their ferocity in battle. Brian's strategy was to rely mainly on his vastly experienced and trustworthy Dalcassians positioned in the front lines.

As the sun rose over Clontarf on Good Friday morning of 23 April 1014 the forces engaged in a confrontation that was to last from morning until sunset. In the relentless close quarter fighting where heavy axe and sword were the favoured weapons, it was no place for the untried. The bow and arrow was not a weapon of the day so this meant that all killing was done at close range. Strength, aggressiveness, alertness – not to mention savage ferocity – were attributes which the Dalcassians displayed aplenty.

As the battle raged, King Brian prayed in his tent behind the lines. His son, Morogh, fighting bravely in the van of the Dalcassian forces, broke through the Norse lines when he killed their leader, Sigurd. His ally, Sitric, had taken no part in the fighting but followed events from the safety of his castle ramparts. When Maelmora fell the allies were routed and Brian's forces chased in hot pursuit. Morogh, who was the hero of the day, was unfortunate in that his hand became locked to the hilt of his sword in a grip spasm after 12 hours of continuous fighting. The distraction of undoing the locked grip while attempting to slay a fallen adversary was his undoing when he suffered a fatal stabbing.

The retreating Norse made for the weir on the Tolka in a frantic effort to get to their ships anchored at Clontarf. The tide had filled and created such a flood that many of them drowned while scrambling to their boats. Brian's grandson (Morogh's son), Turloch, also drowned as he pursued them into the water.

One of the fleeing Norse, Brodar, on seeing king Brian in his tent, slew him in a treacherous act. A number of the Brian's bodyguards gave chase and caught up with Brodar. The raging Dalcassians savagely killed and disembowelled the Norse leader before he could flee the battle site.

Thus it was the Norse tyranny was utterly destroyed at Clontarf by Brian Boru's army. Although his forces did not go on to take Dublin due to loss of leadership they did return victorious to Kincora under the guidance of another of Brian's sons, a man called Taigh. Brian's body was brought to Armagh where the clergy buried it beside the high altar with the utmost honour and dignity. And so ended the reign of one of the greatest monarchs in Celtic history.

Inside Brian's tent at the Battle of Clontarf in 1014.

16. One of the retreating Norse, Brodar, enters the tent of King Brian Boru, and slays the defenceless monarch before taking flight. He was quickly overtaken and killed by the Dalcassian forces.

(From Cusack's 'History of the Irish Nation')

The proud Dalcassian king had restored culture, order and religion to a land laid waste by the ruthless invaders. During his reign Brian had encouraged the adoption of surnames which gave us the now world famous family names such as O'Brien, O'Connor, MacNamara, indeed all of the names we now have. Brian left a noble heritage, which if it had continued and been built upon would have made the country a truly strong and prosperous nation. Unfortunately, leaders of his quality were a rare occurrence. The strife and the turmoil which came after his death was effectively a step back in history.

The following poem, attributed to MacLiag in 1015 [translated by James Clarence Mangan (1803–49)] is indicative of the eminence of Brian and his kingdom centred at Kincora.

Kincora

Oh, where, Kincora! Is Brian the Great?
And where is the beauty that once was thine?
Oh, where are the princes and nobles that sate
At the feast in thy halls, and drank the red wine?
Where, oh, Kincora?

Oh, where, Kincora! Are thy valorous lords?
Oh, whither, thou hospitable! are they gone?
Oh, where are the Dalcassians of the Golden Swords?
And where are the warriors Brian led on?
Where, oh, Kincora?

And where is Murrough, the descendent of kings
The defeater of a hundred – the daringly brave –
Who set but slight store by jewels and rings –
Who swam down the torrent and laughed at its waves?
Where, oh, Kincora?

And where is Donogh, King Brian's worthy son?
And where is Conaing, the beautiful chief?
And Kian, and Corc? Alas! They are gone –
They have left me this night alone with my grief,
Left me, Kincora!

And where are the chiefs with whom Brian went forth,
The ne'er vanquished sons of Erin the Brave,
The great king of Onaght, renowned for his worth,
And the hosts of Baskin, from the western wave?
Where, oh, Kincora?

Oh, never again will princes appear,
To rival the Dalcassians of Cleaving Swords!
I can never dream of meeting afar or anear,
In the east or the west, such heroes and lords!
Never, Kincora!

Oh, dear are the images my memory calls up
Of Brian Boru! – how he would never miss
To give me at the banquet the first bright cup!
Oh, why did he heap on me honour like this?
Why, oh, Kincora?

I am MacLiag, and my home is on the lake;
Thither often, to that palace whose beauty is fled
Came Brian to ask me, and I went for his sake.
Oh, my grief! That I should live, and Brian be dead!
Dead, oh, Kincora?

17. *Ui Briain (O'Brien) Arms.*

(Ballinakella Press)

Chapter 4

Dalcassians at war
(1014 – 1168)

After the death of Brian the high kingship slipped from the Dalcassians back to Malachy of Leinster. Clan strength had been further weakened by the losses of Brian's son and grandson at Clontarf. Even as the survivors of Brian's army marched home after Clontarf they encountered more hostilities. Such assaults from native clans were unbefitting an army which had just rid the country of its worst menace; however it does serve to illustrate the petty-minded avariciousness of the times.

While traversing through Ossory in the midlands, MacGiolla Phadraig attacked them in overpowering numbers. Undaunted, the Dalcassians fixed stakes into the ground to which they tied their wounded for support. An able-bodied soldier was posted by each one for protection. This act of determination so gripped the attackers that they withdrew with an even greater respect for the Thomond warriors.

Once back at Kincora the usual squabbles broke out. Dissension erupted between the brothers Taigh and Donogh as to who would sit on the throne of Munster. The clan members for the most part favoured (if agreement could ever be found) Taigh for the kingship. However he still faced the sizeable task of overcoming the usual incumbents namely the Eoghanachts of south Munster who disputed every leadership issue with vigour.

Taigh and Donogh defeated Donal of the Eoghanachts in a decisive battle at Limerick. By so doing they established their claim to the Munster throne. The end of 1014 also saw the clans of Connaught striking at the weakened Dalcassians. Their palace of Kincora was subsequently assaulted and laid waste. However the men of Thomond managed to muster a raiding party to venture as far north as Lough Ree and return with considerable plunder. On a national scale events quieted somewhat for the Dalcassians but this did not deter the brothers Taigh and Donogh from squabbling over the kingships' of Thomond and Ireland.

The death of Malachy in 1028 prompted Donogh to make a bid for the High Kingship of Ireland. When his brother Taigh opposed him Donogh connived with the forces of Ely O'Carrol and together they murdered Taigh rather shamefully – an unbelievable internecine act. It was another example of the depths to which status-seeking individuals were prepared to sink in order to win out in power struggles.

Afterwards, Donogh gathered under his banner those who had served his father Brian to march up through Meath and onwards to Dublin. When he had asserted himself on that trip he returned through Leinster and Ossory where he took many captives. En route he attacked and subdued all who did not render him immediate recognition. He gained grudging national acknowledgement after this campaign, but it was shown only when the southern half of the country (Leath Mogha) was assigned to him.

Donogh occupied himself with much hostilities about Ireland until he was generally recognised as High King of Ireland in 1049. However the domestic state of the country had become deplorable after the upheavals of widespread war. With fighting and bustling for positions of power coupled with widespread disagreement and strife it was no surprise to learn that living conditions were at their lowest level. Crops and husbandry did not receive the required attention to maintain adequate living standards for the general populous. Also, the climate had turned particularly bad which gave rise to failing crops and poor growth. Fruit, fish and milk were hard to come by; it resulted in people turning to stealing and plunder. Living conditions became so wretched that Donogh (at a Killaloe conference) enacted special laws of order in an effort to maintain a basic level of stability.

From the example he gave it would appear that Donogh was more of a law breaker than most others in his kingdom. He raided the territory of Diarmuid in Leinster simply to assert his position. His action was quickly repaid by the Leinster king who retaliated by attacking Thomond from end to end. Such was the thoroughness of the raid that the castle of Dun-tri-Liag near Corbally in Limerick was levelled. It was an important fortress built by Cormac Cas and later enlarged and fortified by Brian Boru.

While Donogh was interfering in south Munster his own territory suffered another attack. On this occasion it was Aedh O'Connor of Galway who carried away great spoils from the territories of Corcobaiscinn and Tradraige in the south west of Thomond. Continuous hostilities prevailed throughout this period resulting in no obvious gain for anyone.

In an attempt to demonstrate contempt for his enemies Donogh sent his son, Morogh of the Short Shield, to the northern part of the country to chastise his enemies there. However, Turlogh in the north (who was an ally of Aedh O'Connor) gave him more than he had bargained for. It was reported that 15 of Morogh's chiefs were killed and 400 more of his men were left dead on the battlefield.

If Donogh thought that staying within his own boundaries in Thomond would win him some respite he was badly mistaken. Aedh O'Connor sent another raiding party into Thomond within a year. The kingdom stronghold at Kincora along with the village of Killaloe were plundered and destroyed. His final disastrous defeat came in a fierce battle near Tipperary town where he lost many of his best fighting men. The Leinster king then installed his own foster son, Turlogh (who was Donogh's son-in-law), as King of Thomond. This arrangement seemed to satisfy all concerned – relative peace was to reign for a number of years in the Kingdom of Thomond – an unusual situation. Certainly, Donogh had displeased many people. He appears to have been a man of little virtue which is why we are surprised to learn that he went to Rome where he spent the rest of his troubled life doing penance for his foul deeds.

The above-mentioned Turlogh O'Brien was given further room to manoeuvre politically when two powerful Irish princes, Diarmuid King of Leinster and Aedh O'Connor of Connaught were slain in battle. Because there wasn't any other serious contender for the High Kingship it left the way open for Turlogh who needed at least one significant ally to make his bid credible. When that was not forthcoming he gathered up a large army of Munster and other allies. In 1075 he marched to the north of the country. Once there he demanded hostages as tokens of submission. Instead of submission he was met with violent opposition. He was either a poor judge of the political climate or rather pig-headed. His forces were subsequently defeated in a hard-fought battle in County Louth. He was more successful in the province of Connaught where he formed an alliance with the king, Rory O'Connor. As a result he gained loose recognition as the High King of Ireland even if it was under stern opposition from the powerful clans in the north. Such was the uncertainty of his position that he was obliged to keep up his attacks on the many who disputed his claims. We note that in AD 1080 he was in the field again this time sacking Dublin.

During 1084 the people of Thomond were assailed once more by the Connaught clans. They looted and burned around the districts of Tuamgraney, Moynoe and Killaloe which was the pivot point of the Kingdom. Turlogh and his warriors were busy fighting in Meath when the attacks took place. Of course this act would not be left unpunished by Turlogh who shortly afterwards plundered the Kingdom of Leitrim (Muinter Eolais). Turlogh was at that time well advanced in years and it may have been his last major campaign. He died peacefully at the palace of Kincora in 1086. Turlogh was in his 70th year when he succumbed (it was an advanced age for those times).

A son of Turlogh, Murtagh More O'Brien, was next to take over the Dalcassian and the Munster kingships. Murtagh was duly installed when he received the Wand of Power from the MacNamaras at Maigh Adhair in 1086. He also conformed to the time-honoured custom of establishing his position by making raids outside of Thomond. He scored a number of small successes in the Kingdom of Leinster. Next we find Murtagh attacking Connaught by the novel method of using boats on the Shannon and on the sea. Rory O'Connor defeated him and captured many of his vessels. Murtagh himself was taken prisoner and was kept captive for some time.

Donal MacLaughlin O'Neill, High King of Ireland, and Rory O'Connor teamed up to spend considerable time and energy in plundering the Kingdom of Thomond. They raided as far south as Emly and Bruree, both of which are situated in the present county of Limerick. On their return they ransacked the palace of Kincora, capturing many Dalcassian princes and their Danish allies. Further incursions by the Dalcassians into Connaught proved futile and disastrously resulted in the plundering of East Thomond (currently called North Tipperary) by the Connaught men.

Murtagh was a warlike individual as is demonstrated by many more accounts of his hostilities about the country. An example of the callousness of his character may be gleaned from the fact that he delivered a chief, MacCoirten (whom he captured on a northern raid) to his most bitter enemy the O'Learys. The deliverance of hostages over to their enemies was often a fate worse than death. For his underhand act Murtagh received eight other hostages in return, 100 cows and 30 ounces of gold.

His burning ambition was to achieve the High Kingship of all Ireland. After some spluttering successes he finally won a notable victory in the north of the country. It was enough to give him majority support. Like his grandfather, Brian Boru, he immediately set out on a victorious circuit of the country. He was received everywhere without resistance. There was

18.
Magh Adhair
This site is situated near the village of Quin. It was the inauguration place of the Gaelic chiefs of Thomond.
The Wand of Power was there bestowed by the MacNamara chief on the incoming O'Brien king.

(Royal Irish Academy)

much rejoicing when he and his army returned in triumph to Kincora.

In 1114 Murtagh was laid low by a bout of illness. His brother Dermot took advantage of the situation and immediately assumed control without being asked to do so. When Murtagh recovered his health he quickly deposed Dermot and then set about consolidating his position of power in the Kingdom. A direct attack was launched on the palace of Kincora in 1116 by a Connaught contingent. The fortress (which had been erected by

Brian Boru) was destroyed and much booty seized. Dermot died shortly afterwards in the year 1118. One year later Murtagh died; he was buried in the church of his ancestors in Killaloe.

Dermot's son, Donogh, was later installed as Bishop of Killaloe. At that time bishops were usually selected from the noble or ruling class, often having close relationships with the king's family. Such appointments were as much political as they were religious.

Sensationally, two sons of Murtagh gained power. Conor-na-Cathrach was installed as King of Munster (a notable feat for a Dalcassian prince), while his brother Turlogh assumed the kingship of Thomond in the family tradition. As was a necessity for acceptance and success Conor then waged war in Leinster hoping to cement his position. During this campaign he subdued the Danes in their settlements at Waterford and Dublin.

By this time the Connaught kings were really thriving on the diversions of the Munster clans with their internal squabbles. Once again they captured Killaloe in 1119; in 1124 they went over the falls of Doonass in their boats to plunder along the banks of the lower Shannon. They sailed down to the island of Foynes before successfully returning homeward and showed much skill in sailing against the Shannon current.

Thinking that something might to be gained from naval excursions Conor tried his hand at attacking Connaught by using the Shannon. His fleet was still in Lough Derg when he encountered the Connaught vessels. The opposing forces obliged us with the unusual spectacle of a naval battle on the Lough. Long boats were used and were powered by square sails and banks of oarsmen. No doubt the expertise came from the Norse who were dispersed about the country and had many affiliations with the various clans. On this occasion the Connaught forces were victorious – an advantage they were to hold for some time. It kept the Thomond fighters pinned and constrained within their own territory .

Conor's brother, Turlogh Prince of Thomond, was by no means idle at this time. When Cormac of Cashel (a bishop) attacked the city of Limerick he was duly assassinated by Turlogh O'Brien. Conor died at the royal residence of Killaloe in 1142.

The next ruler on the throne of Munster was his brother Turlogh. Conor's only son, Murtagh, was installed as King of Thomond while his brother, Teigue Gle, had to be satisfied with the lower ranking of Prince of Ormond – the smaller Kingdom of East Thomond.

Soon after Turlogh acceded the throne of Munster he heralded the occasion by setting off on a raiding mission in Leinster. It would appear that the only way to power as far as the Dalcassians were concerned was to first subdue Leinster. Then they usually went about conquering either Ulster or Connaught. Success in those areas sometimes rewarded them with the high kingship of all Ireland. It was a tactic that worked for recent descendents of Brian Boru so they were happy to follow best examples.

Turlogh fought wars with such adversaries as the king of Meath, Diarmuid McMurrough and the usual Connaught chieftains. He also became a huge antagonist of the MacCarthys in south Munster. While he and his battalions were battling the latter in the south his brother, Teigue Gle, was once again turning against his kin and finding no difficulty in allying with the King of Meath and with the notorious Diarmuid McMurrough in a bid to depose Turlogh.

Even as Turlogh returned from raids on MacCarthy's territory in south Munster, he encountered allies of Taigue Gle who ambushed him in Emly in the south of County Limerick. The overwhelming numbers vanquished the Dalcassians in a crushing defeat. Some of the notable chiefs who fell in that battle came from the O' Briens, the O' Kennedys, the O' Deas, the O' Shannons, the O' Quinns, the O' Gradys, the O' Hogans, the O' Lynches, the O' Hehirs, the O' Hearns, and the Dalcassian O' Neills. This victory gave Turlogh O' Connor undisputed control of Munster. Turlogh O' Brien was forced to flee to the north to preserve his own life. Teigue was made Prince of Thomond while Dermot MacCarthy became Prince of Desmond in the south Munster kingdom.

Shortly afterwards Murtagh MacLaughlin of the northern Hy Nialls marched south and recorded some victories en route before entering the Kingdom of Munster. He restored Turlogh O'Brien once more as Prince of Thomond. Teigue hastily left Thomond for he feared an encounter with his brother. Unfortunately for him another brother, Dermod, caught up with him and rendered him ineffective by the barbarous act of having his eyes pulled from their sockets. Teigue died in the following year of 1154 as a result of his injuries.

In a jostling for positions between the northern O'Neills and O'Connor of Connaught, the powerless Turlogh was deposed and restored a few more times in Thomond; towards the end of his career he was known to have ruled with a very stern hand. He launched a final attack into south Munster in 1161 where he slew many chiefs of the O'Donohues and O'Keefes as well as a son of Cormac MacCarthy who was Prince of Desmond.

When his own son, Murtagh, came of age he banished his father (Turlogh) from the head of the clan. In 1167 the stormy career of Turlogh came to an end when he died at Killaloe. Murtagh did not last long in office because he was killed by his cousin Conor O'Brien a year later. This cleared the way for a powerful man by the name of Donal More (The Great) O'Brien who received the Wand of Power from the MacNamaras at Maigh Adhair in the year 1168. From the preceding accounts we note that the main preoccupation of the chiefs, princes, kings and nobles alike was constant warfare to assert their authority. Local clans had laws – the Brehon Laws – for appointing their own rulers. Those laws could extend to areas as large as Munster. The main trouble stemmed from the fact that to achieve the high kingship of Ireland the pretenders felt obliged to march on a circuit of Ireland to enforce their authority by garnering or cajoling support from other powerful clans. Such support was not always forthcoming so alliance had to be formed by fair means or foul.

Then there was the unique Irish system of clans banding together to support the principal clan, eg the MacNamaras supported the O'Briens in Thomond. Such a system was not good enough on a national scale when a chief of the O'Briens was attempting a bid on the high kingship (Ard Righ). Long alliances with clans from other districts usually proved troublesome and unreliable. Quite often a king would have to subdue, time and time again, the same usurper in order to maintain his position. This practice was to be the main reason why the Normans were able to establish themselves in Irish society after they invaded the country in AD 1169.

Except for some churches and monasteries all other habitations were constructed from wattle, wood and straw. Due to almost continuous warfare, the time and energy needed to develop more sophisticated buildings never materialized. Communities gathered around ecclesiastical buildings in somewhat primitive shelters which were often little more than lean-tos or small wooden huts. Scattered about the countryside were a number of large duns which were strongholds specifically for the Ui Briain and other powerful clans.

The vassals (many were descendents of original primitive cultures) were used as tillers of the soil and providers of food to the nobler class. This allowed the clan members of standing to have leisure time for such pursuits as hunting, socializing and entertainment. Banquets were a favourite pastime of the Gaelic nobility. Wine, beer and other exotic items were supplied to the Clare ruling class by the Danes of Limerick. Produce of the county at that time would have been wool, hide, tallow and timber from the extensive forests of Clare with oak being much sought after especially for roofing and for the building of ships.

The art of writing and learning was confined mainly to the monasteries which were then springing up around the country. The vassals, craftsmen, and petty chiefs had little use for this important skill. In the monasteries they kept the valuable records of the history, lives and events which were important to the supporting clan. Thanks to such records complete histories have been pieced together. Even though the Norse burned and destroyed the contents of many monasteries a number of valuable books and documents have survived. Historical records have been drawn from such books as *Annals of the Kingdom of Ireland* and *Annals of Inisfallen*.

Religion had a somewhat different impact on the people than we might expect from today's perspective. At that time, war, murder and cruelty were all pretty common. The O'Briens had a particularly effective though very barbarous way of dealing with people who were likely to hinder their aspirations. It was the custom of pulling out the eyeballs of their enemies – an act which rendered the unfortunate ineffective for life. When Donal O'Brien came to power his first inhuman act was to deprive his own brother, Brian-na-Sleibhe, of his sight. Any candidate for power who left himself vulnerable was in a very precarious position indeed.

During the 12th century the first semblance of villages and towns (outside of the Norse settlements) appeared throughout the land. We are told of Kincora (near the town of Killaloe) being burned and looted by the Connaught clans. The reason for the growth of Killaloe as a town was due to two things, first the palace of Brian Boru upriver and secondly the weir or crossing point in the river around which toll collectors and other 'service' providers congregated.

We note also that Tuamgraney was a population centre from quite early on. It had a monastery and round tower since the 10th century, indicative of a significant social centre for people to gravitate towards. Indeed many centres grew in the same way eg the town at Inis-an-Laoigh (Ennis) was to spring up around the 13th century monastic settlement on the Fergus.

Returning to more testing matters we are reminded of the propensity of the Gaelic lords to engage in hostilities therefore a look at the makeup of the Gaelic fighting man might be opportune. A soldier of the period was equipped with a light axe, a sword and perhaps a knife and spear. Such weapons were in daily use whether in time of war or peace; most clansmen were quite adept at using them. In close quarter fighting a soldier would have to be quite skilful to overcome an enemy similarly equipped.

The armour of the early Irish was discussed by one Joseph Walker Cooper in findings that he made to the Rt Hon Ely, Countess of Moyorre. His observations were based on coins and other data found in Queen's County in 1786. He noted that the helmet was of the open variety, possibly with ear flaps. It could have been a general purpose piece of head gear used to keep the hair in place when travelling through thick forest, just as much as for deflecting blows during combat [One wonders how it would have fared under the blade of a war axe]. Before the 10th century helmets would have been made of animal hides. With iron working in use for a thousand years previously, one is inclined to think that the leather helmets may have been encased inside steel straps at least to begin with. In general though, metal body armour was not commonly used until the Normans arrived in 1169, and even then in limited situations by the Irish.

A second defensive devise used by the early Irish was the shield. Many of the illustrations of shields which have come down to us are seen to be circular in shape, and often embellished with Celtic designs brocaded on them. The rim could be protected with a band of iron or bronze. Another type of shield was long and rectangular in overall shape but curved for added protection – somewhat like those the Roman soldiers used. Both types would have been gripped by leather thongs attached to the inside.

Prior to the 10th century body armour was not in use, at least no evidence of such has been recorded. We can assume that metal body armour was not in use by the Irish prior to the 12th century, this is in spite of folklore relating the exploits of Oisin of the Fianna in shining armour and Brian Boru being depicted in elaborate body armour in some 19th century illustrations.

Weapons used for offensive purposes were developed from standard working tools such as the spear and axe. The spear (then called a *friach* or *crannuibh*) resembled a javelin in modern day terms. It was approximately five feet in length and was pointed with a sharp flint stone or fabricated metal point. It was fixed to the wrist by means of a long leather thong. The thong facilitated in recovering a thrown spear for immediate re-use.

The axe was an ancient weapon adapted from primitive tools when it was a crude implement with a heavy stone head fixed to a wooden handle. By the 11th century the axe was being made from sharpened and polished metal; its large chopping area gave it a fearsome appearance. Skilled axe men could deliver a devastating blow that would sever a limb with a single strike. And again the axe handle would have been attached to the wrist by means of a strong leather thong which was a crucial feature where loss or rapid recovery was vital during close quarter fighting.

A weapon developed solely for human combat was undoubtedly the sword. It was a long double edged knife of the single hand and double hand variety that was used as a slashing weapon during crowded fighting conditions. Brian Boru himself wielded a two-handed sword which could have been up to six feet in length. Swords of all types were prized possessions and would have been passed on to favoured clan members.

The Celts had a reputation as ferocious fighters and would not shirk their duty in time of battle. Certainly, the Dalcassian clans had a long history of daring warfare; they would not easily yield on the battlefield. They were fierce skirmishers and frenzy fighters but did not get involved in elaborate campaigns. When more sophisticated fighting methods came along (like those employed by the soon-to-arrive Normans) they had to change their fighting tactics or be defeated.

All the above-mentioned characteristics of the Irish kings and soldiers were detrimentally important factors when the Normans did invade the country. The lack of one central authority, individual greed, primitive warfare tactics, an unsophisticated infrastructure and clan squabbling at all levels all contributed to the slow fall from power that the Irish chieftains were to suffer. Ferocity in fighting was not enough to ensure that the clans would get their way. As we shall see, allies and strong political connections were vital.

When Donal More O'Brien became king of Thomond in AD 1168 he immediately engaged in the usual civil strife as practiced by his predecessors. He gave warning of his determination to succeed when he deprived his own brother, Brian na Sleibhe, of his sight. Such barbarous acts by the O'Briens at this time were not uncommon. He fought numerous battles with the King of Connaught, Rory O'Connor and they proved to be of a nature that was more than distasteful for O'Brien. O'Connor allied himself with O' Ruairc and came into Thomond to extract revenge for the earlier slaying of his half brother. Donal More was forced to pay 720 cows for the injustice he had committed and was left in a substantially weaker position than when he first campaigned against the Connaught allies.

Looking around for allies of his own Donal More O'Brien turned to a recent invader capable of supplying the military support he needed. This turning to the invader (nothing new) was not considered a threat to the country as a whole, simply because the vision of most chieftains did not extend beyond the borders of their own territories. Their ambitions were polluted by personal greed.

With regard to the coming of the Normans, the clans would have to deal with a more sophisticated force who once having conquered a territory did not simply lay the land to waste and ride off – they built fortifications with the intention of permanently colonizing the place.

The question arose, how would the Dalcassian clans of Clare fare against the sophisticated fighting machine that was the Normans from Wales and England? This coming of the Normans was the next highly significant event in the course of Clare's and Ireland's history.

Chapter 5

Kings and Normans
(1169–1342)

Although not strictly Clare history the following overview of Ireland's history does have a distinct bearing on subsequent events in Clare. For that reason it will now be lightly touched on.

Dermot MacMurrough's squabbles with O'Ruarck, Prince of Breffney, ended in the former fleeing to England for military assistance. Indeed he travelled through England, Wales and Normandy in search of Henry II of England to cajole him into supplying an army of invasion. Henry had more pressing distractions but with one eye on his Welsh Normans he thought it prudent to supply a small speculative force to keep his hand in. He provided 60 men in armour who landed in three ships at Bannow in Wexford under the knight, FitzStephen, on the first day of May in 1169. They were to remain camped there until support arrived.

The first contingent of Normans stormed Wexford with overwhelming success. Maurice FitzGerald soon supplied reinforcements. With more urgings from Dermot MacMurrough, Strongbow who was based in Wales sent over another contingent headed by Raymond le Gros, and they landed near Waterford on 1 May 1170. Further military successes were to follow this speculative expedition.

Strongbow, on the approval of Henry II of England, brought a large force of Welsh Normans and others to Ireland and landed at Passage near Waterford on 23 August 1170. The combined Norman forces along with MacMurrough and his allies stormed the Norse towns of Waterford, Wexford and Dublin. This consolidated the invaders' positions – the Irish lacked both disciplined troops and military organization on a grand scale to thwart them – if indeed they had any interest in doing so at all. The mail-clad knights on well-bred war horses looked and certainly were a superior fighting force. One sight of the knights by a bedraggled band of Irish skirmishers was enough to convince them of the futility of engaging in a head-on confrontation. The Irish soon learned to attack only when they could bring their guerilla/ambush tactics into play.

It is worth noting at this point the introduction of skilled archers for the first time in open warfare in Ireland. The Normans had at their disposal the longbow as well as the crossbow – both lethal weapons. Traditionally, the Irish fought with axe, lance and sword; they regarded the shooting of arrows as being beneath them. A small skilled fighting force of Normans would always gain the upper hand when it came to structured confrontation in an open space.

So, the Normans made quick inroads in the southeast of the country. The high king Rory O'Connor did not fight them on a large scale, preferring instead to test their mettle in skirmishes of little importance. However, he was hampered in his efforts by the troublesome O'Brien of Thomond. In order to chastise O'Brien, High King Rory O'Connor attacked Thomond from end to end, aided and abetted by lesser Connaught clans who ravaged the kingdom from Galway Bay to the River Shannon. Some of the clans who fought valiant rearguard actions on behalf of the O'Briens included the MacNamaras, the O'Liddys, the O'Gradys, O'Moloneys, MacInerneys and MacGraths along with many others. Those defensive clashes did inflict many casualties on the Connaught clans. During a desperate retreat they burned the bridge at Killaloe.

Henry II of England set sail from Milford Haven with a fleet of 240 small vessels containing up to 4,000 men. The force, which included knights, archers and war horses made landfall near Waterford on 18 October 1171. Strongbow (who had already rendered the garrison ineffective) handed the city over to Henry to set up a series of acknowledgements to consolidate Henry's standing in Ireland.

With Waterford secure Henry marched on Cashel where he produced a Bull from the Pope which more or less authorised him to conquer the Irish on behalf of the Church. Most of the local princes submitted to him, including O'Brien of Thomond. In fact, Donal More formally handed over control of Limerick city to the foreign king – an act which acknowledged Henry as his liege. Seemingly, O'Brien did not place undue importance on this submission for we note that life continued much as before in Thomond. Perhaps, Irish provincial kings saw no great difference in submitting to an English monarch over an Irish one. Whatever way O'Brien saw it this first English foothold in Munster was a critical step in the breakdown of Gaelic order. After establishing his authority in Dublin, Henry returned to England to answer a summons from the Pope regarding the murder of Thomas Becket. He left his Norman barons and knights in Ireland to keep matters in check – in fact they took a free hand in all matters.

Strongbow was determined to establish his authority in Munster as he had done in Leinster. With this purpose in mind he marched into Munster at the head of a large force of Normans and Danes. Donal More O'Brien and his contingent of Dalcassians waited for him near Thurles (seemingly he had quickly forgotten his allegiance to King Henry of England). The forces fought a head-on battle in which four Norman knights were slain and some 1,700 fighting men perished in this major conflict. It turned out to be a momentous victory for O'Brien who benefited from the support (for once) of the powerful O'Connor clans of Connaught.

The significance of the victory should not be overlooked – had the Irish princes capitalised on the Thurles achievement the course of Irish history might have turned out much differently. Alas it was not to be.

The resounding defeat shocked Strongbow. He recalled Raymond le Gros and his army from Wales and immediately dispatched them to O'Brien's stronghold in the city of Limerick. The intrepid Raymond le Gros forded the River Shannon in the shallows where King John's Castle now stands. The defenders, thinking they had gained some measure of safety by felling the bridges were dismayed to find le Gros and his men pouring into the city. Panic ensued and many fled their posts. The garrison quickly fell to the superior Norman strategy. Donal More O'Brien beat a hasty retreat to the safety of a clan fortification at Castleconnell where he accused his cousins of treachery. For this alleged betrayal he put out the eyes of his kinsmen, Dermot and Turlogh O'Brien. He also killed an O'Connor (the son of the prince of Corcomroe) who happed to be present.

Following those events Rory O'Connor, the generally recognized King of All Ireland, paid tribute to Henry of England as his king with certain rights in Ireland. Rory was not pleased with the support from Donal More so in retribution he once again ravaged Thomond and finally chased Donal More to Limerick and from there to Cashel. He was intercepted near Cashel by Raymond le Gros with supporting clans from Ossory. Although they fought gallantly the Dalcassians had to submit to le Gros who returned to Limerick with Donal More in a bid to arrive at an amicable solution. They received word that Strongbow had died; it prompted le Gros to return to Dublin. O'Brien was left in charge of Limerick. He soon became disenchanted with foreign interference in the administration of his own territory. Consequently he set the city alight stating that the place was only a stronghold for foreigners and as such was better destroyed.

In the year 1178 the Dalcassians saw fit to resume their ancestral struggle with the Eoghanachts of south Munster. The Thomond warriors scoured the province in search of their traditional enemy. As well as fleeing into every corner of Munster, the MacCarthys, the O'Collins and the O'Donovans escaped even into west Thomond in a bid to save their lives. Some of their surnames survive even to this day in Clare and are perhaps descendants of the above-mentioned clan members. It is interesting to note that individual clans were located in particular districts within Thomond. Clan territories can be identified with some accuracy since the time when various families adopted their own distinguishing surnames.

The O'Briens as the dominant clan had secured lands in many parts of Thomond but principally the territory around Killaloe and along the

Fergus towards Miltown-Malbay and up to Ennistymon. The MacNamaras (whose chief was later hereditary Lord Marshall of Thomond) owned nearly all of the eastern part of Thomond from Tulla down to Broadford, from the north of which they drove the O'Kennedy's across the Shannon. In their days of high power under the Gaelic system their own chiefs were styled the princes of East and West Clancuilean.

The O'Deas owned the country called Dysert O'Dea. Between them and the O'Brien's territories at Kilfarboy, along with the mighty MacGormans and O'Donnells of Clonderlaw, through to Inagh, Clouna, Kilnamona, Kilmaley (called Breintir, meaning no man's land) were fixed the MacClanchys at their traditional stronghold at Caher MacClanchy. Also there were the O'Hehirs and the MacBruidins or Brodys who were hereditary historians of Thomond.

The O'Quinns had the beautiful though not extensive territory around Corofin, while all the rest of north-west Clare out to the ocean belonged mainly to the O'Loughlins and the O'Connors. The O'Hallorans owned the country south-west of Tulla towards Ennis, while the O'Moloneys had the district north of it towards Galway. Between these and the O'Briens at Kincora, along the Bay of Scariff to the south and south-west of it were the O'Liddys as well as the O'Grady clan. In the same territories were the MacInerneys, the O'Malones and others of less note simply because they were fewer in number.

The family name of MacMahon (Mac Mathúna) of Thomond comes down from Mahon O'Brien a grandson of the legendary Brian Boru. The family territory was principally that of Corcobaskinn in West Clare. At least two of their once-held strongholds, Carrigaholt Castle and Clonderlaw Castle, stubbornly stand as prominent landmarks even to this day. Their chiefly line ended when their last chief would be killed at the Battle of Kinsale in Cork in 1602. The MacMahon family name is presently one of the most distinguished and numerous in the county.

We arrive at the year 1185 before the next event of significance is recorded. At that time, John (Lord of Ireland and a son of Henry II), came into Ireland at the head of a large well-equipped army. He was to have no direct bearing on events in Thomond and indeed left for England towards the end of that year without doing much except having annoyed many people in prominent positions.

However after John became king in England in 1189 he showed a more professional approach to administrative duties. One of those resulted in the orders for the construction of a castle at the Viking holding in Limerick; this structure is now known as King John's Castle. His action was instrumental in unseating the O'Briens who held Limerick as their capital. Consequently they moved the seat of Thomond to the remote Clonroad.

Although the Norman-English were gaining in power in the eastern part of Ireland they had yet to establish themselves in the Kingdom of Thomond. They began their western campaign by meddling in the affairs of the claimants to the Connaught throne. Donal More O'Brien was induced to side with them against his old enemies – and foolishly he was only too glad to oblige by participating in the plunder of Connaught

The Normans being wise to the ways of the Irish clans made a truce with the O'Connors in the province of Connaught shortly afterwards. They then turned and marched into Thomond where they burned and plundered Killaloe, and ransacked houses and churches. The tactic of switching allegiance to different Irish chieftains who were at loggerheads with each other was used to devastating effect by the Norman-English. In this way the foreigners generated much strife amongst the Irish thereby weakening them into fragmented and leaderless bands. The inability of the Irish princes to unify for the collective good was a byproduct of the clan hierarchical system. It was to have a truly disastrous effect on the development of the country as a whole.

To demonstrate what could have been accomplished by forming alliances, one incident is worth noting. John de Courcey (a prominent Norman) crossed the Shannon at the head of a powerful army, his objective being to subdue the entire western half of the country. Such was the alarm of the clans that they forgot old enmities and grouped together in defence of their territories. Without hesitation the Dalcassian and Connaught clans allied themselves to ambush the invading army in the Corlieu Mountains. This spontaneous force of fierce fighting men who were pitted against a better-equipped army literally slashed the Norman forces to pieces. Those that retreated were indeed lucky to escape with their lives as the Dalcassians and their allies made a bold bid to cut off their escape.

In spite of such reversals the invaders from Wales and England were not going to be shut out of the west especially when they had already brought the east of Ireland under control. By 1192 all Norman-English fighting forces had been mustered to overwhelm Ormond. Once that territory was secured they surged across the Shannon at the ford of Killaloe. Their plan was to sweep through the heartland of West Thomond in order to penetrate and subdue the kingdom by wrecking its very core.

In the flat plains south of Killaloe the Dalcassians regrouped and stood fast. After stern resistance they succeeded in pushing the Norman forces back across the Shannon. The Normans made a hasty retreat towards Thurles where the Dalcassians had earlier routed them in a fierce battle. Once again, the Thomond forces repeated their earlier success with another crushing defeat of the foreigner. The Thomond army did not pursue their enemies into Leinster because they feared that their Irish allies in there would attack them. Had the Irish of Leinster fully appreciated the significance of the event they might have sided with the Dalcassians; the foreign threat could have been broken at that point, although it is hard to refute the organization and military prowess of the Norman-English. On the other hand the small-minded attitude of the Irish chiefs was close to barbarism and did not augur well for compromise in the common interest.

However, one supposes that the concept of an all-Ireland nation was not as well formulated as it is today. Therefore, Donal More O'Brien had to be satisfied with ridding his Kingdom of Thomond of the Norman-English menace. He returned with his forces to the land of Thomond where a reasonable level of stability pertained for a short while.

19. The Franciscan (Abbey) Friary at Quin, County Clare. Pope Eugenius IV permitted friars of the strict observance there in 1433. It was built by the MacNamaras on the site of an incomplete Norman castle. (SFADCo)

Towards the end of his 26 year reign as king of the Ui Briain (O'Briens) of Thomond, Donal More Ua Brian (O'Brien) contented himself with the building of churches for his people. It was about this time that he commissioned the cathedral of Saint Mary in Limerick with the expectation that it would provide a burial place for him and his family.

When Donal More died in 1194 his eldest son, Murtagh Dall, took his place. Unfortunately, Murtagh was soon captured by the Norman-English and was deprived of his sight by them (hence the appellation 'Dall' from the Gaelic which means blind). Murtagh's brother, Conor Roe, was next inaugurated at Magh Adhair as the new King of Thomond.

It appears that there was no person strong enough to hold the position of ruler; we note that in 1198 that Conor Roe was dethroned. Finally, it was Donal More's third son, Donogh Cairbreach O'Brien, who finally established himself in the Thomond seat in the year 1201.

20. ***Ennis – its south-east prospect***

B. Lenthall's, the chief inn. D. Hall of Assizes. A. The Abbey or Friary
This is a view of the emerging town of Ennis drawn in 1681 from Dineley's Journal.
It was Donogh Cairbreach O'Brien who founded the Friary and consequently the town.

(Frost's History of Clare)

The Norman-English still endeavoured to gain a foothold in the Kingdom of West Thomond. Some minor incursions were made with a view to establishing a fortress in the district. In an effort to strengthen his forces in Ireland and to finally conquer the country King John landed at Crook near Waterford on 20 June 1210. He received submissions from a number of Irish chiefs though not all. The *Book of MacCarthaig* tells us that King John knighted Donnchad 'Cairbre' O'Brien, bestowing a lordship on him in return for an annual rent and securing the liberation of his brother and rival, Muirchertach Finn. The *Annals of Inisfallen* place stress on the fact that King John made a deal with the Ui Briain more than anything else (perhaps indicative of O'Brien's dominance).

The tribute that O'Brien reputedly paid to King John for recognizing him as supreme king in Ireland was 1,000 marks and a yearly sum of 100 pounds. That led King John to 'bestowing' the Kingship of Thomond on O'Brien. It must have seemed like a win-win situation to O'Brien because he was to retain his lands and gain an English title to boot. He could continue doing as he always had done – extract wealth from the lower ranking chiefs in servitude to him. Another concession given was that the Norman-English would be allowed build two castles in Thomond, one at

Roscrea and the other at Killaloe. Donnchad found it necessary to have a strong ally like King John because of the challenges from his brother Murtagh on the Kingship of Thomond. However, the presence of the English administration in Limerick was repugnant to Donnchad so he moved his place of royal residence to Clonroad on the banks of the Fergus near the present town of Ennis.

The Ennis area was not a significant place until Donnchad moved there around 1216. Therefore it could indeed be claimed that Donnchad Cairbreach (also 'Cairbre') O'Brien was the founder of the town. He built a large earthen and stone fort on a site near where the present Clonroad bridge now stands. Donnchad, by virtue of the title bestowed on him by King John is the direct ancestor of the titled earls and lords of Thomond, the Viscounts of Clare and the titled families of Inchiquin. He could be termed the first of The O'Briens or Royal O'Briens as we understand the term in modern parlance.

In 1224 a raging civil war erupted in Connaught between members of the O'Connor clans who fiercely contested a leadership power grab. It happened that Donnchad was an uncle of Hugh O'Connor who was one of the pretenders to the Connaught throne. The Dalcassian clans allied with Hugh's soldiers were strongly supported by a Norman-English contingent who jumped at the chance to instigate chaos. The opposing O'Neill clan were forced to retreat because of the strength of the alliance formed by O'Connor and the Dalcassians. It was an easy opportunity for the Thomond forces who plundered widely before returning home; no doubt they felt fully vindicated in getting revenge at the Connaught clans who were a constant thorn in their side.

In a retaliatory action some years later the Connaught clans, aided and abetted by the Norman-English, launched an assault on the Boirenn (Burren – stony place) district of Thomond. The most potent part of the military expertise came from the Norman-English contingent whose soldiers wore armour, had some mounted cavalry and possibly a number of archers in their midst. With such an advantage they easily overpowered the Thomond clans. Donnchad's tactics and leadership was criticized but he was at a disadvantage in such an open standoff engagement. He was not involved in anything more of note before his death in 1242.

Conor, who was a son of Donnchad Cairbreach O'Brien, became King of Thomond after his father's death. With the Norman-English in permanent garrison at Killaloe (the old seat of the O'Briens from the time of Brian Boru) Clonroad became the established royal residence of the O'Brien hierarchy.

Reputedly founded by Donnchad Cairbreach in 1240 the Franciscan Friary of Inis (Ennis) was certainly enhanced by his son Conor in 1247. As can be seen from the present-day ruins in Abbey Street in Ennis; it must have been an imposing structure in its time. During the centuries after its foundation it not only served the local community as a church but it also became a renowned centre of learning as well as a place of worship.

The commissioning of the monastery at Inis (Ennis) by Conor ensured the growth of a population centre there. At this time street towns were beginning to form around churches and other social centres; thus it was that the first streets of the town of Ennis came into being. Inis Cluain Ráda (meadow of long rowing) can be regarded as the capital of the county ever since. An explanation of the term 'the meadow of the long rowing' may be of interest. The River Fergus spilled into the low-lying marshy area at Clonroad and Ennis where there was no clear cut channel for rowing boats amongst the reeds and meadow grass . Indeed it was a long hard pull to get from one end to the other and as such it was memorable to boatmen as the meadow of the long rowing.

Neither did Conor O'Brien have an easy passage as Lord of Thomond – next we find him engaging the Norman-English (who were now active in his kingdom) in battle skirmishes throughout 1257. He is credited with killing a number of them in various sorties. We pause to wonder what happened to his pledge of allegiance to the English monarch and the pact between them? We can only conclude that such treaties were little more than 'holding strategies' while they regained positions of supremacy. Surely, Conor's warlike stance would have influenced other Irish chieftains? Irish history would suggest that little was learned from the stance taken by this leading Irish monarch who if allied with the northern O'Neills would have achieved national success as his ancestor Brian Boru had done before him.

A meeting was convened by all the Irish provincial kings at Cael Uisce on Lough Erne in 1258. This was a significant attempt to agree on a combined strategy against the common enemy. Conor was unable to attend so he sent his son, Teigue. It was agreed by the assembly that the country would benefit best from having one supreme ruler – one who would have at his command a national army. The two obvious contenders for the position of supreme commander were O'Neill from the north and O'Brien from the south – both traditional antagonists in vying for national leadership. O'Neill was favoured by the assembly but young Teigue of Thomond would not yield his father's claim. This was a momentous stance in Irish history – it was to have far-reaching significance for the ultimate control of the country.

Had Teigue O'Brien supported the selection of O'Neill it might have resulted in them ridding the country of the Norman-English powerhouse, although this is far from certain given the history of fragmented warfare in

Ireland. In any case it could not have been easy for the young son of Conor O'Brien to relinquish the O'Brien claim (effectively the High Kingship of Ireland) of his own volition. The most genuine explanation would be that it would be difficult for any O'Brien to accept that they were unworthy of the High Kingship given their historical association with that office. A more shallow reason for his decision is that he would have been aware that men were dying daily for far less-serious discretions. How could he have faced home with a creditable explanation? The tendency of the time was to act first and to perhaps ask questions later. He acquired the cognomen Teigue Cael Uisce after the event and died one year later without gaining any position of power in Thomond.

Hoping to take advantage of the confusion amongst the O'Brien ranks the Norman-English in south Munster crossed the Shannon and came into West Thomond (then a separate kingdom from East Thomond). They were intercepted by Conor and his Dalcassian allies at Kilbarron near Feakle. The foreigners were routed after many others had died in the fray. A son of Conor, Brian Roe, further avenged this latest assault by wiping out to the last man the Norman-English garrison at Castleconnell near Limerick.

Conor next saw fit to reduce to submission some of his Dalcassian clans in Thomond. He called on the clans of northeast Thomond and Ormond;

21. The reclining effigy of Conor O'Brien (Conor-na-Suidaine) in Corcomroe Abbey, slain at the Battle of Suidaine, 1267. Corcomroe Abbey (Cistercian) dates from the late 12th century when it was founded by Donal More O'Brien (Conor's grandfather).

(Brian Dinan)

this calling only meant one thing – the handing over of tributes. He then went into the Burren country where he met stern resistance from the O'Loughlins, the O'Deas, the O'Connors and the O'Hehirs. When he next encountered Conor Carach O'Loughlin at the wood of the Suidaine in the now parish of Drumcreehy a violent battle ensued. Conor O'Brien lost the battle and his life and from it gained the appellation Conor-na-Suidaine. He was buried (1267) in the Abbey of Corcomroe which had been built some time previously by his grandfather, Donal More O'Brien. In a monument placed over his tomb his reclining effigy is carved in limestone and may still be seen there in the ruins of Corcomroe Abbey.

Brian Roe O'Brien was quickly installed as the next King of Thomond. He, like most of his predecessors, busied himself chastising friend and foe alike. By now we assume these events to be commonplace and we will out of interest dwell a little more on foreign acquisitions in the Kingdom.

The Norman-English built a castle at Clarecastle on a strategic fording of the Fergus estuary situated in the flat plane where the river shallows. It is likely that both Clarecastle (then called Clár) and the county of Clare both take their names from this feature in the central part of the Kingdom of Thomond. The ruins of this castle are clearly visible near the current bridge there. The term 'clár atha' likely referred to the crossing point in the river in this flat plain of Thomond. It is the one feature that strikes occupants of river craft as they sail from the wide estuary into the narrowing river meandering through the flat marshland.

A nephew of Brian Roe O'Brien, a man called Turlogh was next to assert his right to the throne of Thomond. Brian Roe was forced to seek military assistance from Thomas de Clare, a son of the Earl of Gloucester. De Clare and Brian Roe marched a considerable force on the castle of Clonroad but they found that Turlogh was away soliciting support in the territory of Corcobaiscinn. Finding that he had now gained a foothold in West Thomond, the Englishman, de Clare, set about building Bunratty castle (1277) to hold and consolidate the lands he had acquired. Later that same year, de Clare enticed Brian Roe on some pretext or another to Bunratty castle where he was treacherously and cruelly killed. Religious oaths were sworn by de Clare that no harm would come to Brian Roe, but once inside the walls of the castle, the Dalcassian prince was immediately imprisoned. Brian Roe was subjected to the cruellest torture imaginable until he endured the horrific death of being drawn between horses until his limbs parted from his body.

In the following year the then ruling king, Turlogh, routed the Norman-English from the kingdom with the exception of a small contingent who held Bunratty. It was tragic that in doing so he was forced to burn St Finghin's Church in Quin where a party of them had taken refuge.

Something of particular interest was undertaken by Turlogh at this time. He constructed the first stone castle built by an Irish lord in Ireland. It was made in the Norman fashion, on the peninsula near the island of Inis (now Ennis). Even though the strategy of securing territory with a central impregnable stone fortress had been obvious to the Irish chieftains for at least 100 years, this was the first time that one of them adopted the practice. Regrettably, that very same castle of Clonroad was deliberately taken apart some 300 years later and not a single discernable trace of it remains today. Stones taken from Clonroad castle were used by the Gore family when they constructed their grand house at Derrymore, Tulla, some ten miles distant. Continuing in the building vein, Turlogh made many improvements to the 'convent' of Clonroad, always it seems with a view to enhancing the royal burial tomb where he and many of his lineage are entombed. It should not be forgotten that the chieftains' wives (the Queens of Thomond) were buried in the same vaults when they died.

During the years that followed there were many internecine struggles between members of the Thomond nobility to include Donogh and Donal Bawn O'Brien against de Clare and his Irish allies. Both suffered heavy defeats in battles at Dysert O'Dea at the hands of Murtagh O'Brien.

In 1311, Dermot, a grandson of Brian Roe, was inaugurated at Magh Adhair in contravention to the claim of his cousin Murtagh, the legal heir. The Norman-English knight Thomas de Clare continued to stir up the pot of Irish turmoil, but his day of recompense was soon to arrive. While leading a large contingent of well-armed Norman soldiers through Thomond they became ensnared in the difficult terrain around Dysert O'Dea and were subsequently assaulted by an impromptu alliance of local clan members. The Irish won a decisive victory over the foreigners on 13 May 1318. One of the local chiefs slew de Clare, and it is said that de Clare's body was hacked to pieces in a fit of rage. De Clare's widow burned Bunratty Castle (mostly a wooden structure at the time); she then fled to England with as many valuables as she could carry and did not return to Ireland again.

It was this action that broke the Anglo-Norman dominance in Thomond for the next two centuries. After the crushing defeat at Dysert O'Dea the English rulers realised that Thomond was not the easiest place to conquer. Brian Bawn O'Brien and Mahon of Inchiquin retired to East Thomond (or Ormond which is now North Tipperary). Meanwhile Murtagh reigned on as the undisputed prince of Thomond (the present county of Clare). He died in 1343 after a successful and relatively long reign of more than 30 years. All along the O'Briens were ably supported by the second most powerful clan in Thomond, the MacNamaras, who held much of East Clare from Tulla down to the mighty River Shannon.

How had the local clans fared against the sophisticated fighting Normans from England and Wales? Truth to tell it was a mixed bag really. The Dalcassians got the upper hand in most of the contests, but this was probably due to engagements in small pitched battles and frenzied ambushes – and certainly not in any large formal confrontations. The Normans were heavily armoured and employed well-drilled tactics, often supplementing their arsenals with crossbows and longbows. The Irish clans, who dismissed arrows as being little more than a nuisance, had scant regard for their personal protection. Most refused to wear iron helmets, mail or other body armour. Their hearts' delight was a good old fashioned hand-to-hand battle fought in a large clearing until they were exhausted or killed. Nevertheless they were adept at melting into wooded terrain and periodically breaking out in devastating ambush.

*22. **Armoured Norman knight on horseback, c 1225.***
1. Norman knight on horse back. 2. Irish wood kern flings spear. 3. Foot soldier.
(Wikipedia)

According to one historian, when the Irish fighter encountered a man in armour on horseback he preferred to use his polished iron axe. The axe was held in one hand with the thumb extended along its shaft. Because they were unable to reach to the head of a soldier advancing on horseback they would strike a swift downward blow into the rider's thigh. A well-delivered blow would sever the leg from the body. This resulted in the limb falling to one side while the body fell lifeless to the other side of the horse.

Irish fighting men of the time also carried a few short spears and two javelins. When all else failed they would not hesitate to use stones picked from the ground. Instead of body armour the Irish soldier fought mostly in linen and woollen tunics.

In sharp contrast to the Irish the Norman soldier came well equipped with body armour, large pikes, heavy swords, cavalry and backup units of archers. Little wonder then that the Irish were reluctant to employ structured military formations against them.

The Normans first conquered territory and then held it from the central vantage points of castles and fortresses, which were situated in elevated or difficult-to-reach locations. Later, the Irish but especially the MacNamaras in Thomond, adopted the use of stone castles to good effect. County Clare was eventually to become the county with the most castles in Ireland. The MacNamaras were pre-eminent castle builders; even to the present day their name is associated with similar large-scale constructions both in Ireland and abroad.

Getting into the middle of the 14th century the Norman-English presence had, after 175 years , been well established in Ireland if not in Thomond. It was obvious that the foreigners were not about to quit to the country any time soon. The fact that the Normans had often intermarried with the Irish made the situation more complex. The English/Normans were by then installing their administration and getting to grips with ruling the country. For the next 200 years or so ruling structures moved inexorably towards England gaining total power in the country; those events will be highlighted in the coming chapter.

Chapter 6

English takeover
(1343–1580)

During this period of Clare history the usual local disorders took place but much of it is without significance; so only events which impacted the course of Clare history will be looked at.

On the death of Murtagh, Brian Bawn O'Brien took over as the new king in Thomond. He ruled peacefully until he was treacherously slain in 1350 by clan Keogh in a place east of the River Shannon. Dermot reigned next without registering anything of note until Mahon Moinmoy wrested the seat from him by force. Mahon wore the crown with some dissension but most notably he was responsible for imposing a yearly levy or 'Black Rent' on the English of Munster. We can tell from this occurrence alone that the O'Briens were still the power masters in Munster.

When Mahon died in 1367 his brother Turlogh Maoel became the next king. His reign lasted barely three years before he was driven out by Brian Catha-an-Aenagh.

Another O'Brien pretender, Turlogh, crossed into Limerick to seek aid from Garrett Earl of Desmond who received him favourably. Before Turlogh with his Irish and Norman-Irish allies could invade West Thomond he found Brian at the head of a large force of O'Briens and MacNamaras advancing to cut him off at Croom (in County Limerick). Many of the Desmond men were slain in a battle in which their army suffered a heavy defeat. John FitzNicholas, Sir Thomas FitzJohn, the Earl of Desmond, as well as many other nobles were taken prisoner. The Dalcassians further sacked Limerick city and left Sheeda Cam MacNamara in charge of it. He was later murdered by some of the English who had remained on in the city.

In 1394 Richard II of England landed in the east of the country with a force of 34,000 fighting men. With this huge army in evidence the Irish princes (Brian O'Brien included) showed good sense in paying mock homage to Richard. No material effect was made by Richard's army in Thomond and seemingly life went on as before. When the English king paid a second visit in 1399 he made an even lesser impact in the country. Brian O'Brien, King of Thomond, died in that same year. His reign was thought to be a peaceful one but most notably his death was not marked by violence of any kind. His brother Conor then took over and he reigned without anything of note happening until he died in 1426.

The year 1433 is given as the year of completion for the beautiful Franciscan Friary (Abbey) at Quin. Its well preserved ruins are a singular attraction even to the present day. The cloister was commissioned by Sheeda Cam MacNamara who requested that the friary was to be his preferred burial place. The same Sheeda Cam was also responsible for additional construction at Ennis Friary including the cloister there.

After Conor O'Brien's death in 1426, Teigue-na-Glenmore became the new prince; he managed to govern without us learning anything more about him. There was a juggling for power during the next few years between first, Mahon Dall (the blind) and Turlogh Bog (the soft) which continued intermittently until 1459. A two year reign by Mahon's son, Donogh, ended with Teigue-an-Chomhaid (of Coad on the lake of Inchiquin) in control. It was Teigue who built the beautiful castle residence by Lake Inchiquin.

During this particular period the English presence became weak in Thomond. The O'Briens continued to enforce the Black Rent on the English which their ancestor Mahon Moinmoy had first imposed on them. The rent was in payment for land occupied. The O'Briens felt themselves in such a position of power that Teigue considered himself ready to challenge for the High Kingship of the country.

The time-honoured way to challenge for the high kingship was that which their glorious ancestor the great Brian Boru had perfected when he marched on circuits of the country to bring all subservient kings and their clans to heel. Teigue's campaign began when he brought a huge army of followers into south Munster. En route he took control of the entire present county of Limerick. He imposed a yearly rent of 60 marks on their chiefs there to be payable forever to him. Being satisfied that Limerick was well and truly subdued he moved on to the old battle grounds of Ossory and Leinster where he scored more successes. When a hard winter began to draw in he was obliged to return to West Thomond by way of Limerick. This campaign established him as the strongest ruler in Leath Mogha, which was recognized as the southern half of the country. Had he not died that year we might very well have seen a return of an Ard Righ (High King) to Ireland and to Thomond.

Conor-na-Srona (of the great nose) who was a brother of Teigue became the next King of Thomond. His reign kicked off when he and his relative, MacWilliam of Clanrickard, waged war against the O'Kellys of Hy Many, the O'Donnells and the MacWilliam Eighter. Conor's Dalcassians won a major battle against their neighbours near Galway. Unbelievably, peace prevailed for more than 20 years thereafter in the Kingdom of Thomond.

In 1483 Mahon O'Griffy, who was Bishop of Killaloe, died and was buried on an island at the mouth of the River Fergus. His body was interred in the Abbey of the Canons Regular of St Augustine on that island in the

Fergus estuary. It was from that time onwards that the island became known locally and popularly as Canon Island.

As the 15th century drew to a close the Earl of Kildare became enraged with the Dalcassians of Thomond. They were, it seems, guilty of supporting a spurious claimant to the Ormond seat in preference to the legitimate heir who happened to be married to the Earl's sister. The Earl brought a large army to the Shannon at Killaloe where he crossed into MacNamara territory in the east of Thomond. They first captured a castle at Ballycullen and placed a garrison there. Then they marched on Conor O'Brien's fortress at Clonroad. However the hastily-summoned Dalcassian clans intercepted the Earl's forces and confronted them and their allies near Quin. It was at Ballyhickey Castle that the forces met in a head-on battle. After a protracted encounter the Thomond forces eventually came out on top. This routing of such a strong invader left Thomond without threat of takeover for some years to come. The last important act of Conor-na-Srona was his capturing of Fineen MacNamara's castle near Quin. After a reign of 30 years, Conor of the Great Nose eventually died in the year 1496.

As we move into the 16th century it becomes noticeable that the original Dalcassian clans continued to retain possession of their long-held clan homelands. The O'Briens and the MacNamaras were the principal clans both in strength of numbers and in ruling authority. Much of Thomond belonged to the Ui Briain (O'Briens), to include the district around Inchiquin, some parts of Tradaree, lands on the west coast around Doonbeg, Miltown, Ennistymon, Bunratty, Dromoland and lands around the islands of Ennis in the centre of their Kingdom.

By this time the MacNamaras had become adept at building stone castles which were sprouting up in all territories. They became the possessors of the greatest number of castles in West Thomond. Timber (which was still very plentiful) would have been the material used by the lowly clan members to construct crude and easily-moveable dwellings. Although the design of castles and churches had grown in physical size they were without the elaborate ornamentation seen on the continent. The Irish churches and castles were more practical than ornate.

The next monarch of Thomond after Conor-na-Srona was Turlogh Gilla Dubh. His reigned lasted for the short period of three years and three months with nothing of note being recorded of him. Gilla Dubh was succeeded by his nephew, Turlogh Don (of the yellow hair) who was a totally different prospect to his uncle. He was immediately at war with the rulers in Limerick, a settlement which he promptly burned and looted with impunity.

Some time later an uncle of Turlogh O'Brien, a man called MacWilliam of Clanrickard, seized a number of castles belonging to the O'Kellys of Hy

Many. The O'Kellys called on the Lord Justice Kildare (who had no great affection for Clanrickard) to assist them. Garrett, the Lord Justice Kildare, brought an army from the east and north to include the forces of Hugh Roe O'Donnell and his son. Also present was MacDermot, Lord of Moylurg, with his followers. They and many lesser clans made a forced march on Clanrickard. MacWilliam then urgently requested assistance from Turlogh O'Brien and his Dalcassian clans and also from Mulrony O'Carroll who was Lord of Ely – and from many more of the Ormond clans. Everything was set for the mother of all battles.

The forces met at Knockdoe eight mile north-west of Galway city on 19 August 1504. An estimated 2,000 Thomond troops were killed in a bitter and protracted struggle. Little quarter was given or taken during the course of the battle. The small number of English archers in attendance stayed well clear of the main fighting arena. The English did not suffer casualties but no doubt they were delighted at the sight of the Irish weakening each other in so terrible a feud. Such were the cries and clamour from the hotly-contesting armies that the din of battle was heard a number of miles away. Finally the Dalcassians and Clanrickard were forced to withdraw even though losses on both sides were roughly equal.

The effect of the Battle of Knockdoe was to greatly weaken the Thomond Kingdom. The clans realized that they had put their territory in great jeopardy by the wasteful reduction of their numbers. Fortunately, the English were also without strength in depth so they did not contemplate mounting an attack on the territory of Thomond for some.

By the year 1508, Lord Kildare was back campaigning in Munster in an attempt to consolidate English rule in the province. Having subdued Cork without undue effort he marched on Limerick. From their peninsular kingdom north of Limerick the Dalcassians carefully monitored Kildare's movements. Massed on the northern banks was the massive contingent of MacNamaras, proud, fierce and chanting war cries in readiness for battle. The O'Brien fighters were also strong in attendance as were the O'Deas, the O'Hehirs, the O'Quinns, MacInerneys and indeed all of the other clans of the West Thomond Kingdom. MacWilliam of Clanrickard, as well he might have, assembled his entire fighting force and came to the assistance of Turlogh O'Brien and his allies. This should be considered a formidable gathering of warring parties.

From the south came Lord Kildare to destroy the wooden bridge at Portoroise which was a fording place in the Shannon at Castleconnell. Not to be outwitted the Dalcassian army crossed the Shannon higher up at Killaloe and made a day-long march down the south bank towards Castleconnell. When they came near to Kildare's forces at dusk they made camp for the night. The opposing forces were billeted so closely that they

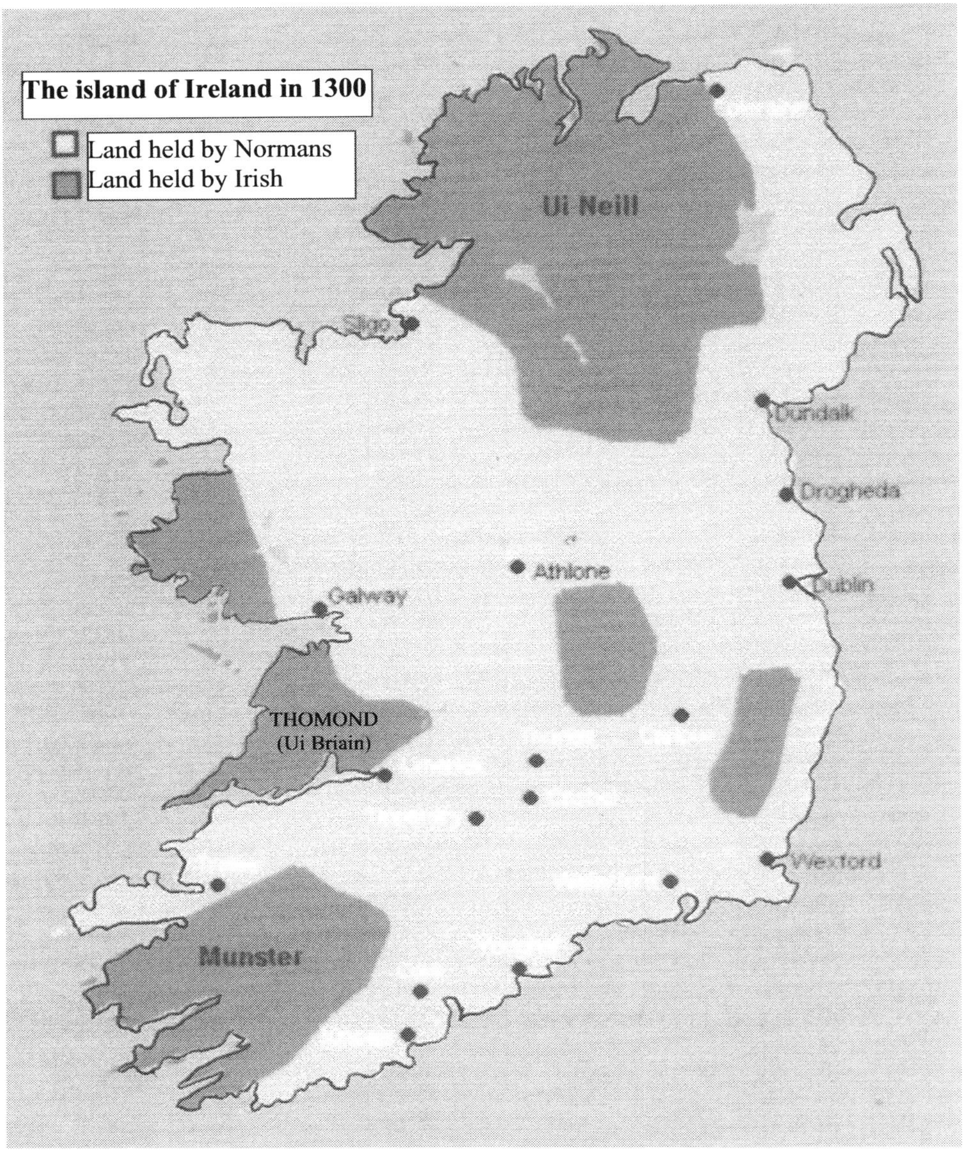

23. ***Norman control of Ireland is indicated on the above map for the year 1300.***

The darker areas show the territories held by the native or Gaelic Irish princes. The Normans had annexed most of the country. Most significantly the Thomond territory (the present County Clare) belonging to the Ui Briain is held by the Irish. This is in spite of the Normans constructing castles in Clare most of which the Irish either confiscated or demolished.

(Wikipedia)

could hear each other speak during the night. Early in the morning Kildare withdrew abruptly towards Limerick, probably seeking a vantage point from which to make his main stand. Before Kildare's men could settle the Thomond and Connaught clans overtook them. After a long day of heavy fighting the English and their Irish allies suffered a narrow defeat at the hands of O'Brien's forces. The encounter left a lasting impression in the mind of Kildare to the extent that in the future both he and his son who succeeded him avoided all situations where an engagement with O'Brien of Thomond and his allies was likely.

From 1510 until 1522 life was comparatively uneventful in Thomond under the kingship of Torlogh Don. In 1523 a speculative contingent of Dalcassian fighters went to the north of Ireland to assist O'Neill against O'Donnell. The forces failed to combine in forming an effective fighting unit which resulted in O'Neill losing 900 men. The Dalcassians effected a hasty if unlikely retreat back to the safety of Thomond. No doubt O'Neill would not have been enamoured with O'Brien's contribution.

It is worth recording a signal event which took place around 1524. Prince Butler, Lord of Ormond, made war on a force of Dalcassians under Teigue, son of Turlogh Don, near Cashel in Tipperary. During the fray the young prince was struck down by a shot of ball resulting in him being carried from the battlefield. Presumably the shot was discharged from a musket and it was the first time that the use of firearms was recorded in Irish warfare. Teigue's body was returned to the Friary (Abbey) of Ennis where it was interred in the vault of his ancestors. Teigue's father, King Turlogh, died in 1528 and he was laid to rest beside his son in the Royal O'Brien tomb in the chancel of Ennis Friary.

As well as Teigue, Reignault who was the wife of Turlogh and therefore Queen of Thomond, also had many more sons. The most famous of the sons was Conor the succeeding prince and Murrogh-par-Excellence who was the Tanist. From Conor are descended the Earls of Thomond. It is from Murrogh that the Barons of Inchiquin, the titled O'Brien Princes of Dromoland, and those of Blatherwycke, Glencolumbkille (and many other significant branches) are descended.

Conor then became King of Thomond and married twice. Donogh the Fat was the only son of his first marriage to Arabella de Burg, a daughter of MacWilliam of Clanrickard. From his second marriage to a sister of the Earl of Desmond he was father to Sir Donal O'Brien and to Sir Turlogh.

About this time, Henry VIII of England was becoming concerned about the close relationship that the Earl of Kildare (now considered Norman-Irish) was fostering with the Irish. He summoned the Earl to London and then imprisoned him in the Tower of London. His son, Silken Thomas FirzGerald panicked and organised a rebellion in support of his father. The rebellion was badly supported by the Irish so when Sir William Skeffington the Lord Deputy came to Ireland in 1529 he had little difficulty in quelling the revolt. Silken Thomas fled to Thomond for his own safety. Such was the strength, independence and remoteness of the kingdom that he felt it was the surest place of refuge. His family and friends were guests at Clonroad Castle for six months, surely an indication of the grandeur, independence and safety of Clonroad Castle at that time. Alas no vestige of Clonroad Castle now remains.

In time Silken Thomas surrendered to Lord Grey whereupon he was also sent to the Tower of London. After a long internment he and five of his uncles were executed. A 12 year-old son of Silken Thomas remained on in Clonroad Castle under the protection of Conor O'Brien. This purge of Geraldine power considerably weakened the overall position of the Irish nobility. More than ever before they were in danger of being completely subjugated by the English forces in Ireland.

Henry did not take kindly to the contempt shown to his rule in Ireland by the O'Briens. He ordered the Lord Deputy, Lord Leonard Grey, to move on Thomond and to extract some measure of submission from the Dalcassian clans. The Lord Deputy came as far as Limerick and captured the castle of Carrigoguinnell in 1536. Lord Grey received token support from Donogh O'Brien in capturing that fortress. Noticeably, some of the Irish nobility were beginning to show a willingness to declare for the English side. The following year witnessed the English forces once again campaigning in Thomond. The adjacent territory of Ormond was relinquished without resistance and in June of the same year the Danish and English settlers of Limerick gladly handed over that city to Lord Leonard Grey.

Conor O'Brien met the Lord Deputy at Limerick where some tacit arrangement was settled upon. O'Brien undertook to chastise his rebellious brother, Murrogh the Tanist, who was probably being supported by the MacNamara clan. Again, it may have been a stalling tactic by O'Brien because we know by now his modus operandi with the English was always one of intransigence.

Seemingly as part of the 'arrangement' Grey's forces were allowed march into Thomond and on to Clare where they took possession of Donogh's castle there. It was the first occasion that the local clans had seen that fearsome war machine – the cannon – and perhaps because of it resistance was practically non-existent. The English contingent pushed on towards Galway, notably bypassing the O'Brien palace at Clonroad, which may have been part of the 'arrangement'. Further on, Grey's army passed unmolested across the O'Dea lands in north Thomond.

In spite of all the jockeying for position this was the first substantial footing gained by the English in West Thomond since the days of Thomas de Clare back in the latter part of the 13th century. Conor O'Brien had in effect given a partial submission to the English ruler. With the Ormond princes capitulating in East Thomond it had become increasingly difficult for the O'Briens to hold West Thomond. Conor died two years later in 1539 barely holding on to the title of King of West Thomond but significantly with the distinction of being the last descendant of the great Brian Boru to have that honour.

Up until this point in history the people of Thomond enjoyed freedom in their territory within the clan system. The Church also had its own measure of independence with the right to receive gifts of lands from the nobility. In order to gain complete control of people's lives the English administration introduced their own system of land ownership and a Protestant Church as the 'official' religion – just as Henry VIII had done in England. On 1 May 1537 the English monarch was officially declared to be head of the church in Ireland.

As happened in England monasteries were sacked, closed or converted for other use; this was the case with Ennis Friary. While O'Brien did his best to keep the Friary functioning as a Catholic church offering spiritual services to the people the new administration continually pressurized him. O'Brien and Henry never really saw eye to eye so O'Brien allowed the friars to remain in the abbey and practice their religion in spite of Henry's edicts. This they did intermittently for many more years.

Eventually, Murrogh the Tanist O'Brien surrendered his Kingdom to the Lord Deputy and gave his allegiance to Henry VIII when he went over to Greenwich where he was made Earl of Thomond on 1 July 1543. For the first time control of Thomond had been transferred to the English administration. Henry made him Earl of Thomond and Baron Inchiquin. That enactment demolished the Brehon Laws and Irish control over the administration of the Thomond Kingdom.

Donough O'Brien, 4th Earl of Thomond, was known as The Great Earl. He later abandoned Clonroad Castle for the secure Bunratty. Was married to Helen Roche, also to Elizabeth FitzGerald. His actions spelled the end of Gaelic Thomond.

The custom for 20 or so of the previous kings of Thomond was to be buried in the Friary which they had founded at Inis-an-Laoigh (Ennis). Donough, having been reared in the Anglican faith in England, choose to be buried in St Mary's Protestant Cathedral in Limerick.

24. Donough O'Brien, 4th Earl of Thomond, known as The Great Earl.

('The Franciscans in Ennis')

Murrogh, like all the other Irish princes had been bribed with gifts of lands and titles for himself for his extended family and for his descendents 'forever'. The supporting Thomond monarchs then realised that their days as local chiefs and rulers were also numbered so they followed the example of the O'Briens. Sheeda MacNamara requested a peerage and asked that his lands be transferred over to him in the English system of fee simple. The latter wish was granted but he was knighted instead of receiving the higher title of peerage.

Grants of church lands were made by the English to its new nobility, the land having been acquired by the recent suppression of abbeys and monasteries. Yet up until Murrogh died in 1551 the English made no other impression in Thomond. However, the structure for change had been put in place when the English titles were accepted. The big change from clan ownership of Irish land to individual titled ownership which the English controlled paved the way for a complete English takeover.

When Murrough O'Brien's title of Earl of Thomond was made hereditary by King Henry VIII in 1543 his relatives realised they would have no chance of assuming power on his death. The English arrangement of titles descending through the eldest son would see an end to that.

Donal and Turlogh O'Brien attacked Donogh in his fortress at Clonroad during the dead of night. Donogh scrambled to the safety of his tower but he did suffer some grave wounds in the process. The enraged brothers then plundered and burned the town of Ennis. A few weeks later on Passion Sunday Donogh died; he was immediately succeeded by Donal O'Brien who was ancestor to the Ennistymon O'Briens. No sooner had Donal taken control when he struck out to re-assert Dalcassian (ostensibly now O'Brien) authority. He made raids into Leinster and returned home by way of Clanrickard where he did considerable damage to castles and livestock. Donald's usurpation did not go unnoticed by the English administration. In 1558, the Earl of Essex with a very well equipped army marched into Thomond hell bent on teaching the troublesome O'Brien a lesson. Donal O'Brien then realised that he had been out manoeuvred so he did not resist when Essex confiscated the castles of Bunratty, Clare, and Inis (Cluain Ramhfhada). He knew then that his days were also numbered.

Donal and his family were forced to flee to Maguire of Fermanagh in the north of the country for protection. His nephew Conor, who was an old protagonist, was installed as the next Earl. Conor complied with the English stipulation of renouncing all the ancient Dalcassian rights in return for the English feudal rights of Thomond. This official act of renunciation was performed in the Cathedral of Limerick after High Mass on 10 July 1558. The event really brought home to the other chiefs the significance of the new position. No longer would they have power over their own lands and people. Instead they would now be ruled by an agent of the English monarchy – the Earl of Thomond – who was determined to invoke English law for his own personal benefit.

Many native rebellions and disgruntlements arose as a consequence. The most prominent dissenters in Thomond were Donogh of Inchiquin and Teigue who called for assistance from his kinsman, the Earl of Desmond. Conor laid siege on Donogh's castle at Inchiquin. Before he could make any impression on the fortress the siege was lifted when the Earl of Desmond arrived with his army. Conor withdrew to Clanrickard where he received succour from the Earl there. Eventually both forces engaged in a dour encounter at Spancilhill resulting in both the Earl of Thomond and Clanrickard jointly suffering a heavy defeat. Many of the O'Briens and MacNamaras fell at the battle of Spancilhill which was fought in June of 1559. After Spancilhill, Donogh and Teigue were restored to Inchiquin and to their other properties.

In the interim and to sustain himself Conor had to content himself with raids outside of Thomond. When he learned that Donal had returned from Fermanagh he immediately rushed back to Thomond. On his arrival Donal was supported by the brothers Teigue and Donogh in raids throughout West Thomond. Their most notorious action was an attack on the castle of Rossroe in Clancuilean (Sixmilebridge) where the Earl happened to be staying at the time. The nearby town was looted and burned with up to a hundred of the Earl's men being killed in the ensuing skirmish.

A great outcry of disgust arose from every corner of West Thomond so much so that the enemies of the Earl were pursued from all sides. Donal and Teigue escaped across the Fergus and felt so pressed that they had to employ mercenaries from Clan Sheedy and Clan Sweeney in order to save their skins. When the Earl of Thomond – with the assistance of English artillery – bombarded and levelled the castle at Ballyalla the county was divided between the two forces. The Earl held Ennis and the lands to the east as far as the Shannon. Donal and Teigue (Murrogh's sons) on the other side held all of what is now west Clare. It was not surprising to learn that the O'Brien feuding only weakened Thomond further.

Turlogh O'Brien who was bishop of Killaloe at the time had not been leading an exemplary life by all accounts. Merchants in Galway went on record to complain that, 'on the borders of Thomond, certain outlaws, being bastards of the Bishop of Killaloe, robbed all travellers'. Consequently when the said bishop died in 1569, the English were delighted to receive a request from Mac O'Brien of Ara to have his son appointed to the bishopric. That petition was granted with letters patent and writs issued. It was the first attempt by the English to install a Protestant bishop in West Thomond. They also thought it opportune to have a public display of their new-found authority in the district. With this in mind, Sir Edward Fitton, who was President of Connaught (Thomond was administratively attached to Connaught at this time) proclaimed that an assizes was to be held in Ennis in February 1570.

Teigue O' Brien, a son of Murrogh of Inchiquin who was the first Sheriff of Clare, arranged for the hearing to be held in the Franciscan Monastery [sic] of Ennis. The court went into session without Conor the Earl of Thomond making an appearance – it was much to the consternation of Sir Edward Fitton to say the very least of it.

On the third day of the sessions a cavalry detachment was sent to his castle at Clare (Clarecastle) some two miles away. When the military detachment entered the castle's courtyard the gates ominously closed behind them. Those captured within the courtyard were detained while those left outside were killed. Facing such outrageous behaviour from the Earl it was little wonder that Sir Edward beat a hasty retreat back to

25. The old Franciscan Friary (The Abbey) of Ennis. Founded by the O'Briens in the 13th century. The South transept and central tower were added in the 15th century.
(SFADCo)

Galway. Not to be denied, the Earl gave hot pursuit and would have killed more of Fitton's party only for they reached the safety of Gort Castle before the quarrelsome Earl could get his hands on them. It would seem that the unpredictable Earl was either displaying great patriotism or that he did not have a clear-cut view of his true predicament. His position of authority was a perilous one and would not be allowed to remain as we shall soon see. Not at all pleased with the Earl's conduct the English administration decided to chastise him for his outrages by sending a large army led by the Earl of Ormond into West Thomond in a desperate attempt to bring the non-conforming O'Brien to heel.

Due to the fact that both earls were related it was easier for them to parley rather than fight. The outcome of the talks was significant and indeed may have been to O'Brien's advantage in the long run. O'Brien surrendered all his castles without a whimper. He immediately went into exile in France while the Earl of Ormond subjected O'Brien's territory to English control. It would seem that such a humiliating defeat may have been too much for O'Brien to stomach.

However, the durable Conor was not done yet. In the following year he is in the court of Queen Elizabeth of England begging her majesty's pardon for past misdeeds. He appears to have won her over for in 1571 we find that he is re-installed as Earl of Thomond and this time with a more favourable outlook towards the Crown. When Sit Edward Fitton came down from Connaught in 1572 to hold his assizes, Conor was much more co-operative than at any time previously.

To give a more 'atmospheric' snapshot of this period, the following extracts from *Frost's History of Clare* are included here:

QUARRELS OF THE O'BRIENS

In 1573, for some reason not known to us, a war broke out between the O'Briens themselves. It is needless to say that the quarrel was taken up by their partisans on all sides, and that a general plunder of the country was the consequence. What the dispute was about is of very little importance, but in their description of the fighting, the Four Masters give the names of several places in the county, according to their original spelling, which we here reproduce as illustrative of its topography. One of the belligerent parties assembled at Ard-na-Cabóg, near Clare Castle. Thence they marched through Drumcliff, Kilnamona, and Dysert, and 'over the same road of Coradh-Finne (Corofin), by the gate of the Castle of Inchiquin, and by Bothar-na-mac Riogh' (the road from Corofin to Killinaboy, called the road of the king's sons, for some reason with which we are unacquainted). They despoiled the church of Cill-inghine-Boaith (Killinaboy) and proceeded in a north-westerly direction, by the confines of Corcomroe and Burren; spreading themselves about, they plundered the country in all directions. Their opponents mustered their forces at Carn-mic-Tail, now Carn-Connachtach, but they had to retire from that place early next morning, their invaders then approaching by way of Slaibh-na-ngroigheadh, keeping Bél-atha-an-Ghobhain (Smithstown), on their left. Both armies – one in pursuit of the other, then marched by Cill Mainchin to Bél-an-chip. There a skirmish took place and one party retreating before their antagonists, by way of Beann Formaile, both arrived at Caherush (Cathair Ruis).

ANOTHER ASSIZES AT ENNIS

Having in view the final subjugation of the Irish of Munster, the Lord Deputy, Sir Henry Sidney, made a progress through that province in 1576. He abolished the ancient customs of 'Coigny, Kernetty and Bonaght', and ordered that the rules of English law should be substituted for them. He made Donal O'Brien of Ennistymon, Governor of the County of Clare and the new ruler signalled his accession to the office by hanging refractory rebels and malefactors. In this year, Thomond was separated from Connaught and joined to Munster, at the solicitation of the Earl of Thomond. In the following year, Sir William Drury, who had been recently appointed President of Munster and who had, at Limerick, hanged several of the gentlemen and common people of the O'Briens, held an assizes at Ennis which lasted for eight days. He left the county, after he had appointed a marshal to compel the inhabitants to pay tribute of ten pounds for each Barony to the Queen, an impost wholly unknown to the Dal gCais up to that time. The lands of the Earl of Thomond were not exempt from payment, although he had proceeded to England to obtain that favour, as well as to complain of the injury and injustice done to him by his kinsmen. His journey, however, was not quite unproductive of advantage. He obtained from Elizabeth a renewed grant of all his lands, pardon for his people and a patent conveying to him most of the church lands and livings of the county. He did not long survive his return home, for his death occurred in 1580, his age being forty five years, during twenty two of which he enjoyed the chieftainship of his race. He was buried in the abbey of Ennis, and his eldest son Donogh succeeded, as fourth Earl of Thomond.

[End of transcripts from 'Frost's History of Clare']

The new Earl had been educated in England so not surprisingly he proved to be pro-English in outlook and in his activities. Both he and his father, Conor, had deviated from the spirit of the clans that had supported their kin down through the generations. When they accepted the new system it made them agents of the Crown and banished forever the Gaelic Brehon Laws.

It was at this time that the capital of Thomond was decided upon. The English queen instructed the President of Connaught to divide the county into baronies and to nominate a capital town. Clarecastle would have been the most suitable location but the Earl of Thomond insisted on keeping it for himself. Ennis was chosen because it came to prominence during the assizes and the location was developed when the O'Briens had their seat of power at nearby Clonroad.

An incident then occurred which warrants special mention. Donogh Beg O'Brien who took part in the Clanrickard rebellion fell into the hands of the Sheriff of Clare. Cruise, the Sheriff, delivered Donogh Beg to the new Lord Deputy, Sir John Perrot, who was in Quin receiving submissions from insurgents. As an example of his justice he first half hanged Donogh Beg

O'Brien from the shafts of a car. His body was then crushed and mangled by blows of a heavy axe. Most of his bones were broken. Next, his battered and bleeding body was carried to the tower of Quin Abbey and was fastened high upon it as a feast for the birds of the air. It is not recorded how long the corpse remained upon the tower.

As the 16th century drew to a close administration in West Thomond underwent traumatic structural changes. It saw the beginning of governing the territory like an English county. The land of Thomond became officially known as County Clare and consequently was reattached to its historic base of Muma (Munster). This indeed did signal the end of the 2,000 year old system of the Brehon Laws of succession. In its place came individual ownership, parchments and letters patent, lawyers and administrators all to bewilder the native Irish. Thomond and the Gaelic clans started to fade away forever.

It could be said that clan ownership of lands, rulers whose succession was decided by the sword, pillage and plunder as a means of maintaining positions of power had all retarded material progress. Savagery and the battle axe had been the instruments of rule and as such they had left the vulnerable without protection. For who would farm extensively only to have his crops destroyed by marauders? Who would build a better house only to have it burned to the ground by pillage?

The Irish chiefs and fighting men were not beaten for lack of courage or strength of hand. Tellingly, they were overwhelmed by cunning and superior organisation. Sadly, this particular shortcoming was also to work against them in the centuries ahead as they strove for independence. Yet, their struggle continued on through further centuries of suffering all in a bid to secure the greatest prize of all – true nationhood and freedom.

Chapter 7

English rule
(1580–1640)

The Lord Deputy, Sir John Perrot, convened a parliament in Dublin on 26 April 1585. The outcome of this meeting was that the country would be governed more in keeping with the English administrative system rather than the haphazard Irish method which had been in use up until that time. As a result the Governor of Connaught and Clare, Sir Richard Bingham, imposed new taxes in his district. It meant a levy of ten shillings had to be paid yearly for every quarter of 120 acres (old English/Irish acreage). This was payable to Her Majesty's Government and it was sanctioned by the nobility of Clare on 17 August 1585. The following is a 'verbatim' extract taken from the agreement:

Indenture, dated the 17th. August. 1585, between Sir John Perrot, knight, of the one part, and the Lords spiritual and temporal, chieftains, gentlemen, etc, of that part of the province of Connaught called Thomond, that is to say, Donogh Earl of Thomond; Murrogh Baron of Inchiquin; the Reverend Fathers in God, Mauritius (Murtagh O'Brien Ara), Bishop of Killaloe, Daniel, Elect-Bishop of Kilfenora, (Daniel O'Griffy, Vicar-General); Donogh O'Horan, Dean of Killaloe; Daniel O'Shanny, Dean of Kilfenora; Denis Archdeacon of the same; Sir Edward Waterhouse of Doonass, knight; Sir Turlogh O'Brien of Ennistymon, knight; John MacNamara (Finn) of Knappogue, otherwise called MacNamara of West Clan Culein; Teige MacMahon of Clonderlaw, otherwise called MacMahon of Corcobaskin East; Turlogh MacMahon of Moyarta, chief of his name in Corcobaskin West; Murtagh O'Brien of Drumline, (brother of the Earl of Thomond); Mahone O'Brien of Cloondovan, gent.; Owney O'Loghlen of Greggans, otherwise called the O'Loghlen; Ross Loghlen of Glencolmkille, Tanist to the same O'Loghlen; Mahone and Dermot O'Dea of Cragbrien, chief of his name; Turlogh, son of Teigue O'Brien of Ballycorick, gent.; Luke Brady, son and heir to the late bishop of Meath; Edward White of Cratloe, gent.; George Cusack Dromoland, gent.; Boetius Clancy of Knockfinn, gent.; John MacNamara of Mountallon, gent.; Henry O'Grady of the island of Inchicronan, gent.; Donogh MacClancy of the Urlan, chief of his name; Donogh Garv O'Brien of Ballycessy, gent.; Conor O'Brien of Cahircorcran, gent.; and George Fanning of Limerick, merchant, of the other part.

Witnesseth, that all Irish titles shall be abolished; the inhabitants are to grant to the Queen ten shillings a-year for every quarter of land containing one hundred and twenty acres that bears either horn or corn, in lieu of all other demands, save the raising of horse and foot for her Majesty. The Earl of Thomond is to surrender all claims upon Inchiquin in favour of Baron Inchiquin, but he is to have five shillings per quarter of annual rent out of Clonderlaw, Moyarta, Burren, and part of Tulla, except such lands as belong to the See of Killaloe. Out of other parts of Tulla, Lord Inchiquin is to be paid a yearly rent of five shillings for each quarter, the bishop of Killaloe's lands to be exempted; and out of Corcomroe, he is to receive five shillings per quarter, but his claim is not to extend to the denominations owned by the bishop and dean of Kilfenora, nor the property of Boutius Clancy, 'in consideration of his birth, learning and good bringing up'; nor to that of Sir Turlogh O'Brien of Ennistymon.

There were 20 prominent signatures to the document which enforced this new system of land tenure. Significantly, the powerful MacNamaras flatly refused to have anything to do with it. In addition to the ten shillings it was also required of the landowners that they provide 40 horsemen and 200 footmen for the service of the Crown when required.

To ensure that things would go smoothly the English showed generosity towards the Earl of Thomond. He was entitled to five shillings rent for every quarter of land in his possession. Most of the church lands belonging to the various abbeys had been confiscated (eg the 16½ quarters in Corcomroe under the bishop of Kilfenora). This newly-acquired land was used by the English to bribe the Irish nobility. The Earl received large tracts of land in the baronies of Islands and Bunratty as well as all of Ibrickan.

The baronies of Inchiquin and Tulla were bestowed on the Baron of Inchiquin. The Bishop of Killaloe received five quarters around his house in Killaloe, while the Bishop of Kilfenora was presented with four quarters adjoining his house in that parish. An attempt to grant lands was made to the MacNamaras, but the English had to acknowledge in the grant that the MacNamaras had challenged their right to do so. Provision for this claim had to be inserted in the wording of that document. Had the O'Briens been as obstinate at this stage, who knows, events may have turned out differently. In any case the MacNamaras showed remarkable insight, integrity, pride and self belief in their heritage as a distinct race of people.

Others of note to come into special favour were Dr James Neylon of Ennis and Boetius Clancy of Knockfinn. When it came to choosing the better option it would appear that the redoubtable Boetius had no peers. Most people in possession of castles/tower houses and land were made official grants of them by the Crown.

Bingham came down from Connaught at the head of a strong military force bearing firearms and cannon. When he arrived at Cloon Dovan in Kilkeady, six mile north-east of the village of Corofin, he met with a strong stone castle well fortified and prepared for siege. With cannon and and military hardware Sir Richard immediately assaulted the ramparts.

26. ***Restored 15th century Norman style tower house at Dysert O'Dea.***

Such tower houses were built prolifically by the MacNamaras of Thomond. Most had their roofs and staircases demolished by the Commissioners for overthrowing and demolishing Castles in Connaught and Clare.

(SFADCo)

He soon realised that it would be difficult to storm the fortress. Such was the strength of the structure that the cannon balls did little more than bounce off the solid limestone walls. The English general spent three fruitless weeks at the gates of Cloon Dovan and it seemed with little hope of success. In desperation Bingham positioned sharpshooters all around the fortress, covering every conceivable angle, thereby making it perilous for the defenders to continue flinging out missiles.

One of the sharpshooters mortally wounded Mahon O'Brien on the battlements of his castle. Panic ensued amongst the defenders and they quickly surrendered. They had made a fatal error of judgement for the cruel Sir Richard Bingham never took prisoners. All the defenders were callously put to the sword. The English forces demolished the castle as much as they could. Only one bare wall of Cloon Dovan's once stout castle remains today.

Of course there were many other smaller acts of defiance about the county during this phase of English takeover. The English administration had become so intent on maintaining control that they hanged approximately 70 men and women in Ennis. They found it necessary to establish a jail there (possibly in Ennis Abbey) in 1591 and to appoint a Patrick Morgan as jailer. This act clearly augmented their settlement in Clare for the very first time.

On another front the remains of the disastrous Spanish Armada which had assaulted England was then floundering off the Clare coast. During September of 1588 seven Armada ships sheltered in the Shannon estuary and anchored near Carrigaholt. The Coroner for Thomond, Nicholas Cahane, boarded one of the ships to carry out an inspection. He did not speak Spanish but he understood that the crew were in dire need of fresh water. To get this vital commodity the Spanish sent a longboat to Kilrush with an offer to exchange a barrel of wine for every barrel of water supplied. However, Sir Richard had warned the people not to assist the Spanish so the offer was refused. After refitting on Scattery Island the ships moved into the open seas and turned south for their homeland.

A day later another vessel was seen at anchor off Liscannor. The purser (whose name was Pedro Baptista) came ashore and explained that the master of the ship and some of the men had already died of thirst. Another vessel was wrecked just off Doonbeg with some 300 men going down with her. A small number struggled to the beach where they were killed by the local inhabitants (surely a sign that many Irish had swung to the English side).

One of the larger vessels went aground between Mutton Island and the shoreline resulting in the death of a 1,000 more men. The wreckage was the scene of much plunder for many days with the natives from all around converging on the disaster area. All that remains of the vessel is a large table now on display in Bunratty Castle. The Spaniards who managed to get ashore and escape being harmed by the natives were taken into custody by the high sheriff, Boetius Clancy, who immediately put all of them to the sword.

Returning to the machinations of the Earl of Thomond we find him now so much in favour of the English that when Bingham needed assistance to quell the riotous Burkes in Galway he could confidently call on O'Brien to assist him. This he did with enthusiasm in 1593, 1596 and again in 1597. It will be remembered that in earlier history the Galway clans spent much of their time plundering the O'Brien homeland; perhaps the Earl felt some justification in paying back his old enemies for their past transgressions.

After a sojourn in England we next find the Earl and the Baron of Inchiquin joining forces with the English against Hugh O'Donnell. An outright revolt erupted in the north of Ireland at that time. While crossing the River Erne a member of O'Donnell's army shot Murrough MacMurrough O'Brien (4th Baron Inchiquin) which penetrated his mail through an opening under his arm. He died from his wound and he was buried nearby in the Abbey of Assaroe. The campaign against O'Donnell was unsuccessful and it forced O'Brien's army and the English forces to retreat across the Erne and abandon their valuable artillery.

Red Hugh O'Donnell took a very dim view of the Earl of Thomond's stance in joining forces with the English side. To discourage such future alliances and possibly as a measure of retribution he led an army from the North down to Thomond in 1599. When the northern army arrived at the Clare border, O'Donnell split his forces into three sections. One group went into the Burren to plunder it. Another detachment raided around Ballyogan, Cailmore, Tullyodea, and as far as Ballygriffey. The main force marched into Rockforest and Kilnaboy. They gathered much spoils until eventually all raiding parties regrouped and departed northwards out of the county through the territory of Clanrickard. Token resistance came from scattered individuals but no organised defence was evident from Thomond as a whole.

Seemingly, O'Donnell was not happy that he had done enough to convince the Clare people of his hatred for allies of the English because in the following year of 1600 he returned to plunder the county. His army entered Clare near Moyroe and Tuamgraney and went down as far as Ennis from where he sent out raiding parties all across the county. Crops were despoiled in the countryside while much of Ennis was torched;

residents sought refuge in Ennis Friary. On the following day O'Donnell camped overnight in Clarenbridge after despoiling Thomond. Soon there was open conflict in the county between those who supported the English and their religion, land tenure and language, and those who would not. The nobility in Clare were by then conversing in English even though the majority of the ordinary folk spoke Gaelic. Under King James of England the Earl of Thomond was expected to enforce laws and impose fines to compel Catholics into attending Protestant services. The Anglican Church of Ireland had been designated the establishment church. Even more ridiculous was a stipulation to enforce the cutting of their long hair and to dress after the English fashion.

Religious persecution took place on a grand scale. The Protestant bishop O'Brien was able to collect his tithes only with assistance from the Earl himself. His counterpart, the Catholic Bishop O'Mulryan, did not feel safe in living within the county. Such was the severity of the victimization that a group of priests requested a ship in order to flee the country. One such vessel was provided at Scattery Island where 46 religious individuals boarded her. When the ship was well out to sea it was claimed by some that the Catholics on board were thrown overboard and left to drown.

With all Catholic priests on the run the church buildings were neglected and fell into disrepair. Many of the fine old abbeys and churches were rendered roofless and useless. The Protestant ministers who officiated had very small congregations to attend to because the Gaelic Irish did not take to the new religion. The old Franciscan Friary at Ennis may have been used as early as 1615 for Protestant services. After its structural conversion in 1622 it was then used right up until 1871 when it was abandoned as a functioning church. During its Protestant tenure it was known as the Parish Church of Drumcliff (previously a Catholic parish).

The end of 16th century and much of the early part of the 17th century saw many inquisitions held at Ennis, at Sixmilebridge and at other population centres throughout the county. Such legal hearings were primarily concerned with the transferring of inheritances when land owners died. Records of the transactions were written in Latin; they are since stored in the Irish Records Office in Dublin. The real purpose of the hearings was to establish clear ownership of property so that appropriate taxes could be levied.

Many of the Ennis sittings were held before local juries; some of the chairmen who presided included: Nicholas Kenny; Sir John Denham (Knight); John, Bishop of Killaloe: John Evans, and as always the redoubtable Boetius Clancy. Not surprisingly the Ennis proceedings were held in the Franciscan Friary (commonly referred to as 'The Abbey') – that imposing structure which still stands on the street of the same name in Clare's capital town.

An entry of inquisitions (of which there were many) and fairly typical of the times reads as follows:

Inquisition, taken at Ennis, on 19th March 1619, finds that Donogh Grana (The Nasty) O'Brien, late of Mogowna, died on 22nd December 1612, being owner of Ardcarney, of three bedrooms in the castle of Mogowna, to with the 'white chamber, the 'guard chamber', and one other near the court; of the land of Inchicolaght, Drumboige, and Deeroolagh; finds that he held these lands from Dermot, Baron of Inchiquin, finds that Syra is the widow, and that Conor is the son and heir of said Donogh, finds that the lands of Teeronaun are now in possession of Sir Roger Shaughnessy in his capacity of Guardian of William Neylon (his stepson); finds that Brian NaMacoiree (The Early Riser) O'Brien, had conveyed the lands of Ardcarney to Turlogh NaMacoiree, by deed of 1616; finds that Marcus O'Griffy and his wife enjoyed the produce of this land, and that the fee simple was claimed, as his right by James, son of Nicholas Neylon.

Only occasional resistance was offered in the county against the complete takeover by the Crown. Organisation like theirs had not been known hitherto fore. It appears to have been accepted as inevitable by the Gaelic Irish. With the principal clan leaders the O'Briens acting as English Earls, leadership and lack of direction was missing. It was no surprise therefore that a united Irish front was not put up against alien domination. Internecine warfare between the Gaels was nothing new so this latest 'intrusion' did not seem to be all that threatening.

By the time the 4th Earl, Donogh, died in 1624 and with the coming of his son, Henry, into the 5th Earldom they had contributed much to English rule and the implanting of Protestantism in Clare. It must be said though that the native Irish never relinquished their Catholic religion. Perhaps it was this more than anything else that bound them together as a unified people who were to persist through the centuries and emerge as a distinct nation in the end. On the other hand, because the O'Brien nobles were educated in England and spent much of their time there they became intrinsically English in outlook and behaviour.

When the English crown passed from the Catholic James 1 to the Protestant Charles I in the year 1625 Ireland was not as well settled constitutionally as the Monarch would have wanted. Charles therefore encouraged his agents in Ireland to proceed with the plantation of Clare in whatever way they could. Plantation meant the removal of the Irish from their historic lands and the placing thereon those loyal to the Crown ie adventurers, soldiers, and supporting dignitaries. In a letter from the Lord Deputy in Ireland in 1637 instructions were issued to go on with the plantation of Clare. It further added that 'from His Majesty you may expect encouragement and support'.

So beaten down was the populous that in the year 1640 it was recorded in a parliament convened in Dublin that 'the many grievous, exactions, pressures, and vesicatious proceedings of some of the clergy of this kingdom and their officers and ministers against the laity, especially the poorer sort, led to the great impoverishment and general detriment of the whole kingdom'.

As bad as conditions were in Clare they were much worse in some of the other counties of Ireland. Little surprise therefore to find rebellion in the north of the country spreading south to the ancient Kingdom of West Thomond (but alas now labelled County Clare).

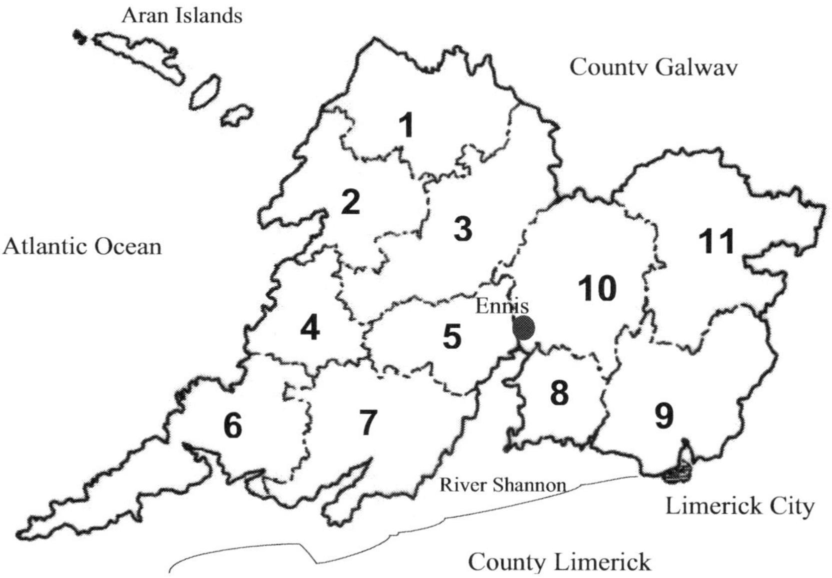

27. Clare (Thomond) was divided into 11 baronies (designed after the English system of administration) in the year 1579. Many of the old territorial names and districts were supplanted by the new designations.

The baronies are as follows:
1. Burren. 2. Corcomroe. 3. Inchiquin. 4. Ibrickan. 5. Islands. 6. Moyarta. 7. Clonderlaw. 8. Bunratty Lower. 9. Tulla Lower. 10. Bunratty Upper. 11. Tulla Upper.

Chapter 8

Rebellion and oppression
(1641–1800)

It was not totally unexpected when a bitter revolt broke out in Ulster in 1641. The province had been heavily planted with impoverished settlers from Scotland. News of the outbreak of the 1641 rebellion was first received in Clare at the great fair of Quin. It was enthusiastically adopted in the county as a signal to strike a blow against all English settlers.

Because the English gentry had secured themselves in most of the Irish castles it was not surprising to find that they became the immediate target of attack from the native Irish. Ballyalla castle, situated a few miles north of Ennis, was the first to be put under serious pressure. All the local Protestants and loyalists of the Crown had fled there for safety.

In a prelude to storming the castles many native leaders drove off the stock belonging to local farmers. The Earl of Thomond, Barnabas, judged and proclaimed that the culprits should be hanged. Most other leaders did not agree with Barnabas so they put up bail for the accused. For two unfortunate individuals who could not put up bail their immediate fate was to be hanged from the battlements of Bunratty Castle.

On or around 9 December 1641, Oliver and John Delahoyde of Fomerla, drove away the herds of John Ivisden, Thomas Pandell and those of many other English planters. This angered the Earl so he sent mounted and foot troops to arrest the brothers Delahoyde. John was found to be dying but Oliver was brought before his lordship the Earl. With oaths and tears did Delahoyde swear that he was innocent of all charges. Falling for this dramatic plea Barnabas not only released him but further empowered him with martial law to apprehend any offenders he might find in his own district. Delahoyde was not long returned to his home place when he went about driving off English cattle as before.

When many of the poorer English settlers had gained admission to Ballyalla Castle it was found that provisions there were not adequate. Some women who were sent out to collect eggs, geese, lambs etc were waylaid on their return to the keep. They were attacked and beaten and had their goods taken from them. The attackers warned them if they were caught again they would be hanged. This drastic action by the rebels discouraged further relief from entering the castle. Those inside were then forced to make do with what was already gathered in.

By early February in 1642, Captain Dermot O'Brien and other Clare notables had raised an army of about 1,000 men from south Connaught and Thomond. The Captain sent a letter to the Cuffes who were responsible members inside the castle (it was Maurice Cuffe, a merchant of Ennis, who wrote down all that happened during the siege of Ballyalla). In the letter, O'Brien threatened to storm the keep if they did not wilfully surrender. The Cuffes replied that they would hold the castle for His Majesty's use until their lease expired.

28. Leamaneh Castle, a stronghold (tower house and fortified house) belonging to a section of the O'Brien clan. One of its most famous residents, Máire Rua (who was the wife of Conor O'Brien) lived there in the 17th century. (SFADCo)

Dermot at once instructed Turlogh O'Brien (the first prominent rebel in the county) to lay siege on the fortress at Ballyalla. The stronghold was surrounded with men from each Barony who took turns in keeping watch and thus preventing the defenders from sallying forth for provisions. During the cold weather the men built huts in the hedgerows in an effort to keep dry and warm. In the interim one of the MacNamaras had gone to the north of the country to procure a cannon which would be suitable for bombarding the castle walls. From time to time the defenders would steal out to surprise and harangue the besiegers. During some such sorties they grabbed the temporary wooden roofing and returned safely with them to the castle where they burned them as firewood. Presently, MacNamara came back from the north with the news that a cannon could not be got. This resigned them to settle in for a protracted siege.

Besides Turlogh and Dermot O'Brien there were many more O'Brien clan members in the rebel grouping. This shows the amount of dissension within the greater O'Brien clan when they were prepared to go against the clan leader, Barnabas, even though he was Earl of Thomond. The rebels included Sir Daniel O'Brien, Knight of Carrigaholt; Daniel of Carrowduff; Conor, eldest son of Sir Daniel; Conor of Leamaneh, as well as many more of this ancient clan. The MacNamaras who were also there in numbers could always be relied upon to support the traditional clan structure as they had done down the centuries, especially when the O'Briens were involved. Flann and David Neylon of Rosslevan and Andrew Burke of Ennis, along with numerous others from far and near joined in supporting the cause.

On 6 February 1662 safe conduct was offered to those inside Ballyalla Castle if they would surrender. They flatly refused the offer. Thereafter the besieged were verbally abused with threats and oaths from their assailants. The soldiers outside warned them that Turlogh O'Brien had in mind using some fearsome instrument of war that would destroy the castle and leave them no option but to surrender without conditions.

Turlogh might have been a student of ordnance engineering because he built a leather cannon which was supposed to launch a keg of powder at the castle. His intention was to blow down the castle walls; instead the explosion blew out the cannon's breach – an act which came close to killing his own men.

He next turned to his second device, a pitched roof shelter covered with many layers of hides and designed to withstand flying musket balls and steel arrows. The 'sow' (as the structure was called) was rolled up against the castle walls with a number of the rebels crouching beneath the hides. The hide canopy protected them from being molested while they attacked the walls with picks and crowbars. It was a slow and tiresome endeavour but it did have some effect. Those inside the castle ran short of water forcing them from time to time to venture out in search of some. During such sorties they killed a few men guarding the sow as well as seizing tools and firearms. Their successes took the sting out of the attackers thrusts. However, after an initial surrender on 12 March 1642 the Protestants once again seized the castle and defied the Irish chiefs by remaining within.

Throughout all of 1642 the rebels constantly harassed the ranchers by driving off their cattle. They believed this to be the best way to prevent the confiscation of their lands. Its immediate effect was to leave the English settlers short of food which caused them to strike back with their own raiding parties. Soon, the defenders of Ballyalla had regrouped to the extent that they sallied forth to recover stolen cattle; they became strong enough to engage the rebels in skirmishes.

The rebel leaders, Donal O'Brien of Leamaneh and Teigue Roe O'Brien, soon tired of such haphazard 'warfare' and finally resolved to put Ballyalla Castle under the severest siege yet. They sealed the castle to such an extent that no supplies got in and nobody could steal out. The garrison was soon in desperate straits for the want of supplies and provisions.

When a 'brass gun' was sequestered after the surrender of Limerick, the threat of using it was enough to effect the surrender of Ballyalla castle on 12 September 1642. A happy outcome of the siege was the decision by the rebels to allow the castle defenders to go free and unmolested.

A second successful siege was laid on the castle of Inchicronan by the O'Gradys and the O'Shaughnessys. Gradually the rebels had by now thrown the English administration into such dire straights that they became desperate for any kind of a short-term solution.

The English quickly turned to their administrative structures to resolve the property war. The claims or 'depositions' were taken so seriously that special courts were set up to administer them. By the end of 1642 the English settlers had submitted many claims to the Crown for property lost. Either the claims were greatly exaggerated or the English had become extremely rich in their new lands. We note that James Vandeleur, a Dutch Protestant made a claim for £1,836; he personally named many of the Irish rebels whom he asserted owed him money. He also put in for the loss of his house and mills, some outhouses, and four quarters of land.

William Chambers, who lived in Kilrush, claimed that his losses amounted to £1,519. He swore he was robbed of his cattle, goods and chattels. Ann Asher of Killimer made a deposition for £994, claiming that the O'Cahanes were the culprits. Perhaps the greatest request for loss was that of Gregory Hickman who was an English Protestant in Barntick. His deprivations came to £3,672 in cattle, sheep, horses, and furniture. He named many who were debtors to him, including Laurence Rice and another Ennis merchant who allegedly ran off with 18 packs of his wool. He further broadened his demand when he took the opportunity to name some Protestants who had allegedly turned Papist and had been seen going to Mass – an allegation that could bring fatal results.

[The following extracts from Frost's *History of Clare* give two snapshots of events at the time]:

(1). *Edmund O'Flaherty of Connemara came, in April 1642, with a fleet of boats to the coast of Clare, having for his object the expulsion of Peter Ward, an Englishman, from the castle of Tromroenear Miltown-Malbay. He was joined by the following viz:- Donogh O'Brien of Newtown, Turlogh, Conor, and Mahone, sons of Dermot O'Brien of Tromroe; Richard Fitz Patrick, Seneschal and Receiver of the Earl of Thomond in the Barony of Ibricken; Hugh McCurtin; Daniel, son of Scanlane MacGorman; Teige Fitz Patrick of Fintrabeg; Teige Roe O'Brien, son of Sir Daniel O'Brien; Mahone and Donogh McEncarriga of Cloghaneinshy and Fanore; James and Teige, sons of Donald Mergagh Gallery of Poulawillin; Daniel and Mahone MacGorman of Cahermurphy; Hugh Hogan of Ballyhehan; Edmond Oge O'Hogan of Moyhill; Dermot MacGorman of Knockanalban; Gillabreeda MacBrody of Knockanalban; Loghlen MacCahane of Doonbeg.*

(2). *They laid siege to the castle, and in a few days compelled the garrison to surrender. In the progress of the contest, Peter White and his wife Alison, and his son George, were killed. Their bodies were removed to the graveyard of Kilmurry by order of Daniel O'Brien of Dough, but they were disinterred by direction of Daniel, son of Scanlane MacGorman of Drumsallagh, 'a mass priest', and again buried outside the churchyard, for the reason that no heretical corpse of a Protestant should be allowed to repose in consecrated ground. All this is stated in the deposition of John Ward, son of Peter, who swears that his father's property, worth £871 was plundered. The younger Ward then repaired to Bunratty, to complain to the Earl of Thomond, whose tenant his father had been, that in the act of spoliation, the Earl's confidential agent, Richard FitzPatrick had been a prime mover. All redress he got was a cell in the prison of the castle. Having expostulated with the Earl for the hardship of this treatment, he was threatened with a box on the ear. He goes on to declare that, at Newmarket-on-Fergus, he met Teige Roe, son of Sir Daniel O'Brien. That young gentleman, in the presence of Cormac Hickey, of Bunratty, surgeon, and of several others, imprecated the curse of God upon any one who did not join in the rebellion. He mentioned that, after the surrender of the castle of Limerick, on 23rd. June 1642, part of the garrison repaired to Bunratty to offer their services to the Earl, and that they were refused. He intimates that, with the connivance of the Earl, a brass gun was sent from Limerick, by water, to Clare, and that the piece of ordnance in question was mainly instrumental in capturing the castle as well as Ballyalla. Nothing was easier than to intercept this gun, seeing that a Dutch ship, well armed and laden with rape seed from Limerick to London, then lay in the Shannon, and might have been used for that purpose. Ward was present one day, when the Earl exclaimed to Dermot O'Brien, 'By the Lord of Heaven, cousin Dermot, if I be not paid my rents, I will retake the castle of Clare, in despite of all your forces. I shall bring Forbes' ships to the place'. Another day he said to John MacNamara, that his countrymen mightily slight him in not paying his rents. 'By G— were it not for me Lord Forbes would have spoiled the whole country, and I am nothing better for it, and nothing the nearer to receive my rents'. His Lordship entertained at Bunratty, with eating and drinking, the most notorious rebels of the country, every one being freely welcome. Ward adds, that Mathew Hicks, who held the castle of Tuamgraney, surrendered it on quarter, and on his way to Bunratty would have been robbed only for the intervention of the English garrison at Cappagh, near Sixmilebridge.*

One of the little Protestant garrisons founded by the Earl of Thomond was situated at Doonass, then called Annaghmore and Annaghbeg. Several of the Clare Depositions have reference to the expulsion of these people by the Irish gentry of the surrounding countryside. They were for the most part small farmers or mechanics, and their names were: Roundtree, Pitch, Norman, Cobb, Drury, Capel, Wilkinson, Meale, Culliver, Brine, Derby, Church, and Edwards. Motivated by terror, some members of the colony turned Catholic, amongst whom were: French, Roane of Coollisteigue, Haddock, and Dyer of Doonass. Those who drove them out included; Lord Brittas, John M'Namara of Neadanura (Newtown), Geoffrey Burke of Errinagh, and the MacNamaras of Cragleigh.

Every Protestant settler in Clare was either attacked or had his lands and goods stolen. Some of them converted to the Catholic religion to avoid being molested. Most eventually retreated to the Protestant-held castles of Bunratty (the Earl reluctantly received them) and to Limerick.

The Anglo-Irish who were Catholics sided with the old Gaelic Irish. From this allegiance came the Confederation of Kilkenny at which Lord Mount-Garrett was chosen as President. They organised an army across Ireland to which General Barry was elected commander in Munster. Sir Daniel O'Brien (an uncle of the Earl of Thomond) was assigned command in Clare. All these developments unsettled the Protestant people to such an extent that they pressed for assistance of any kind from England.

General Barry and Lord Muskerry took Limerick and its castles as an opening gambit. With the exception of Bunratty Castle the whole of Clare was now in the hands of the Confederate Catholics. The Parliamentarians (Protestant alliance) had firmly entrenched themselves at Bunratty and would not be easily dislodged. To further strengthen their position at Bunratty a fleet of ships with supplies and troops from England sailed into the Shannon estuary. The fleet was commanded by Sir William Penn (father of William Penn, founder of the State of Pennsylvania in America). [It seems that the Penn family were career administrators and adventurers in the service of the Crown].

The ships entered the estuary on 11 March 1646 and eased their way up towards Bunratty; they took time out to assail and molest the inhabitants along the banks. In an escalating move some 700 soldiers from the fleet were put ashore and landed on a small island adjacent to Bunratty. In the meantime negotiations were taking place between the Earl and a Captain Huntly. The talks eventually resulted in the cautious Earl agreeing to allow the Parliamentarians to occupy the fortress. Wisely, the fleet stayed out in the estuary to give added assurance to those defending the castle. To cause further disruption the Parliamentarian fleet blocked trade between the Confederate-held city of Limerick and the open sea.

This new development troubled the commanders in the city of Limerick. In order to re-assert their position it became necessary for them to take the castle at Bunratty. They knew that the garrison consisted of about 800 foot and 60 horse and cannon. Bunratty was under the command of a very able Lt Colonel MacAdam. To strengthen the castle MacAdam had earthen fortifications erected on the north and west perimeters which were the sides not afforded the natural protection of the river.

Lord Muskerry rode into Clare at the head of an army of 3,000 foot and 300 horse. He had very experienced field officers in General Purcell, General Stephenson and Colonel Purcell, all of whom had seen action in the German wars. Soon after arriving at Bunratty the Confederate army entrenched around the castle. The river Raite (from which Bunratty Castle takes its name) protected the fortress on the east and south prospects. The Confederates concentrated their forces on the north-western side. No great impression could be made on the massive stone structure even when two field pieces were put into action. In fact the besieged sometimes charged out to engage the Catholic Confederates in skirmishes.

When Cardinal Giovanni Battista Rinuccini arrived from Rome with aid the Confederates gained great heart. Amongst the large store of supplies he had with him 20,000 lbs. of powder and six small trunks of Spanish gold. He spent much time in the trenches encouraging the troops. Bunratty greatly impressed him; he wrote to his brother in Italy that there was nothing in their country to compare with the palace of Lord Thomond. A vivid description has been placed on record of the beautiful gardens, ponds and parks with its 3,000 head of deer.

A constant fusillade was kept up by the attackers throughout each day and night. The Parliamentarians began to feel strained from the pressure applied by the attackers. A fateful break came in the action when a chance shot from a field piece passed through a window and killed Lt Colonel MacAdam. It greatly shook the Parliamentarians to such an extent that they surrendered shortly afterwards.

Those who remained of the garrison were allowed to board their ships in the estuary and set sail for Cork. Some of the standards taken from the castle were paraded through Limerick city (headed by Rinuccini) to St Mary's Cathedral where a *Te Deum* was sung to celebrate the victory.

The joy of the Confederates was short lived because Lord Inchiquin (aka Morogh of the Burnings) fighting on the side of the Parliamentarians, commenced a campaign of ravaging destruction throughout the province of Munster. He slaughtered some 3,000 persons in Cashel Cathedral – splattering the blood of priest and laity alike even on the holy altars. Lord Taffe for the Confederates attempted to intercept him before he reached Cork. Inchiquin's skilled troops, although less in number, reduced Taffe's army by half in a torrid engagement near the town of Mallow.

Morogh of the Burnings was to later change sides and ironically ended up dying a Catholic in 1674. He was buried (at his own request) in Saint Mary's Protestant Cathedral in Limerick.

Worse was to come in this civil war. At the time the most brutal war monger in England was a man called Oliver Cromwell. At the head of a large well-equipped army Cromwell landed in the southeast of the country in 1649 and immediately assailed the fortified towns. He never gave quarter not even to those who surrendered without resistance. Before he could reach Limerick he was recalled to England to deal with more pressing matters. Ireland was spared from further atrocities but Cromwell left much bitterness behind him in the east of the country.

He also left a large well-equipped army led by able and experienced generals. His son-in-law, Ireton, was given overall command of the troops. Ireton's aim was to get into Connaught and in particular into Clare so that he could come at Limerick from the northern side. Although Confederate forces under Lord Castlehaven had fortified the Shannon at Killaloe and at O'Brien's Bridge it wasn't enough to deter Ireton. The English managed to ferry troops across the river in spite of the absence of a bridge at O'Brien's Bridge. Surprisingly the Confederates retreated without offering resistance.

Down from the north of Ireland came General Ludlow at the head of a strong contingent of Parliamentarians. He swept through the Burren area, gathering up provisions as he went to finally link up with Ireton on the Clare side of Limerick ; this action locked the city under tight siege.

English ships had menacingly entered the Shannon; a few days previously they had bombarded the castle of Carrigaholt and placed it under their control. After Carrigaholt they threatened Limerick's walls. The Parliamentarian English sent a large detachment of 2,000 foot, 12 horse troops, and eight troops of dragoons commanded by Ludlow in sweeps across Clare. They destroyed Carrigaholt, killed a small Irish contingent near Ennis and slew Conor O'Brien of Leamaneh. Ludlow then quickly returned to assist Ireton at Limerick's walls. Meanwhile the Confederates of Clare were standing by at Sixmilebridge awaiting communication from the garrison commander, Hugh O'Neill, in Limerick. It was unfortunate for the Confederates that no such communiqué came.

The city of Limerick was bearing down under much despoliation from the ravages of the plague. The defenders lost heart when they realised that relief was not forthcoming. Finally on 27 October 1651 the Confederate Irish within the city walls had no other recourse but to surrender.

The English forces soon established their authority in Clare. The castle of Clonroad quickly fell to them and they also kept the castle at Clare under constant siege. On 8 September, Ireton entered the fortress of Bunratty. Only because he was aware of the capitulation of all the other strongholds did Captain Butler surrender Clare Castle on the first day of November in 1651. The 'Cromwellian' war came to an end with this action.

County Clare was ravaged and utterly despoiled by the English under Ludlow. The only harm that the county could inflict on him was the discomfort of its climate from which he contracted a bout of sweating. It is to him also that the following regarding the Burren is attributed: 'It is a country where there is not enough water to drown a man, wood enough to hang one, nor earth enough to bury him which last is so scarce that the inhabitants steal it from one another.' Ludlow died of his fever (which may have been pneumonia) in the winter of 1652.

The Ten Year War had so completely reduced the population that it was sometimes hard to find people in most townlands. In June of 1653, out of 1,300 townlands only 40 were inhabited, mostly in the Barony of Bunratty. A census revealed that there were only 16,474 Catholics and 440 English Protestants in Clare in 1659. Many hundreds were taken to Cork harbour from where they were transported into slavery to Barbados. By 1680 the population did creep up to 30,000 inhabitants in Clare.

It was reported that people fed on horse meat and even on their own kind in order to sustain their miserable lives. All churches and castles not held by the English were demolished. Priests were hunted down and dared not show their cloth. An example of the cruelty of Cromwell's soldiers may be gleaned from the from the fact that two of his officers, Captains Stance and Asper, put 500 families to death in the Baronies of Islands, Ibricken, Clonderlaw and Moyarta.

The second consequence for Clare after the surrender of Limerick was the defenceless nature of the county. The surrender left Thomond wide open for English takeover. The population had been decimated; those who survived were left destitute and hungry which effectively cleared the county for English settlers. With Irish leadership non-existent confiscation was merely a matter of procedure.

There was much doling out of confiscated lands from 1667 onwards, mostly to prominent people who helped bring down the Gaelic system. Recipients included Daniel O'Brien (Lord Viscount Clare), the Earl of Thomond, Baron Inchiquin, and the Protestant Bishop of Killaloe; this action clearly showed the importance of English titles. Final settlements were made during the reign of William of Orange.

Because William was a Dutchman we find a number of Dutch settlers also obtaining grants of land. A Joost Van Keppel received Lord Clare's property near Carrigaholt. Lord Clare had sailed to France with the 'Wild Geese' after the siege of Limerick. A Dutch family (Vandeleur) gained much property around Kilrush and elsewhere; deed titles of their properties are on legal documents down to the present day.

Where were Clare's leaders during this worst ever disaster to befall the country? Barnabas, the Earl of Thomond, who was meant to be the leader of his people, retired to England and died there in 1657. Morogh whom we referred to earlier in regard to this war fought some of his best battles for the Parliamentarians against his clansmen, who were the native Irish and the Anglo-Irish. He would have been better employed protecting his own homeland no matter what his religion. It was unfortunate for the Irish cause that he did not do so for he was a most able general. He had been educated in the best military schools in England and he proved to be a ruthless commander. When he retired to France he was offered high positions in their forces. As was mentioned earlier he died a Catholic and he donated £20 to the friars of Ennis Friary to say masses for his soul. [He may not have left enough money].

Towards the end of the 17th century Lord Clare's Dragoons (who were formed from soldiers from the Carrigaholt area in west Clare) saw much action in the north of Ireland but might have been better employed in Clare. They helped King James II storm the city of Derry which was being defended by the followers of William of Orange (a Dutchman). The Dragoons as well as James' army suffered a decisive defeat at the Battle of the Boyne in 1690. This was a major turning point in the war. The Irish forces (minus King James who had fled) retreated west of the Shannon. While Limerick was under siege Patrick Sarsfield led 500 men at night through Clare to cross the Shannon at Killaloe and go into Tipperary. There he successfully blew up a supply train of munitions at Ballyneety. He returned as he came to make an undetected re-entry into the besieged city of Limerick. That action has been dubbed 'Sarsfield's Ride.'

During the assault on Limerick's walls a hasty command by a French officer to close the drawbridge at Thomond Gate in the city resulted in many Irish soldiers being trapped outside on an open access bridge. The enemy slew them without quarter so that the bodies were piled five and six deep on the bridge. After six weeks of relentless defence the spirits of the defenders sagged. Supplies had run low and there were no prospects of relief. Negotiations began on 3 October 1691 resulting in the Treaty of Limerick being signed by both parties. This second surrender ended the war.

The implications for Clare out of the surrender of Limerick meant two things. Firstly, nearly all the Irish soldiers (many of whom came from Clare) took the option of emigrating to France where they served in the French forces. Presumably they hoped to have another day against the English from within the ranks of the mighty French army. Indeed it became their privilege in that army to serve in the front lines whenever they were pitted against the English – and they did so quite willingly whenever the occasion arose.

Before leaving the odious conditions of the 17th century for the those of the 18th we might glimpse at general social conditions of the time. Commerce had previously begun to develop when Donogh Earl of Thomond obtained a grant in 1609 to hold a market on Tuesdays in the town of Ennis. Incidentally, with the influx of English and Irish settlers from Limerick the shape of a town began to grow west and south from the Friary (Ennis Abbey) grounds. The three original streets were Abbey Street, Gaol Street (O'Connell Street) and Mill Street (Parnell Street).

Fairs were also permitted in the town, one on Easter Monday and on the following day. A second fair took place on 24 and 25 August each year; it was held on the old fair green of Clonroad. Ennis had been constituted a borough on 26 September 1612. The town was managed by a provost and 12 burgesses. The provost was empowered to make bye-laws, he had a mercantile guild and a common seal. He was also clerk to the market

29. Clonroad Castle as it appeared in 1680 to the English traveller, Dineley. Regretfully, the entire structure was dismantled in the 18th century by the Gore family.

(Frost's History of Clare)

supplemented by two sergeant at arms and two inferior officers attending official functions.

The town traded extensively in hides, tallow and butter which the buyers transported on light craft using the river Fergus. There were around 120 houses in the Ennis of 1680 containing an estimated population of 600 people. Twenty of the houses in the town were slated and the rest were thatched. The principal buildings were The Franciscan Friary (or Abbey), the Hall of Assizes, Lenthall's Inn, and of course, Clonroad Castle. In fact, the oldest building in the town is and always was, the Franciscan Friary, around which the town grew up. A Denis Casey was town clerk in 1687.

The 1700's blew in the cold harsh Penal laws to devastate the Irish people. An estimated 60,000 souls populated Clare when the century unfolded. The ravages of the Cromwellian war, the confiscations and the deportations had reduced living conditions to wretchedness. Most of the populous lived in the inhuman conditions of mere slaves. To further aggravate their plight the English Penal Laws pounded the bewildered people into deeper subservience. Although the Gaelic Irish had been promised freedom and religious tolerance under the Treaty of Limerick they saw very little of that.

Laws were passed to 'banish all Papists and regulars of the Popish clergy out of the kingdom.' Clerics of any hew if found anywhere in the country could be either imprisoned, transported or executed. The authorities were unrelenting in pursuit of priests. The Clare members who sat in the parliament which passed the Penal Laws were Sir Donogh O'Brien and Sir Henry Ingoldsby. Representing the Borough of Ennis at the same parliament were Francis Gore and Francis Burton, all of whom were avowed Royalists and anti-Gaelic activists.

Laws enticing Catholics to become Protestants soon came into force. An example of such laws was the one concerning automatic possession of property. If any member of a known Catholic family had converted to Protestantism then he or she immediately became the legal owner of the family property. One can immediately see the machinations that this divisive legislation did lead to. Another law: if a Protestant took up the Catholic religion his or her belongings became the legal possessions of their nearest relative. Heavy fines fell on practicing clerics and on those who would not disclose the names of priests. A redeeming feature of the times was that many local Protestants became unwilling to enforce the Penal Laws on their Catholic neighbours. We can deduce from this that all humanity and decency had not been eroded by the cruel administrators. Unfortunately by the time Queen Ann's reign had passed in 1714 too many oppressive laws had been written into the statute books. A vast amount of damage had already been done.

The greater part of the 18th century was taken up with the enactment of further oppressive acts and laws to prevent the growth of 'Popery'. In spite of the poverty and cruelty the Catholic population in the county showed a steady increase during the course of this century.

Much of the countryside was still wooded at this time. Even on the western seaboard large forests could be seen. Folklore has it that when cattle strayed in Tulla and Quin they would not be easily found due to the thickness of the woods thereabouts. The territory between Kilkishen, Tulla and Quin was a sea of trees. During the time of the foreign administration most of the fine forests were stripped to supply the lucrative English market. It was said that the majestic oaks near Killaloe were felled to build some of the finest ships in the English navy.

Roads which had developed spontaneously and irregularly were of the roughest order. Invariably they meandered over the high ground which might be durable enough to support some summer and occasional winter traffic. Goods had to be brought to market on pack horses, or even on crude sleighs pulled by animals and pushed by humans. Most could not afford a

30. Dineley's sketch of Bunratty Castle as it was in 1680

(Frost's History of Clare)

horse so walking was the only option available to them.

This state of affairs made the horse more prized that it had been throughout Irish history. The breeding of such animals was a significant undertaking but mostly for landowners of some substance. From ancient times fairs were part and parcel of the old Gaelic way of life. Horse fairs in Ennis, Spancilhill and Kilrush amongst many others are steeped in Irish history. Fairs and markets were some of the few places where ordinary folk could enjoy distractions from their miseries.

By the end of the 18th century it was noticeable that the oppressive Penal Laws were not being rigidly enforced anymore. Some priests were allowed build thatch roofed churches – provided they did not look too ostentatious. A better working relationship developed between the Catholic and Protestant communities as some measure of enlightenment crept in. Clare's landlords would not have been the worst in Ireland; some had Gaelic blood coursing through their veins so they were sympathetically disposed towards their neighbours.

31. The Fair of Spancilhill as seen in modern times. Ireland's oldest horse fair has been ongoing since ancient unrecorded times. It is held on 24 June each year.
(Clare Champion)

Some measure of parliamentary progress was noticeable at this time. Sheriff Poole Hickman convened a meeting on 6 April 1782 in Ennis of gentry, clergy and free-holders. The outcome was that they enthusiastically supported the Irish Parliament in their recent resolutions. Essentially the declarations meant that the Commons of Ireland should have the right to make laws for their own people in their own country. They further claimed that for any body of men, other than King, Lords and Commons of Ireland to make laws for the country was unconstitutional. A vote of confidence was given to Clare's representatives in Parliament who were were Sir Lucius O'Brien and Edward Fitzgerald.

A particular feature towards the conclusion of the 18th century was the attempted 'risings' throughout Ireland, especially in 1782, 1798 and 1800. There weren't any such rebellions in Clare but the people did experience some of the fringe activities. The English Yeomanry searched about the county for any who might sympathise with rebels and United Irishmen. The Yeomanry were a cruel force who inflicted instant punishment if they did not get the co-operation they sought. For those who came under suspicion it meant being brought to Limerick to stand court martial. Whipping and transportation to Australia – or even hanging on the bridge at Limerick – were the usual punishments.

Although times were particularly difficult a love of learning and music was evident in the people. Hedge schools were well attended. Those 'masters in the ditches' were more than mere teachers, many were literary men of distinction. Some of the poets who lived in the early part of this century in Clare included Hugh and Andrew MacCurtin. The poet James Considine came from Mullagh. Brian Merriman taught school in Feakle, although he was reputedly born in Kilmihil. Irish was the language of those poets mentioned, but the Ennis man Thomas Dermody wrote in English.

32. Clare Castle in 1680. [Taken from Dineley's Journal – note similarities with the Lawrence photograph on page 120 in Chapter 9]. (Frost's History of Clare)

Undoubtedly, Dermody was a literary genius for he knew Greek and Latin and taught in his father's school at a young age; he wrote good poetry when he was ten years old. At 11 years he ran away from home and ended up in London. He served in the British army, was wounded in Flanders and died in miserable conditions in London at the young age of 27.

To add to the list of notable characters who seemed to flourish at the time we look at MacNamara of Moyreisk. The duelling pistols appear to have been his answer to most problems. It was a practice which gained for him and his kin the colourful appellation, 'Fireball' MacNamara. No direct descendant of his has come down to present times. He is buried in the transept of the historic Quin Abbey.

In the 18th century only two factors checked the unleashing of famine and starvation all across the country. The main food of ordinary folk of the time was the potato. Many failures of the crop occurred in the 18th century.

In 1740 an entire failure of the crop was widely reported. The 1793 crop was completely lost due to blight. Again in 1800 widespread loss was suffered. It is not fully understood how the populous lived through such deprivations. There seems to have been an acceptance that the potato crop was vulnerable to unspecified 'diseases' and it was thought that very little could be done about it.

The unusually low population of less than 4,000,000 people at the worst stages of the 18th and beginning of the 19th century was a major factor in avoiding widespread famine. Also, the Irish Parliament's influence in tempering the British Government's stringent rule was the second significant factor in staving off famine.

If the population were to increase significantly and the Irish Parliament were rendered ineffective in influencing the British Government then the gates of starvation would be thrown open. This very scenario arose towards the middle of the 19th century when the Irish population was estimated to have risen to more than 8,000,000 souls.

The population of Clare doubled in the 50 years before the famine. It stood at 286,394 in 1841, two and a half times the present figures. They made up a total of 48,981 families. Apart from a small number of professional people and craftsmen all of them earned an existence from the land. The great challenge of that time was the provision of food and work for such a teeming population.

The structure of Clare society during the period was not conducive to widespread industry. The upper class such as landlords and business people were low in numbers and because of that employment was not being generated to any great extent; the infrastructure wasn't there to match the available labour force. To aggravate matters further the labouring class were prolific breeders and suffered from lack of opportunity because many landlords had literally deserted the country. An oversupply of labour and an undersupply of food meant only one thing, and that one thing manifested itself to an alarming degree in the middle part of the 19th century – it was to be famine on an unprecedented scale.

Chapter 9

Famine fever
(1801–1900)

The most significant political event to occur in the early part of the 19th century was undoubtedly the Union of Ireland and Britain. With Scotland already united with England since 1707 and forming one 'arrangement' (Britain) with England, they felt it was time for the Crown to subjugate Ireland. This they did with the Act of Union which came into effect on 1 January 1801. It abolished the Irish Parliament and meant that the Ireland representatives were obliged to sit in the British Parliament at Westminster. But as we shall see even those deputies would not represent the views of the Catholic Gaelic Irish. It was the final injustice in the ongoing subjugation of the Irish nation.

Catholics were without basic freedoms of any kind. The 1793 Act had given all 40 shilling freeholders (landowners with small holdings) the right to vote for Members of Parliament. However Catholics were not allowed to stand for election; therefore the Catholic voters were left with the choice of voting for a suitable Protestant candidate – if indeed they felt like voting at all. More often than not local landlords 'instructed' their tenants as to whom they should vote for – or else. It was clear then to the Catholic majority that the one thing they should be fighting for was Catholic Emancipation.

More in desperation than in hope the Clare Catholics followed the fortunes of the Napoleonic wars in Europe. Hundreds of Clare men and thousands of Irish men stood in the French ranks to fight against the old enemy. Although many Irish men also served in the ranks of the British forces nevertheless the hearts of the people at home lay with Napoleon. There was a vague expectation that if the French Emperor conquered Britain that Irish Catholics would somehow be granted their freedom. Such leanings showed how much the Irish yearned for their independence.

At home Ireland produced an 'emperor' of their own in the person of a remarkable Kerry barrister named Daniel O'Connell. His skill lay not in traditional soldiering but in the law courts and parliaments of the very structures that England had erected. His skill in law and oratory won him many 'a lost cause' by driving 'a coach and four' through any law that the English administration might devise.

Once again we must record that the majority of the Clare Protestants proved to be a humane and fair-minded community. Time and again their members stood up for fair play for their Catholic neighbours. They held a meeting in Ennis in 1807 to demand the liberation of their Catholic neighbours from the yoke of the cruel laws that oppressed them. This was in spite of members of a Protestant Orange Organisation elsewhere in the country asserting themselves over their Catholic neighbours.

Major MacNamara who was an officer from Clare rendered Daniel O'Connell invaluable assistance when he was challenged to a duel by D'Esterre in 1815. O'Connell won the duel because of the expert duelling advice received from Major MacNamara. This act by MacNamara made the people of Clare proud, as if he had resurrected ancient glory.

The year 1822 brought another famine to the county. It was not as widespread as the '46 and '47 famines were to be; no doubt it was just as cruel for those caught up in it. With the population increasing rapidly wholesale disaster was looming, and yet the authorities were doing nothing to avert what was obviously a looming catastrophe.

The dramatic increase in the population is something of a puzzle, especially when the extreme poverty should have been working against such a development. The Catholic Bishop of Raphoe may have had an explanation in part when he told the Irish Poole Enquiry of 1835: 'They (the peasants) cannot be worse off than they are… and they may help each other'. He was referring to the fact that girls married at 16 and boys at 17 or 18. Irish women were known to be exceptionally fertile; 19 in 20 of them bore children at least every second year for 12 years. [Perhaps it is beyond our understanding as to how nature works to ensure the survival of the species].

The 1841 census found that the population of Ireland had reached an incredible 8,175,124. It led Disraeli (the British Prime Minister) to declare that Ireland was Europe's most densely-populated country. He asserted that parts of Ireland even out populated many areas of China.

It is even more astounding to find that those census figures could have been on the low side. A relief officer who wrote about the census of 1841 said it was 'pronounced universally to be no fair criterion of the present population'. He had it tested in Clare to find that the population was actually one third greater than had been recorded. It can be assumed therefore that when the famine of 1845 came the Irish population might have been greater than 9,000,000 souls.

The bulging population led to extreme pressure in living directly off the land but it was the only means of sustaining labourers' families. Holdings had to be split into smaller and smaller parcels to accommodate the burgeoning families. It got to the extreme situation where families were attempting to survive on plots of less than an acre. Rents soared (100% higher than they were in England) and few could afford to purchase or rent land. A system of hiring out land for a short period called 'conacre' arose. It was merely the last stage in a dwindling series of dubious solutions to feed the ever-increasing population.

Conacre was a contract whereby a portion of the land was let out to an individual to grow crops. It was not a lease but a licence to occupy. The owner was obliged to manure and prepare the ground to receive crops. It was the obligation of the hirer to provide the seed, plant it and harvest it. Rent was very high (between £10 and £14 for good ground) with poor ground fetching about £6 per acre. The demand for conacre was overwhelming yet only for its existence many more people would surely have starved.

On the political front the Catholic Association proposed that Daniel O'Connell should stand in the election of 1828 as a candidate for County Clare. At first O'Connell was reluctant to run against the Protestant Vesey FitzGerald who was a fair man and a good landlord. Eventually the renowned barrister was persuaded by his friends to contest the election. From the moment the decision was made the campaign took off with electrifying zeal.

O'Connell had two dedicated and talented men working for him in the county. Tom Steele was a Protestant and a landowner who did much to pacify and unite the people in the cause of Catholic Emancipation. Steele was a landlord of considerable wealth – his country house overlooked Cullane Lake which lies between Kilkishen and Tulla. A second devotee of O'Connell was The O'Gorman Mahon who was born in Mill Street in the town of Ennis. O'Gorman Mahon led the life of a gentleman thanks to the amount of property he inherited from his father who was a merchant in the town. Early in life he adopted the suffix 'O'Gorman' from his mother's side of the family. It was a source of some pride to him; he would not hesitate to challenge those who questioned his right to use it. Being a man given to fighting rather frequently he would call the disrespectful to a duel without too much provocation. One of his favourite weapons was the 'under and over' pistol (it is now on display in the Clare Museum in Ennis). The O'Gorman Mahon was elected MP to the Parliament of Westminster for the Ennis district in 1847 and again in 1879.

Most of the voters in Clare comprised the community of small farmers identified as '40 shilling freeholders'. For O'Connell to win the election he would have to woo the 40 shilling freeholders away from their traditional voting pattern ie voting for the landlord's man. The O'Gorman Mahon and Tom Steele did the rounds of the county to impress upon the freeholders of the necessity of voting and the benefits of voting for Daniel O'Connell in particular. The reputation of both Steele and the O'Gorman Mahon as a duellists ensured that the landlords didn't impeded them in their work.

Polling days – there were two – saw masses of people jammed into the narrow streets of Ennis. The attention of the entire United Kingdom focused on the little courthouse in the square or 'Height' of Ennis as it is known locally (where the O'Connell monument now stands). Police and soldiers patrolled the streets but the mood became more festive than unharmonious and happily their services were not called upon.

In a pre-election speech the outgoing candidate, Vesey Fitzgerald, made a moving and finely-balanced address to the voters. O'Connell, the great orator that he was, commenced his own delivery with a bout of sarcastic humour which won the hearts of the people. He concluded his speech in a thundering voice laying before the unsophisticated Clare peasants what would be in store for them should they fail to elect a Catholic candidate. By the time he had concluded the people were so taken with his words that the impact of Mr Fitzgerald's speech had entirely evaporated.

On the first day of polling Catholics had to produce written evidence that they had taken the oath of allegiance to the Crown. Some confusion arose from this new tactic by the establishment. As a result most of the voting on the opening day was registered by the Protestant people. By the second day Steele and The O'Gorman Mahon had the long lines of Catholic voters well versed in swearing the oath. It was enough to get a large number to cast their votes. The result favouring O'Connell by a margin of 982 votes was received with tumultuous jubilation by the people of Clare and Ireland.

Clare had achieved an all time first by returning a Catholic MP to the English Parliament at Westminster. It reinforced the old title of leaders or banner men (the first into battle and the last out of it) and cemented the title of the 'Banner County'. It was in the true spirit of their ancestors – the ancient Dalcassian fighting men. Was this a glimmer of hope that the Gael was getting off his knees to truly return to the fray and build a nation?

O'Connell went on to fight for Catholic Emancipation and Repeal of the Union of Ireland and Britain. A small measure of freedom was handed to the Catholics in 1829 with the passing by Parliament of The Roman Catholic Relief Act 1829. In Ireland it repealed the Test Act 1672 and the remaining Penal Laws in force since the passing of the Disenfranchising Act of the Irish Parliament of 1728. Its passage followed a vigorous campaign on the issue by Daniel O'Connell. A severe body blow was delivered in the same legislation when the 40 shilling freeholders were deprived of their right to vote. A cynical move surely whereby a potent weapon had been nipped in the bud by a segment of British politicians. A £10 franchise became the new voting requirement. This higher sum eliminated a high number of small land holders from voting, thus helping to sway the election in the direction the authorities wanted ie against the Catholic position.

During the 1830's the landlords and their tenants were constantly at each other's throats. The unfortunate tenants found it nigh on impossible to come up with the exorbitant rents demanded. It led to evictions from their holdings when they were unable to pay. Feelings soon hardened with murders and hangings following in the wake of dispossessions.

By far the biggest landlord/tenant problem stemmed from the absentee

33. Eviction scene at the Birmingham homestead in Moyasta. *The tenants are dragged out by troops and then the 'tumbling' of the house begins.*

(Lawrence Collection, 1777, National Library of Ireland)

landlords who permanently resided in London and did not care a toss for the condition of their estates nor the plight of their tenants so long as agents forwarded rents to their London accounts.

Travellers in Ireland in the 19th century were struck by the number of empty useless mansions. Millions of pounds sterling in Irish rent money was being spent frivolously on the gambling tables of England and throughout Europe. Agents were in place to look after the landlord's interests in Ireland; their only brief was to come up with the rent using whatever means they found necessary.

Holdings were divided again and again to get more tenants on the land so that more and more money could be collected for the landlords. The unscrupulous agents did not care a twig for the plight of the renters so long as they got their commission.

With the size of holdings dwindling, it became impossible for the tenants to produce enough crops to feed their own families never mind have an excess for rents and other necessities.

To illustrate some of the worst atrocities and injustices suffered by the Irish we can go to the writings of Daniel O'Connell MP.

O'Connell's book, *Memoir on Ireland Native and Saxon,* makes for telling reading and demonstrates that the great statesman was under no illusion as to how the English behaved towards the Irish. The following are harrowing extracts which highlight some grievous events in history as O'Connell saw them:

The English domination in Ireland commenced in the year 1172. It was for some centuries extended over only an inconsiderable portion of the island. From various causes the English district or Pale sometimes augmented in size, sometimes diminished. It did not become greatly diffused over Ireland until the last year of Queen Elizabeth, nor universally so, until shortly after the accession of James the First. The success of the forces of Queen Elizabeth was achieved by means of the most horrible treachery, murder, wholesale massacre, and deliberately created famine. Take the last instance; the growing crops were year after year destroyed, until the fairest part of Ireland, and in particular the province of Munster, was literally depopulated. I give here one quotation. It is from the English Protestant historian Morrison: 'No spectacle was more frequent in the ditches of the towns, and especially in wasted countries, than to see multitudes of these poor people, the Irish, dead, with their mouths all coloured by eating nettles, docks, and all things they could rend above the ground.'

And in another extract from O'Connell's book:

Never was a people on the face of the globe so cruelly treated as the Irish.

The Irish people were not received into allegiance or to the benefit of being recognised as subjects until the year 1612, only 228 years ago, when the Statute 11 James I. cap. 5, was enacted. The Statute abolished all distinctions of race between English and Irish, 'with the intent that', as the Statute expresses it, 'they may grow into one nation, whereby there may be an utter obligation and extinguishment of all former differences and discord between them.'

During the four hundred and forty years that intervened between the commencement of domination in 1172 and its completion in 1612, the Irish people were known only as 'Irish enemies'. They were denominated 'Irish Enemies' in all the Royal Proclamations, Royal Charters, and Acts of Parliaments, during the period. It was their legal and technical description.

During that period the English were prohibited from intermarrying with the Irish, from having their children nursed by the wives of Irish Captains, Chiefs, or Lords; and what is still more strange, the English were also prohibited from sending goods, wares, or merchandises for sale, or selling them upon credit or for ready money to the Irish.

During that time any person of English descent might murder a mere Irish man or woman with perfect impunity. Such murder was no more a crime in the eye of the law, than the killing of a rabid or ferocious animal.

O'Connell goes on to extract and quote from official English sources how they set about depopulating the country. He notes 'that there were more than 100,000 persons of every age and sex banished'; of whom several thousand were, as he says, sent to the West India islands. We also learn from the original letter in the possession of Dr. Lingard that the vessels were crowded with the poorer classes of Catholics and sent to Barbados and other West India islands. 'I believe,' says the writer, 'that already 60,000 are gone; for the husbands being first sent to Spain and Belgium, already their wives and children are destined for Americas.' It would be indeed idle to exclaim at any cruelty committed at that time. Those unhappy exiles perished in hundreds and thousands. Of the myriads thus transported, not a single one survived at the end of 20 years.

'Was there any species of crime which was not perpetrated against the Irish by the barbarians of the English Governments?' asked the famous Liberator.

Many of these, of course, refer to the aftermath of the Treaty of Limerick when many Clare people were transported to Barbados and the West Indies.

It is no wonder that the clergy were in constant hiding when we hear of such acts of law put into force by the English as the following:

In the same year (1652) the Parliament commissioners at Dublin published a proclamation, signed Charles Fleetwood, Edmund Ludlow, and John Jones, wherein the acts of the 27th of Elizabeth was made of force in Ireland, and ordered to be most strictly put into execution. By this act, every Romish priest, so found, was deemed guilty of rebellion, and sentenced to be hanged until he was half dead; then to have his head taken off, and his body cut in quarters; his bowels to be drawn out and burned; and his head fixed upon a pole in some public place. (Curry's Review, page 392).

In the last chapter of his book O'Connell goes on to catalogue some of the chiefs and nobles slaughtered by the Protestants. Beginning with some illustrious chiefs from other parts of the country we note that amongst them are Lord Hugh McMahon; Cornelius Maguire; Lord Viscount Iniskillen; the illustrious Felix O'Neill; Henry O'Neill, son of Eugene O'Neill; Thaddaeus O'Connor of Sligo, a descendant of the royal race hung at Boyle in AD 1652.

In relation to some of the Clare chiefs who were cruelly betrayed, the following extract is recorded:

The illustrious Donat O'Brien, descended of the Royal race of the O'Briens, a most generous man and of unsurpassed hospitality, after the Protestants had plighted to him their faith and given him safe conduct in order that he might become their tributary; an attack being made one day by the Protestants against the Catholics, he (O'Brien) relying on his having been received into their friendship, approached, when a certain Protestant knight shot him through the body. Unsatisfied with this cruelty, when the old man (then about 64 years) had entered a hut, half dead, that he might in penitence commend himself to God, a soldier followed, set fire to the hut and burned this noble old man – in Thomond AD 1651.

James O'Brien, of illustrious lineage, maternal nephew of the aforesaid Donatus O'Brien, a youth of high hopes and prospects, was murdered at Nenagh by the Ormonds. They cut his head off and sent it to his uterine brother, Moriarty O'Brien, then their prisoner.

Bernard O'Brien, of the same noble family, a youth of equally fair prospects, was hanged in 1651.

Daniel O'Brien, first cousin of the said Bernard, was hanged, and his head cut off at Nenagh, 1651.

One unusual practice which reached its zenith during the 1820's and the 1830's was the lawless practice of faction fighting. It was little more than groups of families banding together to engage each other in skirmishes with sticks and stones. The venues for those contests were the villages and towns to which the country folk would flock on fair days. Groups, sometimes in the hundreds, confronted each other on the main street on appointed days. With sticks and stones flying in all directions it was a lucky man who came away without injury.

The police and towns' people stayed well clear of the faction fights. All shops and houses were boarded up to minimize damage to property. Faction fighting would appear to have been linked to the old clan wars. Faction fighting began in Tipperary and it was also common in Limerick and Kerry, but to a lesser extent in Clare. A few interesting episodes which occurred in Clare are worth relating.

A fierce fight took place at the fair of Kildysart on 23 May 1825. When the buying and selling was completed and no doubt some refreshments drunk, both factions faced each other. The Kildysart faction was led by Pat Moylan, Mick McInerney and Martin Keane. The stalwarts for the Ballinacally faction were of the O'Donnel, Connor, Quinn and Walsh families. All were formidable combatants.

Moylan struck James O'Donnell the first blow, which was enough to unleash the warring factions on each other. A group of 20 led by Martin Keane of Kildysart found the going tough – at one stage Keane had to face the formidable trio of Quinn, Walsh and Connor. Expert though Keane was, he was hard put to ward off three good men. When the cudgel was knocked from his grasp by an elbow stroke from Walsh he quickly stooped to retrieve it. At that instant Quinn and Connor were in the process of delivering blows which they were unable to check. Keane fielded some heavy blows on the side of his head, fracturing his skull and rendering him unconscious. In the ongoing melee he was trampled on by the crowd.

Towards the evening O'Driscoll of the Ballynacallys stunned McInerney who was a very skilful fighter. Then finally, with an uppercut of his blackthorn stick, O'Driscoll practically lifted Moylan off his feet thereby laying him out on the dust. The contest quickly ended because both factions were falling down with exhaustion. They all agreed that it had been a great fight but regretted that Martin Keane had been badly hurt. In fact Keane later died of injuries suffered in this particular fracas.

Over in Killaloe the Corbans and the Hourigans had a history of some stern encounters. After the big fair of Killaloe on 21 April 1829 three men lay dead in Ballina just across the Shannon from Killaloe. The military made an unsuccessful attempt to stop the fighting there. When they fired their rifles into the crowd John Minogue and Thady Moloney of the Corbans and Stephen Hinchey of the Hourigans (all small farmers) were shot dead.

Sergeant William Browne was convicted of the wilful murder of Hinchey although he was later acquitted at the Clonmel assizes. Four of the faction leaders were also arraigned before a judge and jury in Clonmel. Each was sentenced to two years imprisonment for his part in the riot.

The practice of faction fighting continued on a reducing scale until the middle of the 19th century when it died out almost completely. Strong memories of the factions have lingered in some places. In recent times family feuds have bee re-ignited with little more than the shouting of an old faction battle cry.

34. The Baker rifle was a muzzle-loading flintlock weapon used by the British Army in the Napoleonic Wars and may possibly have been used by them to disperse the Killaloe faction fight. This rifle was an accurate weapon for its day with reported kills being taken at 100 to 300 yards (91 m to 274 m) away.

(Wikipedia)

This century saw events of a more progressive nature (such as the building of schools) taking place throughout the county. It provided a modicum of employment whereby labourers could earn some money in the construction of the schools. Unfortunately, fast on the heels of the schools came the construction of the workhouses – places of death and disease for the sick and destitute. The districts in which the workhouse were located were called unions, initially there were four situated in Clare: Ennis, Kilrush, Scariff and Ennistymon. The first inmates were received into the newly-completed workhouse at Kilrush on the 9 July 1842. A building was erected to cater for a maximum of 800 inmates or 'paupers'. The Poor Law Union was the hinterland for the workhouse whose destitute inhabitants it was intended to serve. Kilrush Union contained a population of 82,353 persons according to the 1841 census; it was spread out over a geographical area of nearly 116,000 acres extending into three baronies.

Daniel O'Connell was of the opinion that if the Union of Britain and Ireland was to be abolished and Ireland left to run her own affairs she would be well able to feed all of her people. To gain further support for his ideas he addressed a series of outdoor meetings around the country. The first meeting was at Ballycoree near Ennis in 1843. Reports of the day told of the roads to Ennis being jammed with enthusiastic Catholics converging on the hill north of the town. Once again Clare was the hub of patriotic fervour with the entire country looking to it as the ashes from which would spring the Phoenix of freedom. 100 bandsmen led the marching procession on that day while brilliant sunshine added to the enjoyment of the huge crowd. It was a successful rally with Clare's contribution to the Repeal Rent fund amounting to £1,200. A celebratory banquet was held afterwards in the Old Chapel located in the Chapel Lane of Ennis.

More 'monster' meetings and rallies followed in other parts of Ireland, but the 'repeal year' of 1843 came and went out without the movement realising its objective. That which was dragging Ireland down – the Union of Britain and Ireland – remained stubbornly in place.

By 1845 three adverse conditions had collided to spell disaster for Ireland. First, the Union had not been repealed which meant that Ireland could not control her own affairs and would therefore be openly manipulated by Britain in all things political. Secondly, the population had increased phenomenally from 1½ million in 1651 to approximately 8–9 million people by 1845. And thirdly, the staple diet of the Irish peasant, the potato, rotted in the pits towards the end of 1845, which left no reserve until next planting time. A wail of despondency went up from the Irish people for they surely knew what was in store for them.

Failure of the potato crop was always a puzzle even in England and on the continent of Europe. Writing from Devon in England, Jas Barnes told of total failure there. After careful examination of his own crop he came to the conclusion that the original cause of the disease was still unknown. He was, however, fairly convinced that the trouble started in the tubers and spread from there. He could not have been more wrong as the following 20th century discovery explains.

The potato crop failed due to an attack by Phytophtora Infestans, more commonly known as blight today. Three quarters of a century later it was discovered that a water mold (a fungus like organism) on the potato leaves which spawned when weather conditions became wet and humid caused the disease. The disease was also capable of being transferred directly to the tubers by being washed down and through the ground from the leaves. The 1845 crop was infected after digging, while the 1846 harvest rotted in the ground. This dramatic failure in the soil meant that the epidemic would be widespread. It proved to be the case.

The *Clare Journal* of 19 January 1846 urged the gentlemen of Clare to grow their potato crops early. Being late in tillage was injurious to the crop the Journal stated. It was further asserted that the gentlemen of Clare should make some exertions themselves rather than suggesting to the government ways in which the land might be improved. As common and as vital a crop as the potato was very little was understood of its peculiarities.

When rents went unpaid widespread evictions followed. Roofs were torn from the tiny cabins in a single sweep with grappling hooks. Sometimes an entire village would be de-roofed exposing all the undernourished occupants to the merciless weather. The despoiled people huddled in dreadfully wet ditches with the remains of their original roofing propped over their heads. Such a 'habitation' was called a scalp. Living in a ditch without a roof was referred to as a scalpeen. A large portion of the population was subjected to those dreadful conditions. It would not be unrealistic to assume that people who were subsequently made homeless

'35. ***The cutting at Ballyhee*** *with finely constructed abutment walls which was the result of famine relief work. A channel was cut from Clonteen Lake, through the hill at Ballyhee to release large volumes of water into the Fergus. It is half a mile long and some 50 feet deep. It is located north of Templemaley graveyard above Ballyalla Lake, north of Ennis.*

(Brian Dinan)

once suffered under scalps and scalpeens and consequently found it difficult to reintegrate into a settled way of life.

When those small tenants looked over their rotted potato fields in the foreboding atmosphere of 1846 surely a mood of utter despair gripped them. A modicum of hope was offered with relief works being put into operation by the authorities. The money paid ranged from six to ten pence per day, but hardly enough to feed individuals let alone their families.

At the Clare Abbey relief works the overseer, a Mr Hennessy, was shot and wounded by an unknown and distraught man. The works were suspended while they attempted to bring the man responsible to the authorities. Much suffering followed in the village of Clare when the people were left without relief. Time passed but nobody came forward to name the assailant. Finally, a Captain Wynne intervened by sending pleading letters to the Board of Works and to Lord Trevelyan. A quote from the documents gives a graphic description of general conditions in Clare at the end of 1846:

Although a man not easily moved, I confess myself unmanned by the intensity and extent of the suffering I witnessed more especially among the women and little children, crowds of whom were to be seen scattered over the turnip fields like a flock of banished crows, devouring the raw turnips, mothers half naked, shivering in the snow and sleet, muttering exclamations of despair while their children were screaming with hunger.

The works at Clare Abbey were at last reopened on 28 December 1846. When the workhouses became overcrowded quite quickly a new one had to be constructed in Tulla. Conditions in those fearful institutions were most unhygienic. More often than not cholera overtook those battling against starvation. The Kilrush Union was particularly bad where hundreds of paupers (inmates of workhouses) succumbed each month. It was little wonder that the people died in droves in those institutions. In the running costs of the workhouse it was calculated that it took 11½d (less than 1 cent in present day currency) to feed a pauper each week. (The term 'pauper' for a destitute person carried well into the 20th century). Children were reared and educated in the unsuitable surroundings of workhouses – an experience that surely scarred them for life. A school mistress in the Ennis Union received a yearly salary of £15, with ration, coal and candles.

Soup and stirabout porridge were dispensed at population centres throughout the county. Although the people were dying on their feet they could not abide the shame of queuing for soup with bowl or pot in hand. The people of Ennistymon said they had no bowls such was their pride. At Miltown Malbay a crowd rushed the kitchen and demolished the boiler in their frustration at the demeaning reactions of the authorities.

Many benevolent better-off people did their best to get food to the hungry. The Society of Friends did Trojan work in their efforts to relieve the starving. Donations came from America and England to buy food for the people. All those subscriptions, although very welcome, were but a pebble to a quarry. For every ship England sent up the Shannon to supply the district with grain, six more left the country bound for England laden with other foodstuffs. Ireland was exporting enough food to feed twice the population. Such was English Government policy!

The Ennis relief fund of 31 March 1846 which was published in the *Clare Journal* showed that there were numerous Clare contributors. Topping the list was a Mr Joseph Gore with a donation of £50. Mr Vandeleur made a similar contribution to the Kilrush Union. Regretfully they saw no other way of solving the dilemma.

36. Daniel O'Connell (The Liberator) *sought Catholic Emancipation for the Irish. A monument erected in his honour by Michael G Considine stands in the centre of Ennis.* *(Wikipedia)*

The famines of '46 and '47 – the Great Hunger – left much hatred in its wake. It cleaved as a sword through the English/Irish connection like nothing before or since. Its effects stretched right up to present times. A century after the Great Hunger, Irish people were still admonishing England for its woeful neglect. Irish people continue to feel the sorrow of that famine right into modern times. The catastrophe so soured English/Irish relationships that Ireland's stance in WW 2 wouldn't allow her to enter that world conflict because it was believed that England's conduct during the famine years was unsympathetic to the plight of small nations.

Political agitation continued and grew apace through the 19th century. O'Connell was prosecuted for holding another of his popular mass meetings in Clontarf, Dublin. His arrest led to his falling from political prominence.

A revolutionary movement, called Young Irelanders next took up the political cudgel. This was a movement more disposed to using violence to achieve their political aims. The British had been aware that O'Connell was not prepared to resort to violence; so they used this limitation in their manipulation of him and his movement. Daniel O'Connell became politically ineffective thereafter. He died on 15 May 1847 at Genoa, while travelling to Rome. A famous Clareman, William Smith O'Brien, was the principal revolutionary after O'Connell's demise.

By the time the famine had ended in 1851 an estimated 2½ million persons had lost their lives throughout Ireland. In Clare possibly up to 70,000 people perished – equivalent to 70% of the current population.

The revolutionary Fenian Movement which began in the 1860's had strong organisations in both Ireland and the United States of America. Many of Clare's sons returned from the American Civil War to give clandestine military instructions to those in Ireland. Weapons of war were secretly imported into the country and put into hiding for the 'rising'.

The night of 5 March 1867 was designated for striking the revolutionary blow. Many thousands of Clare men had mustered to their appointed positions but no weapons or overall plan materialised. At the Kilbaha lighthouse station an insignificant skirmish took place and a small number of volunteers were betrayed in a grove near Ennis when one of their number struck a match to signal the authorities. All-in-all, it turned out to be an unmitigated disaster of planning, which was totally devoid of any organisation and saddled with poor implementation.

The best known political activist of the latter half of the 19th century was Charles Stewart Parnell, leader of the Irish MP's to the Westminster. Parnell made his famous 'boycott' speech at Ennis in 1880. In 1885 he was back in Miltown to address a huge crowd on the much-agitated Land Question while basking in glorious sunshine on the lawn of the parochial house. Banners flew, bands played and Parnell cut the sod to commemorate the official opening of the West Clare Railway. The main objective of the Land League was to obtain Fixity of Tenure for small farmers in order that they might have some stability in the operating of their little farms. The removal of rack rents was one unfair imposition that beset the tenant farmers. However, both Parnell and the 19th century passed without self-government (Home Rule) coming to Ireland.

*37. Jackie Whelan and his West Clare steam engine which he recently rebuilt and put into operation at Moyasta in West Clare.
The original West Clare line was closed down on 31 January 1961 in spite of a local public outcry.*

(West Clare Railway Images)

Many of the fine buildings around Clare were constructed during the 19th century. The Christian Brothers, offering good education for boys, brought their school to Ennis in 1827 and again in 1854. The Christian Brothers School at Ennistymon was founded in 1824, which makes it one of the oldest such schools in Ireland. In 1879 construction work began on St Flannan's College on the Clare Road in Ennis. In 1854 (at the request of Dean Kenny) six Sisters of Mercy came out from Limerick to set up a convent in Ennis. On 29 May the sisters set up St Xavier's Convent in Arthur's Row from where their schools expanded to provide much-needed education for girls in Ennis.

Ennis' original courthouse dating from 1641 was demolished in 1848 and a more imposing building constructed in Lifford in 1850. The site of the old building now accommodates the 74 foot high column holding the statue of Daniel O'Connell. The 'monument' (as it is now known) was worked from limestone by Dublin sculptor, James Cahill. It was unveiled on 3 October 1865 by Dr Power who was the then Bishop of Killaloe.

38. A boat being unloaded at Clarecastle harbour at the end of the 19th century. Note the excellent condition of barracks and castle in background.

(Lawrence Collection 6466 N. L.)

Although Clare and Ireland experienced some slight increases in prosperity after the Crimean War it was mitigated by the famines that befell the country in the wet summers of 1863 and 1864. Those outbreaks did not have the devastating effects of the horrendous '46 and '47 famines had, nevertheless widespread suffering did cause much hardship for the poor.

Living conditions did improve to some extent towards the end of the 19th century mainly because produce like cattle and butter fetched improved prices. However, the commercial structure of the country was quite weak with Britain always calling the tune with regard to commodities purchased and prices on offer. It was then clear to all free-thinking Irish people that Ireland's only hope for improvement was to take charge of her own destiny.

In the last quarter of the 19th century the English Tory Government banned the Land League. This resulted in secret meetings which brought illegal activities into play. Much coercive action disrupted the farming community. In spite of a ban, some meetings took place in Ennis, Kilrush and Miltown Malbay.

39. Turnpike Road, Ennis, c 1900. The dwellings shown were demolished in the mid 20th century to make way for MacNamara and Dalcassian Parks.

(Lawrence Collection, 6265. National Library of Ireland)

The land tenants withheld their rents to protest against coercion. Evictions took place at a number of locations. Tenants in Bodyke barricaded themselves in their cabins and refused to get off the land. The police arrived amid much excitement. In 1887 at least 28 families were ejected from their homes culminating in the infamous 'Bodyke evictions'. At Miltown Malbay a protracted struggle ensued, whereby it was made all the more troublesome by the revelation that the letting agent had already re-let property from which a tenant was being evicted. In spite of all the chicanery the fracas eventually petered out peacefully.

Undoubtedly, the 1800's made up one the blackest centuries in the history of Clare and Ireland. Starvation and loss of land was the lot of a once proud and fighting Dalcassian tribe. Without local rule and national government there was a gnawing desire to achieve some modicum of self government if the Irish were to gain any measure of self fulfilment.

The first step towards native administration was won from the Westminster Parliament in 1898. The Local Government Act of that year gave Ireland her first county and urban councils. The acquiring of local government status became the catalyst for the ongoing building of social houses in the early part of the next century – a very important step going forward with social infrastructure.

Due to the famine and related hardships people poured from the land in droves in search of a better life. Clare people emigrated to America,

40. The 'good ship' Jeanie Johnston, which would have been typical of the ships crossing the Atlantic during the famine. The mortality rate for passengers was 30%, although it is claimed that no one lost their lives on the 'good ship'. Conditions were so awful on most other ships that they were generally dubbed as 'coffin ships'.

(Brian Dinan)

Australia and Britain, many with only their shirts on their backs, so to speak.

Clare was populated by about 130,000 people before the '46 and '47 famines. (This is compared to 119,000 today). With a small measure of local government in place the question became – could a dwindling down-trodden people arise to re-establish themselves as a nation once again? Would the spark of self determination within a native government arise phoenix-like from the depths of those generations of lost, languishing and unfulfilled souls?

The answer was – it had to be attempted – not only for their sakes, but to provide opportunities for future generations of Irish people to better themselves. Surely, some lessons had been well learned?

Chapter 10

Fight for freedom
(1900–1925)

The 20th century began in much the same fashion as the previous one left off. Large families continued to subsist on small patches of land, much of it of poor quality, while landlords still retained the prized land and plenty of it. Poverty and the workhouses loomed large over the populous as may be gleaned from the following *Clare Journal* report of 9 January 1908.

At the weekly meeting of the Board of Guardians of the Ennis Union, the Chairman Mr P E Keanneally presided. A report on the state of the house went as follows:

Admitted 35: Born 0; Discharged 37; Died 4; Remaining in the House 44, at an average cost of 4s.-2½d; Number in Infirmary 96, at a general cost of 5s.-4½d.; In fever hospital 2, at an average cost of 10s.-3d. Tramps admitted 15 men, 4 women and 9 children.

Clare's towns and villages consisted of small merchants and part-time publicans with little else in the way of commercial enterprise. Urban development barely existed and where it did it was at a snail's pace. Employment other than agricultural labouring was scarce and sporadic. Paradoxically, a measure of relief was experienced when the First World War broke out in 1914. The lack of local employment prompted many men in Clare to enlist in the British Army. Wages – for the unfortunate it would be pensions – flowed into the country from the soldiers fighting abroad. It kept many a family in food and shelter.

A step towards normal civil rights was enacted with the 1903 Land Act. This piece of legislation gave a new measure of freedom to tenant farmers. The three major gains for the farmers was known as the 'three F's'; they were, fair rent, fixity of tenure and freedom of sale. The Act enabled the tenant farmers to buy back their holdings from the landlords by a system of annuities. This became an important breakthrough because with fixity of tenure in the holdings it meant that fairer rents could be set and the right of free sale was guaranteed; it was an important step forward for the tenants. However, the landlords had to be accommodated and so they were with the British Government making special grants to compensate them against any losses – we can be sure that the landlords did not lose out on the deal. The 'land war' continued unabated with Michael Davitt in Mayo spearheading the movement. It was the Clareman, William O'Brien, who, in the 1902 Land Conference paved the way for advanced social reform.

POBLACHT NA H EIREANN.

THE PROVISIONAL GOVERNMENT

OF THE

IRISH REPUBLIC

TO THE PEOPLE OF IRELAND.

IRISHMEN AND IRISHWOMEN: In the name of God and of the dead generations from which she receives her old tradition of nationhood, Ireland, through us, summons her children to her flag and strikes for her freedom.

Having organised and trained her manhood through her secret revolutionary organisation, the Irish Republican Brotherhood, and through her open military organisations, the Irish Volunteers and the Irish Citizen Army, having patiently perfected her discipline, having resolutely waited for the right moment to reveal itself, she now seizes that moment, and, supported by her exiled children in America and by gallant allies in Europe, but relying in the first on her own strength, she strikes in full confidence of victory.

We declare the right of the people of Ireland to the ownership of Ireland, and to the unfettered control of Irish destinies, to be sovereign and indefeasible. The long usurpation of that right by a foreign people and government has not extinguished the right, nor can it ever be extinguished except by the destruction of the Irish people. In every generation the Irish people have asserted their right to national freedom and sovereignty; six times during the past three hundred years they have asserted it in arms. Standing on that fundamental right and again asserting it in arms in the face of the world, we hereby proclaim the Irish Republic as a Sovereign Independent State, and we pledge our lives and the lives of our comrades-in-arms to the cause of its freedom, of its welfare, and of its exaltation among the nations.

The Irish Republic is entitled to, and hereby claims, the allegiance of every Irishman and Irishwoman. The Republic guarantees religious and civil liberty, equal rights and equal opportunities to all its citizens, and declares its resolve to pursue the happiness and prosperity of the whole nation and of all its parts, cherishing all the children of the nation equally, and oblivious of the differences carefully fostered by an alien government, which have divided a minority from the majority in the past.

Until our arms have brought the opportune moment for the establishment of a permanent National Government, representative of the whole people of Ireland and elected by the suffrages of all her men and women, the Provisional Government, hereby constituted, will administer the civil and military affairs of the Republic in trust for the people.

We place the cause of the Irish Republic under the protection of the Most High God, Whose blessing we invoke upon our arms, and we pray that no one who serves that cause will dishonour it by cowardice, inhumanity, or rapine. In this supreme hour the Irish nation must, by its valour and discipline and by the readiness of its children to sacrifice themselves for the common good, prove itself worthy of the august destiny to which it is called.

Signed on Behalf of the Provisional Government,

THOMAS J. CLARKE,
SEAN Mac DIARMADA, THOMAS MacDONAGH,
P. H. PEARSE, EAMONN CEANNT,
JAMES CONNOLLY, JOSEPH PLUNKETT.

41. The 1916 Proclamation of the Irish Republic; signed by Thomas J Clarke; Sean Mac Diarmada; P H Pearse; James Connolly; Thomas McDonagh; Eamonn Ceannt; Joseph Plunkett.

(Wikipedia)

The west coast of Clare continued to be inhospitable to seafarers. A shipwreck occurred off Spanish Point on 14 January 1916. The three-masted schooner, *Kelp,* was smashed on the rocks there. Fortunately the crew members received help and support from the locals – this action was in stark contrast to the reception meted out to the soldiers of the Spanish Armada ships some three centuries earlier.

In Easter Week of 1916 the blow struck for Irish freedom reverberated not only around the country but around the world. The American papers in particular followed the event with great interest. It was not a coordinated countrywide rising, indeed the confusion in implementation almost scuppered the entire undertaking. The main action took place in Dublin with the GPO being the focal point and the centre of military action and administration. Inspired by the legendary dead Fenian, O'Donovan Rossa, the commanders Clarke, Pearse and Connolly were inspirational in setting out the Republican ideals as well as putting the 'Rising' itself into action.

The Rising of 1916 brought about the War of Independence of 1919–21; it became the catalyst for gaining freedom for Ireland – although there was still the matter of attachment to the British Commonwealth. To complicate matters the agreement at the end of the hostilities allowed northern Ireland (the Six Counties) to remain within the United Kingdom. It was to become an ongoing sore in the untangling of the Irish/British relationship and has not been properly resolved even at the present day.

That military action in the bid for Irish freedom was not viewed in all quarters with approval if the *Clare Champion* of 6 May 1916 is anything to go by. Most people of the time failed to comprehend the significance of the heroic undertaking carried out by the selfless leaders of Ireland's 1916 'revolution'. 'The Dublin revolution has come and gone – gone to join the shades of many another attempt on the part of desperate Irish men to establish an Irish Republic.' So said the Bishop of Killaloe while preaching at Quin as he bewailed and lamented 'the mad Dublin venture'. He did, however, give them credit for dying bravely even if foolishly.

After the surrender of the GPO by the leaders of the Rising (the signatories of the 1916 Proclamation of the Irish Republic) were summarily executed in Kilmainham Jail. This callous action by the British authorities brought the wrath of world opinion down on the Crown and was to gain much sympathy for the rebels. The Bishop of Killaloe came to reverse his opinion of the 'mad adventure' when he fully understood the significance of the Rising as well as the power of public opinion. World opinion soon forced the British Government to release all Republican prisoners by early 1917. It had the effect of freeing Republican activists to unleash a new wave of political and paramilitary activity. The later hunger strike by Terence MacSwiney totally swung public sympathy to the Republicans.

In Clare on the night of the 23 June 1917 an historic event unfolded. The train from Dublin had on board the hero of Boland's Mills (Easter Week Rising), one Éamon de Valera. He was on his way to Clare at the behest of the Sinn Féin organisation to contest a bye-election caused by the death of Major William Redmond who had been MP for East Clare since 1892. Redmond believed freedom could be gained for Ireland by peaceful means in co-operation with Britain. It seems ironic then that he choose to die on the Western Front fighting for Britain but could not do the same for Ireland.

The de Valera train that pulled into Ennis station was greeted with fog signals, flags and banners. On the roadway outside 1,000 volunteers had assembled to demonstrate their undying allegiance to the cause of self determination. An historic tie was thus forged between war hero and county – de Valera had commenced his campaign for the Sinn Féin party's cause in Clare. It was to be a campaign that would have long and far-reaching consequences.

Commandant de Valera's maiden speech in the political arena was made in Clare on that very night. He addressed a crowd of Sinn Féin supporters at their headquarters in the Old Ground Hotel before retiring for the evening. The assemblage was ecstatic and greeted his every sentence with shouts of 'up dev' and 'we'll put him in'.

A campaign of political rallies began and continued with much fervour right up to poling day on 10 July 1917. A disturbing incident occurred on the first day of the rally when Sinn Féin supporters were motoring between Broadford and Tuamgraney. On stopping to clear an obstruction on the road the party came under gunfire. 15 rounds in all were rained down on them, one of which pierced the vehicle's petrol tank. None of the party suffered injury and after effecting repairs they arrived in Tuamgraney in time for their political rally.

Some prominent speakers who supported de Valera and the Sinn Féin cause in the Clare campaign included; Professor Eoin McNeill, Larry Ginnell MP, Peader Clancy, Arthur Griffiths, Séan Milroy, Count Plunkett, T V Honan as well as many other political and clerical dignitaries.

In opposition to Sinn Féin was Mr Patrick Lynch KC representing the Irish Party. He came from a very well respected and well connected Clare family – in most other circumstances he would have been an excellent representative but after centuries of oppression the 1916 Rising had cast off the yoke of foreign domination and changed the people's mood.

As the campaign begun parades and street rallies (especially in Ennis) became commonplace. The Sinn Féin supporters waved the Tricolour while supporters of the Irish Party and Mr Lynch usually displayed green flags, sometimes the French colours, but notably the British Union Flag. On Monday 25 June a clash between police and supporters occurred at

O'Connell Square in Ennis. The police baton-charged the crowd and as a consequence some civilians sustained minor injuries.

On July 10 voting took place at Ennis courthouse. Early voters included Dr Michael Fogarty, Catholic Bishop of the Killaloe dioceses, and Very Rev Canon O'Dea, President of St Flannan's College, Ennis. In an incident outside the Town Hall pooling booth a number of men suffered injuries in a minor scuffle. Countess Markievicz and Dr MacClancy were amongst those who attended to the injured. Incident after incident occurred right into the night until it became unsafe to walk the streets of Clare's capital town.

Tempers subsided overnight and the count was made known on the following day by the Sheriff, Major F G Cullinan. The result was as follows: de Valera, 5,010 votes; Lynch, 2,035 votes. It was a clear-cut victory for Mr de Valera and the republican Sinn Féin organisation the news of which reverberated throughout the country. Clare had again struck a blow against the old enemy by endorsing the freedom fighters through the ballot box. The victory garnered much support for Sinn Féin and this influenced the neutrals into believing that self determination was not only possible but indeed the best way forward for the Irish nation.

Success at the polls was the signal for further drilling and training of volunteers. In all areas of the county and the country men learned the rudiments of soldiering. It was done in open defiance of authorities such as The Royal Irish Constabulary. Many local military leaders were put under arrest but all to no avail as the enthusiastic volunteers continued to drill, to train and recruit volunteers.

In September de Valera returned to Clare to rally the people after the death of that great patriot, Thomas Ashe, in Dublin. The following famous speech by de Valera was delivered to the people of Clare:

Since I was last in Clare, I have visited many parts of Ireland and everywhere I went I heard the words 'Good old Clare' and 'Brave old Clare'. Everywhere I went I found the enthusiasm and spirit almost as strong as in Clare. The same determination is alive all over the country today as in the brave boys of Ennis and Clare who are bravely and unflinchingly defying the Sasanach in his prisons and it shows that there is no breaking the spirit that is alive in the hearts of Irish men.

As I came along the streets I saw the illuminations and the great enthusiasm displayed by the gathering, but I also observed that the flags were draped in black. I thought of the many times Brian of old went out with his brave Dalcassians to battle and came back victorious but at the same time mourning the loss of brave comrades who fell in the fight. If victory in Ireland has to be purchased at the cost of draping our flags, then let it be so, but victory we shall have and that determination which is in our hearts no enemy can crush.

On the following day a mass meeting of up to 25,000 people assembled in and about the Square in Ennis; there they raised ecstatic vocal support for their favourite commandant. In effect this was recognition of him as the

Commander-in-Chief of the Sinn Féin Republican army. Thereafter he was frequently and affectionately referred to as 'The Chief'.

The year 1918 saw the development of a new activity in Clare as in other parts of Ireland. The Sinn Féin volunteers advocated total severance from British authority – which meant the removal of all vestiges of British rule in the police, the army, and in local government. Because the rebels lacked arms to form any kind of a fighting force the practice of stealing weapons and ammunition became widespread. Irish men home on leave from the British army proved to be easy targets for the volunteers.

Many men were taken into custody during this period of unrest to include amongst others; H J Hunt (Commandant Fifth Battalion, Clare Brigade); Michael Murray (Commandant First Battalion); Art O'Donnell (Commandant Seventh Battalion); Frank Gallagher (Vice Commandant First Battalion); John Moynihan (Captain, A Company, Fifth Battalion); John Murnane (Captain, B Company, First Battalion); J J Liddy (Captain, G Company, Seventh Battalion); Michael Breen (Lieutenant, C Company, Fifth Battalion); Peter O'Loughlin (Lieutenant, B Company, Sixth Battalion); Tom Browne (A Company, Fourth Battalion); James Madigan (A Company, Fourth Battalion); William McNamara (A Company, Fourth Battalion); Thomas Callaghan (C Company, Fourth Battalion); Thomas Marrinan (F Company, Fifth Battalion); Frank Shinners (A Company, Fourth Battalion); as well as Paddy, Michael and Austin Brennan, and Jimmy Griffey. All of the above were imprisoned in Mountjoy Jail in Dublin at one time or another.

Towards the end of 1918 the Westminster Parliament was dissolved with 14 December being fixed as polling day for fresh elections. It became immediately obvious that one person stood out as a likely candidate for election to the East Clare constituency – Éamon de Valera.

At an election meeting in O'Connell Square, Ennis, the Rev William O'Kennedy of St Flannan's College delivered a long address in which he wholeheartedly supported Mr de Valera as candidate. However he did stress the Clare yearning for complete and undiluted freedom and that no representative, not even Éamon de Valera, would be allowed 'sully the flag like the Redmonds and the Dillons'. If that happened he continued: 'The Dalcassians will tear the idol out of their hearts and smash it to the ground because it is contrary to the principles for which our forefathers fought and for which we will fight on, but men of Clare, de Valera is not a man who will massage the body of old John Bull.'

He went on to read a letter of support from the Most Rev Dr Fogarty, who strongly condemned England for 'its plutocratic record of oppression, corruption and chicanery'. This was a significant mood swing by the clergy who had begun to take a stronger stance on the side of Nationalism.

Because de Valera and Brian O'Higgins were the only nominees for their respective constituencies in Clare both were returned without going to contest. Both men were incarcerated in English jails at that time. The absence of the candidates from the campaign field greatly reduced interest and atmosphere in the election proceedings.

The latter part of 1919 saw the people of Clare and Ireland clamouring for the release of Irish prisoners of the War of Independence; most were detained in British detention centres. There was much excitement when it was learned that Clare's adopted hero, Éamon de Valera, had escaped from Lincoln prison and had been spirited to America. More rejoicing followed in west Clare when Brian O'Higgins came home from Birmingham Jail.

Guerilla action continued unabated throughout the County of Clare. The barracks in Newmarket-on-Fergus was raided in August resulting in the RIC men suffering the indignity of being tied to their beds by the Republicans. A small quantity of revolvers, rifles and ammunition was seized. The Newmarket guerilla action was the first of its kind in the county; it was ably led by Michael Brennan, O/C East Clare Flying Column.

The barracks at Broadford was also put under siege. Raids spread to Islandbawn, Kilkee and Ennistymon. A police car was ambushed in the Kilmihil area. In Ennistymon a youth was killed in a raid and two RIC constables were shot during the Islandbawn Protection Hut incident. Other barracks to come under attack included Kilfenora, Doonbeg and Lissycasey RIC Hut. A police patrol was fired on in the Ballyvaughan area.

The British Authorities were by now alarmed at the increased level of guerilla activity in the county. It prompted them to send in reinforcements and backup equipment. Armoured cars and Crossley Tenders appeared more frequently on Clare's roads. By April 1920 most RIC (Royal Irish Constabulary) huts throughout the county had been torched by the IRA rebels as they were then labelled. In Miltown Malbay police fired into a crowd of agitators and killed three people including a well-know Gaelic footballer, Patrick Hennessy. The Protestant church at Clarecastle was burned by 'Home Rule' supporters. As hostilities continued unabated the British sent two destroyers up the Shannon and landed 50 soldiers of the Royal Marine Light Infantry at Kilrush. It seemed to be ineffectual because the rebels continued on as before.

March 1920 saw the introduction of the infamous irregular troops [disaffected individuals de-mobbed after WW 1 who came from many different British cities] known as the Black-and-Tans – named after the distinctive uniforms they wore. This phase of the freedom fight was known as the 'Tan War' and it lasted until 11 July 1921. The Tans became discredited for the indiscipline, cruelty, drunkenness and the many atrocities they committed.

A constable Lockheed was killed during the taking of the RIC Barracks in Ruan in October, 1920. In November three volunteers and a civilian were shot dead 'while trying to escape' on the bridge at Killaloe. Their names: John Egan, age 26; Michael McMahon, age 26; Martin Kildea, age 27; and Alfred Rogers, age 22 years. By early December the authorities were so desperate that they raided Westbourne House, the Catholic bishop's residence in Ennis. As it turned out the bishop was away at the time.

The volunteers grew ever bolder in their exploits – two members of the Black and Tans went missing during the campaign. An original of the note as shown on the next page was taken from the gates of the Old Ground Hotel, Ennis, just before the hotel was ransacked and its furniture burned in the grounds. The original note may be viewed in the *Riches of Clare Museum* at Arthur's Row, near O'Connell Square, in Ennis. Guerilla activity subsequently increased and became commonplace.

42. British Army Crossley Tender transporting 11 Royal Irish Constabulary (RIC). Used in Ireland by both RIC and 'Black-and-Tan'. Two of the RIC Constables are armed with SMLE Rifles fitted with 2.5 inch Rifle Grenade Launcher Cups. Other weapons include SMLE rifles, service revolvers and a Lewis Machine Gun.

(Wikipedia)

LAST WARNING

If the two constables who were kidnapped at Ruan on the morning of the 15th inst. are not returned by midnight the 21st to Ennis those who have received such former notices can prepare to meet their God.

Black and Tan.

Even though martial law was proclaimed in January of 1921 the war action continued without letup. The tension of the times may be glimpsed by relating an incident which occurred during a curfew. A young girl in Ennis was returning home carrying a can of milk after curfew when the can was shot from her grasp by British soldiers. Undoubtedly, nobody could be trusted when no one knew how the next attack might materialize or where it might come from. Shooting at children and indiscriminately into crowds was not a practice which enhanced the reputation of the British forces in Ireland. As de Valera said in one of his earlier speeches, 'If ever a people deserved freedom and the right to live out their lives unfettered, surely it was the Irish.'

On the political front, another election was scheduled for 13 May 1921. Its purpose was to elect four TD's (Teachta Dail) to represent Clare in their new free parliament. The nominees who were elected unopposed and without fuss were: Professor de Valera; John Liddy, farmer, Danganelly, Cooraclare: Patrick Brennan, clerk, Meelick; and Brian O'Higgins, author, Carrigaholt. Peace proposals were also put forward at this time; after much discussion a nationwide truce was agreed and came into effect at 12 noon on 11 July 1921.

Éamon de Valera and the Sinn Féin organisation kept the volunteers on standby in the county while their representatives engaged in tough discussions with the British on the outcome of the war. A peace treaty was signed on 6 December to accept a partitioned country. All republican internees were subsequently released from interment. However, much dissension followed because the delegates had failed to win a 32 county republic from the British. Votes taken at local council meetings throughout the country showed there were divisions but the majority votes cast were enough to legally ratify the treaty. This was accomplished on 7 January 1922 by Dáil Éireann. Éamon de Valera resigned from the Dáil because he disagreed with the vote.

A division occurred in the ranks of Sinn Féin between those who stood for ratification and those against ratification. Those who supported the treaty included Michael Collins, Arthur Griffith, Richard Mulcahy at national level, and Michael Brennan from Clare. Against the treaty stood Éamon de Valera, Cathal Brugha, Liam Mellows at national level, and

Commandant Frank Barrett and Brian O'Higgins of the Mid-Clare Brigade. Heated debates took place both county-wide and country-wide with de Valera strongly urging the Clare 'Dalcassians' to rally round the flag.

An uneasy peace under the truce lasted into April 1922 until an ex-RIC Sergeant, John Gunn, was shot dead in the Lower Market Street in Ennis. Minor incidents continued for some months until the symptoms of civil war manifested themselves in an incident at Carron where a mother of nine was shot and died of her wounds; the killing was without explanation. Fighting broke out in the Four Courts in Dublin causing much concern. Institutions such as the Ennis banks closed their doors to all customers for a short time. Ennis RIC barracks was partially looted on 6 July by a large crowd of women and children.

The Free State Army commenced night patrols whereby the movement of the general populous was severely restricted. Lorries of Free State troops came under attack by a mob in Ennis. All roads and bridges including a railway bridge and the railway line to Corofin were severely damaged resulting in the village being isolated for a time. Free State Army posts taken over from the British military came under constant attacks from anti-treaty irregulars. Skirmishes and personal attacks continued which resulted in more killings, injuries and property damage.

In September 1922 the first Civic Guards (now An Garda Síochána) under the command of Superintendent O'Dwyer arrived in the Clare capital. By the end of October the force stood at 63 men, ten sergeants and three inspectors who were quickly installed in the former RIC barracks in Ennis, Ennistymon, Kilrush, Lisdoonvarna, Sixmilebridge, Tulla, Kildysart, Kilkee and Killaloe.

The famous West Clare Railway was attacked between Kilmurry and Craggaknock and the passengers were made to disembark. Many more attacks by anti-treaty forces were carried out on the railway lines throughout the county and it had the effect of disrupting mail and restricting travel for the civilian population. Although it received many setbacks the old West Clare Railway bounced back anew to provide that timeless meandering service for which it was popularly famous.

Attacks on Free State troops in the Ennis area became ever more frequent, resulting in injuries and some deaths. Fighters on the anti-treaty side executed by the authorities included William O'Shaughnessy, Christie Quinn, and Patrick O'Mahony. The military barracks situated on the Kilrush Road in Ennis was used as a place of execution.

Frank Aiken, Chief of Staff of the Republican Army, ordered a suspension of all hostilities on 30 April 1923. Towards the end of May matters had quieted down considerably with all parties once again turning their attentions to preparing for another election. On this occasion Labour choose two candidates to contest the election, namely Patrick Hogan and P J McNamara. The farmers selected three candidates, while Sinn Féin put forward Éamon de Valera, T V Honan, Frank Barrett, Brian O'Higgins and Michael Comyn KC. Supporters of the treaty operating under the banner of Cumann na Gael (another new political party) selected the following to contest the election for them: Dr Eoin McNeill, P Kelly from Cree, James O'Regan, Michael Hehir and Peader O'Loughlin. The date for the general election was set for 27 August 1923.

The main bone of contention for the election protagonists was partition of the country. The Northern Ireland situation was clearly anti-united Ireland in its makeup. At a Sinn Féin rally on 15 August Éamon de Valera was arrested by the government forces and taken to the Military Barracks

43. *Throughout Ireland the various political parties quickly swung into election mode. The photo above depicts a Dublin hackney driver who allowed his cab to be plastered with election posters – the Irish showing their natural talent for the art of canvassing.* (Wikipedia)

on the Kilrush Road, Ennis. Hundreds of people suffered injuries when a stampede erupted at the appearance of the military who were driving an armoured car upon which was mounted a Lewis machine gun. Happily, a quiet election followed on 27 August in which de Valera headed the poll with 17,762 votes. After many counts under the PR system (proportional representation) the following were deemed elected: Éamon de Valera (SF); Eoin McNeill (CG); Brian O'Higgins (SF); C Hogan (Farmers); P Hogan (Labour).

For the next nine months many of the IRA remained incarcerated in Irish jails, including de Valera and O'Higgins. A massive public campaign got under way to free all prisoners of war; by 16 July 1924 Éamon de Valera had already been released.

On his return to Clare he was welcomed with bonfires and much celebrating on August 15 which was the anniversary of his arrest. He continued to observe that anniversary date down the years by visiting the County Clare Agricultural Show in the Ennis Show Grounds. He always stood tall and defiant as if remembering the old days of confrontation even though his eyesight was failing during his visits in the 1960's and 1970's. At that famous meeting of 1924 in the old town of Ennis, de Valera's words had been received and repeated with great enthusiasm by the massive crowd. He had become *the* man for the people of Clare.

The determined nature of Éamon de Valera was uniquely suited to that brilliant but simplistic feature of the Dalcassian character – their innocent belief in their right to assert their freedom as a people. The Dalcassians had found and adopted a leader to carry out their ultimate wishes; nobody less than de Valera would do for them. Not since Brian Boru did the Dalcassians have such a successful leader – he had helped achieve for them what his illustrious predecessor alone achieved – their much-loved independence.

It mattered not that de Valera's character would not allow him to take a softer position on the treaty debate. He could only be one way – direct, simple, and achieve the goal at all costs. The modern-day Dalcassians would not stand for any other complicated nonsense. He was good enough for them to obtain their freedom from a most belligerent and tenacious oppressor. The time was at hand to move on now that the fighting was over and independence was won.

Appeals from the Very Rev P J Hogan Adm Ennis and from Mr G McElroy RM to remain calm and to conduct the campaign with dignity were heeded. No further incidents of a serious nature occurred. The time had come for moving on to building a modern country.

Chapter 11

Freedom at last
(1925–2015)

After hostilities had abated it became the immediate goal of the new Irish government to maintain and expand the infrastructure already in situ. The country was in an underdeveloped state. It lagged behind Britain in health services, employment, and wages as well as being burdened with woeful industrial and agricultural standards.

Although the motor car had made an appearance on Irish roads the most common modes of transport were the horse cart, pony and trap, and the bicycle. The 'high nelly' bicycle brought young people to work to dances and to matches. The country's economy was almost totally based on agriculture. After many years of foreign rule Ireland was left bereft of a commercial infrastructure. Consequently, Britain could command produce from Ireland at low prices simply because Ireland did not have other markets to use as competitive outlets.

A programme of self-reliance was soon put into practice in an effort to develop an indigenous economy. After many years of protectionism and stifled trade the country had become inept in trading practices. Technology did not spring up in Ireland and that which came in from abroad was of a limited nature and only at the wishes of foreign developers with their own agendas. When the country arrived at the year 1930 it was still mainly depending on agriculture. Even though Ireland was then a self-governing country, development happened at a snail's pace.

44. The 'high nelly' bicycle , the most common form of transport used in the early 20th century.

(Wikipedia)

When the British forces of occupation pulled out of the country there wasn't a national electricity supply service available to private users nor to industrial users. A small number of private electric supply schemes operated in places but none that could be termed 'national' or that had adequate power to supply widespread users. Therefore of immediate concern was the need for a national electricity supply system. The potential of the mighty River Shannon was looked to as the most obvious source for natural power and for its time it was considered quite an adventurous undertaking.

Previous proposals to harness the Shannon came from Sir Robert Kane in 1844 and also by the 'Frazer Scheme' in 1896. Both proposals had shortcomings and we had to wait until 1923 when Dr Thomas McLaughlin set before Patrick Gilligan (the Minister of Industry and Commerce) a scheme to exploit the full height difference (the head) between Lough Erne and the sea. The proposal was accepted because McLaughlin was familiar with the Siemens system of operating. Construction of a power station

45. Ardnacrusha Power Station became the first hydro-electric power station to serve all of Ireland. It was operational on 24 October 1929 with its four turbines of 86 Mega Watts producing 332,000 Mwh of electricity – small by present standards.

(ESB)

commenced at Ardnacrusha in the extremely hot summer of 1925, with Siemens supplying the technical expertise and equipment.

Although there was a strike in the early days of the project it did go on to employ 5,000 men, some at the very low wage of 17s-6d per week. The power station was ready for use four years later and turned its turbines on 24 October 1929. Ardnacrusha's contribution to Ireland's infrastructure has been admirable but there have been consequences to the environment. Recently it has been superceded in size and importance by oil and coal burning power stations throughout Ireland.

46. O'Connell Street, Ennis, before the arrival of the motor car, c 1910. (Note O'Connell Monument in background)

(Lawrence Collection, National Library)

47. Abbey Street, Ennis, c 1910. (Note the Abbey tower in background)

(Lawrence Collection, National Library)

With the advent of the motor car garages opened to create jobs for mechanics, sales personnel, owners and managers. But as an economy almost wholly reliant on agriculture Ireland operated at too a leisurely a pace.

The impact of mechanisation on agriculture worldwide did not significantly effect Ireland until after the Second World War had ended. It was going to be a painful transition.

Living conditions remained difficult right into the 1930s, seemingly with no prospect of improvement. It took three things on the world stage to change living standards out of all recognition in Ireland, especially so in County Clare.

WW 2 brought the need for an airport at Shannon; next came civilian aviation and then the industrial estate at Shannon. It could be said that this sequence of events launched County Clare into the technological age.

Because of the restricted range limitations of piston engines on aeroplanes of the 1930's it was impossible for them to make the 4,947 kilometre sea crossing from America to Europe without landing to refuel. A circuitous route was identified ie Gander in Newfoundland Canada to Rineanna in County Clare. A study found it could be traversed if airports were constructed at both of those locations. Thus it was that Shannon Airport in County Clare became the vital stop-over for all European/American air traffic travelling in both directions. And so it was out of the wetlands of Rineanna (from the Gaelic 'landing point of the birds') that Shannon Airport was born.

In 1936 construction work began on the 760 acre site at Rineanna on a clár (flat place) quite close to the Shannon estuary. The runway had barely been completed when the first aircraft touched down in 1939; it was an

Irish Air Corps Aero Ansen A43. The first commercial aircraft to land at Shannon was the Sabena Belgian Tri-motor S-3. Between the war period of 1939-45 services were confined to the Irish Air Corps who operated daily patrols in the area. By taking a neutral stance for the duration of WW 2 Ireland may have lost much commercial activity by not allowing Allied aircraft to land at Shannon. That business went instead to Northern Ireland and to Scotland. After the war passenger traffic increased dramatically until when in 1947 Shannon became the world's first Duty Free Airport. Many enterprises developed from this small beginning and helped in spawning the fine international airport that is in place today.

From the depths of pauperism in the recent past Shannon Airport launched County Clare onto the world stage. It was the most important event to occur in the county in modern times. It became the catalyst that revitalized the old Thomond Kingdom into a modern-day vibrant society. It infused a new-found hope in the people of Clare. The businessman who did most to pioneer development work at the airport was Brendan O'Regan from Sixmilebridge; he was an innovator and a clever entrepreneur. As comptroller at the airport he initiated many novel commercial practices and set a trend for others to follow.

With the emergence of the long distance jet aircraft in the 1960's the possibility arose that Shannon might be over-flown with a consequent loss of business. The potential loss of revenue and employment caused some concern at first. Shannon Free Airport Development Authority (the company looking after the interests of the old Thomond region and now the Midwest) was equal to the occasion when they established an industrial estate in the immediate vicinity of the airport. The incentives offered to foreign industrialists to establish their manufacturing firms in Shannon proved to be a winning formula. They received grants and tax free concessions to build subsidiaries of their factories at the airport site. SFADCo also offered grants for production machinery, training grants for workers coupled with tax-free profits on all enterprises for ten years after they went into production on Shannon's modern industrial estate.

This new industrial zone was such a successful undertaking that it attracted firms from the USA, UK, Germany, Japan and South Africa who set about establishing manufacturing plants at Shannon. Those foreign factories offered thousands of jobs in production and management so that pretty soon the Development Company found it necessary to build a housing estate on nearby Drumgeely Hill. This was to accommodate the many workers being drawn from all over Ireland as well as exiles who returned from overseas to fill the new posts.

It was from this beginning that the town of Shannon was born. In the centuries prior to the foundation of Shannon no significant new settlement had been established in the county. The foundation and growth of Shannon Town was truly the most encouraging event since the days of Brian Boru. Significantly at the time of writing, Shannon has grown to become the second largest town in Clare with a population of around 9,800 people.

Not content with enticing industrialists the Shannon Development team came up with the idea of bringing tourists to medieval banquets at Bunratty Castle. The ruins of the once majestic fortress were restored to their present splendour in 1960 by Lord Gort. Commencing in 1963 the old halls of Bunratty rang to the sound of music and merriment when the modern-day banquets commenced. Tourists are attracted from all parts of the world to wine and dine in splendour as did the Earls of Thomond in medieval days. Yes, there is much joviality at Bunratty these days – a far cry from times when men were tortured and slain within those same walls.

Under the shadow of Bunratty's ancient walls the village inn also prospers. Durty Nellie's must be one of the oldest and busiest pubs in the country. Cars rather than horses may be seen there daily, patiently awaiting their owners outside the hostelry. It seems to be a case of the modern 'peasant' living it up in way of the long-departed nobility.

48. 'Flying boats' at Foynes County Limerick on the Shannon estuary. This was the forerunner to setting up Shannon Airport at Rineanna in County Clare.

(SFADCo)

Although the ancient field game of hurling was always with the Irish clans it was not organised into a proper field sport until the latter part of the 19th century. The GAA (Gaelic Athletic Association) was founded by Burren man, Michael Cusack, at a meeting held in Hayes's Hotel in Thurles County Tipperary on 1 November 1884. From then on both hurling and Gaelic football were regulated by set rules and played on a standardized playing pitch. Prior to that point the games had been played by pursuing a

49. The layout of Shannon Industrial Estate in the early 1960's. It was the start of concentrated industrialization which brought diverse industries to County Clare. (SFADCo)

leather-covered ball from parish to parish. Clare won four All-Ireland Senior Hurling titles: in 1914, 1995, 1997 and 2013. A senior Gaelic football title has so far eluded the Bannermen [see Appendix 4].

Some traditional customs which have survived and even gained in popularity in the 20th century are Irish dancing and traditional music. The middle decades of the 20th century are renowned for ballroom dancing throughout Ireland. Every town and village in the county had its dance hall, Mega halls like Paddy 'Cons' (The New Hall) in Ennis attracted super showbands which often drew more than a thousand dance goers.

The more traditional dances and music were fostered by far-seeing groups like Comhaltas Ceoltóiri Éireann. Many of the ancient tunes and dances have been recorded and preserved for posterity by such purists as Willie Clancy of Miltown Malbay. County Clare has since become a great stronghold of traditional music with areas like Miltown Malbay and Doolin hosting Irish music lovers from all over the world. The Willie Clancy week is held each summer in Miltown Malbay; it is an event attended by many thousands of music lovers. The 2017 visit of Fleadh Cheoil na hÉireann brought 450,000 people to the county's capital over nine days.

50. Shannon – County Clare's newest town since 1960. The above picture shows early development with the industrial estate and airport runways in background.

(SFADCo)

Ennis's narrow winding streets contained vast crowds during the 2016-17 Fleadh Cheoil as they had done when Éamon de Valera held his political rallies on the 'Height' of Ennis in the 1920's. But behind the charming facade of the town's shops and dwellings lay another story of deprivation, poverty and human struggle. The ordinary people of the town (an 8,500 population in the mid 20th century) for the most part lived in substandard housing. Communities of kind-hearted people existed in hovels and mud cabins located in Turnpike, Bohereen, Drumbiggle, Old Mill Street and the many lanes of the town, especially those leading down to the Fergus at the back of Mill Street (Parnell Street). The tidal Fergus often flooded habitations in the Ennis Quays to make for wretched living conditions. However the Council did act to clear many 'slums' and lanes and build new schemes of houses in the Turnpike, Marian Avenue and Hermitage areas.

The advent and availability of printing presses contributed to the rise of media (specifically newspapers) in Clare. Between 1784 and 1903 at least a dozen newspapers were published in the county. They ranged from the *Ennis Chronicle and Clare Advertiser* in 1784 to the phoenix-like rise of *The Clare Champion* in 1903.

When *The Clare Man* was forced to close down by the authorities, its editor, Mr Tom Galvin, set about re-birthing the Nationalist voice in Clare. He was aided by loyal staff such as Pappy Garrihy when they sequestered typeface from *The Clare Man* on the night previous to it being auctioned off. Galvin literally snatched the body and soul of *The Clare Man* and infused it with Nationalist vigour when his first *Clare Champion* editorial stated: "*The Champion* will stand as the inveterate foe of landlordism, shoneenism, grabbers and castle hacks." Notably, *The Champion* lives on vigorously to the present day.

51. Moneypoint Power Station near Kilrush in County Clare.

(SFADCo)

Perhaps one of the last great reminders of earlier times was the fair held each year in the Fair Green in Ennis. This once empty field (now a sports field and playground) was converged on by cattle which filled it from end to end. From morning until nightfall individual bargains were struck and sealed with the traditional slapping of the palms. The residents of the town gained little respite from the bawling of cattle which could be heard for miles distant. From the old Fairgreen of Clonroad (where the Kings and Earls of Thomond held their fairs) grew the new Fairgreen at Lifford. The tradition was discontinued when the sale of cattle was conducted by Clare Marts on the Quin Road. It was sad to see such historic events abandoned, but the fabric of the town did suffer on fair days with thousands of cattle soiling and damaging the narrow streets.

52. Bunratty Castle and parks still displaying its former splendour. (SFADCo)

The railway which was laid through Clare in the 19th century is still in operation. The main line from Limerick runs through Ennis and northwards to Galway. It is with much regret that the county's narrow gauge artery has long since disappeared. The line of the old West Clare Railway ran on a narrow gauge track from Ennis to Kilkee, calling at Corofin, Ennistymon, Lahinch, Moyasta en route. Some of its crowded Sunday excursions to Lahinch proved to be rather severe 'exertions' for the little steam engine. On the steeper gradients (with the train overcrowded) the passengers might be asked to get out and push. The 'West Clare' has been immortalised in Percy French's famous song, *Are You Right There, Michael, Are You Right?* It was a sad day when Córas Iompar Éireann had the line ripped up and sold to the emerging country of Nigeria in 1960. The reason given for this piece of historic destruction was 'economic viability'.

The recent industrial development also meant that the town of Ennis was to prosper as an indirect result. Large urban development in the way of social housing schemes were built in the Hermitage, Árd na Gréine, Bohereen and other lesser developments. In 1956 during an auction on the first floor of an old historic building in Ennis (Carmody's Hotel) the crowded room suddenly collapsed. Eight people died in the tragedy and a number more suffered injuries. Éamon de Valera had sometimes stayed in Carmody's Hotel when he visited Ennis. The site of the building has since been cleared to make a larger entrance to the Abbey Street car park.

A picture of the commercial state of County Clare may be gleaned from the fact that at around the year 1900 barges on the River Fergus were still plying goods between Clarecastle and Ennis. Those long flat-bottomed vessels (called 'lighters') met the heavier barges at the little quay at Knox's Bridge to transfer the goods on their final stage of the journey. Unloading took place on the quays of Parnell Street and in earlier times at Wood Quay when it was in flood. The system of transporting goods by barge went out when rail and road vehicles came into play in the early 20th century.

The district of Ennis contiguous to the Fergus was much more tidal than it is today. The reason for this is that tidal control barriers have been put in place at Clarecastle to prevent backwater flooding at Ennis. Prior to the erection of the tidal barriers Ennis suffered much flooding on a regular basis. Parnell Street (Mill Street), the Mill Road and the 'Post Office' field regularly went under water after a heavy downpour during spring tides. Town flooding has been significantly reduced – except for one exceptional downpour (the worst for 100 years, it was said) on 5 and 6 August 1986. Once again the residents of Ennis witnessed flooding as in the days of old when Parnell Street, the Mill Road and the 'Post Office' field become awash with flood water.

Another interesting commercial activity of the 19th and 20th centuries was the arrival of cargo boats in the little harbour of Clarecastle. Coal and lumber came from Glasgow, Liverpool and London to supply the merchants in the town of Ennis. It was the custom, even into the 1950's, to haul the coal from Clarecastle to Ennis in high-wall carts drawn by massive Shire horses. As the overloaded carts struggled to make it up the steep hill leading into Ennis their colleagues with empty carts going downhill whipped their horses to achieve a good gait of going – hauliers were paid by the amount of coal transported per day. It is known that a number of families had part of their winter fuel requirements supplied from spillages at Clarecastle docks with lesser amounts from loose coal lumps falling from carts as they lumbered on the bumpy road to Ennis.

In the early 1970's the old Union Workhouse in Ennis was still being used as a hospital for the elderly, the sick and infirm of limited means. Even at that far-removed-time the whiff of famine could be discerned from the demeanour of the 'inmates', many of whom had suffered from losing their holding, their families, and their personal integrity due to land divisions and misuse brought about by the economic disasters of the 19th century. Dressed in rough serge suits, wearing caps woven in similar material and leaning against the workhouse walls they spent their days smoking plug tobacco in clay pipes. It was as if they were still stuck in famine times, looking bewildered, not knowing what to do next, and petrified by the trauma of the catastrophic era from which they had been expunged.

On the one hand it was a great pleasure to witness the demolition of the old County Home when a gigantic metal ball swinging from a towering crane bashed into the old walls of confinement to take them down in a matter of days. The end of pauperism and the genuflecting peasant was finally at hand. A well-designed modern hospital, St Joseph's, was erected in its place. Would that it were as easy to erase the scars from generations of all those oppressed souls.

During the middle part of the 20th century Ennis was fortunate in securing a number of manufacturing industries with many of them giving good employment. The first factory of note to make its appearance in the town was the English company, Braids (Irl) Ltd. It was set up before WW 2 and was operational right through the war era. Braids factory was greatly appreciated by the people of Ennis as a vital employment source. It offered much-needed income for the working class people of the town during the lean '40's and 50's when little else was on offer. Although Braids suffered many adjustments to its output it did survive until the latter stages of the 20th century when the competition of cheap goods from the Far East finally made the firm a cost liability.

With the advent of industrialisation in the 1960's and 1970's about seven major firms set up operations in Ennis with each one giving employment in excess of 100 people. In addition to those mentioned, at least 20 lesser size firms (employing an average of five people each) also commenced operations in Clare's capital. It was encouraging to note that some of the ventures initiated at this time were started by local entrepreneurs.

As if to copperfasten the mid century affluence in the county another important project started in the 1980's soon came on stream ie the ESB generating station on the Shannon estuary. This Moneypoint site, about five miles from Kilrush, was selected by the ESB as being the best location in the country for its biggest coal-burning power station. The steam-driven turbines are powered by vast quantities of coal imported from various countries in huge bulk tankers. The station's total capacity was set at 900 MW in three units of 300 MW each. The first unit was started up during 1985; the station was scheduled to operate at full capacity by the end of

1987. Like Clare's first power station located at Ardnacrusha, Moneypoint has brought much-needed employment to its locality. The building of Moneypoint cost in the region of £730 million and the ongoing benefits are even better with the injection of more than two million in wages going into the local economy each year. Such indigenous development ignited a confidence in the people which had been sadly missing since the days of the old Kingdom of Thomond.

Clare in its long and troubled history has seen Stone Age Man, man in the Bronze and Iron Ages, and adventurers in armour from abroad – yet she has borne and absorbed them all. She witnessed tribes which produced Munster and All-Ireland High Kings. Her fortunes were once redirected by the Christian influence and by the love of learning. The county was attacked many times and it repulsed those same attacks just as often. Internecine warfare coupled with a primitive governing system did for long periods utterly retard her progress. Invasion, disorganisation and defeat occasionally brought the Banner County to her knees. She has been savagely depopulated by systematic transportation of her innocent women

53. Majestic Dromoland Castle was the former home of an O'Brien sept. Is it a dinosaur from the old Kingdom of Thomond? Not at all, it is now a fully functioning 21st century luxury hotel.

(SFADCo)

and children into slavery – not to mention the trauma of appalling and lingering famine.

Yet when native power was restored County Clare (once the heart of the old Kingdom of Thomond) as an integral part of a free country proudly took her place amongst the nations of the free and civilized world.

The narrative of Clare's history, once again, pauses here. Indeed it is at a much happier place than the Rev P White found it at the conclusion of his own very thorough *History of Clare and the Dalcassian Clans.* The author's concluding chapter is worth recording here:

This history of Clare now comes to an end. I shall not deal with the deplorable division caused in the National ranks by the unhappy fall of Mr Parnell. This is for wider ground than is taken up here, and may well be reserved for a calmer atmosphere. While the last lines are being written, Mr. Gladstone is for the second time energetically pressing through Parliament a Home Rule Bill which in substance meets with the approval of all Irish Nationalists. If it gives to Ireland, as it must give sooner or later, self-government, the writer fondly hopes that whoever may in the future take up the thread of Clare's narrative will find in it a subject more encouraging and more inspiring than fell to his lot.

How the wheel has turned!

Clare has its freedom, its right of self determination within a country that has gained independence for the most part from the malevolent officiousness of England. Not only that but she has gained membership of a greater economic block (The European Union) and this should ensure that she continues to prosper at the very least.

It should now be the aspiration of its inhabitants to improve their lot and continue with the recently-begun progress; to enjoy the freedom which was always desired and dreamed of, fought for, suffered and hungered for, and even died for by countless thousands of illustrious, daring and certainly humble ancestors since the very formation of our native land.

An Clár abú.

'Come on the Banner!'

Appendix 1

Personalities from the remote past

The most important person as far as the clan members were concerned was undoubtedly the recognised leader of the most powerful sept. In the case of Thomond it has always been a Dalcassian prince. After Brian Boru's time it would specifically have been an O'Brien.

An attempt is made in the following to form a list of leaders from earliest known times up until such practice fell into disuse. Various sources have been consulted only to find that dates differ quite an amount; so I have compiled what I believe is a fair approximation. [Those undertaking fresh projects should do their own research].

Dates prior to AD 1000 refer to events when individuals came to prominence – not always birth or death dates. As can be expected many dates are prone to variations and are included here as guidelines only.

Eber 560–300 BC
Son of Mil (leader of the Spanish Celts who came to Ireland). Celtic ancestor to all Munster and Thomond (including County Clare) kings.

Mogha of the Silver Hand AD 130–167
Munster king and a direct descendant of Eber. Ruler of the southern half (Leath Mogha – Mogha's half) of Ireland. Slain at Moylea, AD 167.

Oilioll Oluim AD 167–234
Only son of Mogha of the Silver Hand and the progenitor of all the men from whom the Dalcassian leaders are descended. First King of Munster.

Fiacha Muilleathan AD 234–245
Grandson of Oilioll Oluim and his successor as King of all Munster (Munster was called Muma in ancient times).

Cormac Cas AD 240–280
Second son of Oilioll Oluim. Ancestor to the Thomond O'Briens. Married a daughter of Oisin (of the Fianna). First king to be assigned to North Munster (Thomond) region which at first comprised Clare, Limerick and much of North Tipperary. Thomond was eventually reduced to take in County Clare only.

Mogh Corb AD 265
Son of Cormac Cas. King of Munster.

Luighaidh Meann AD 315
Fourth descendant of Cormac Cas. Claimed Thomond for his own.

Conal of the Fleet Steeds AD 325–335
Son of Luighaidh Meann. Succeeded his father as King of Thomond.

Cas AD 330–350
Son of Conal of the Fleet Steeds. The name 'Dalcassian' is derived from him. 7th in descent from Cormac Cas; he was ancestor to all the important Thomond (Clare included) clans. He had 12 sons.

Blod AD 360
Eldest son of Cas, and direct ancestor of the O'Briens, McMahons, Malones, Moloneys, O'Currys, Hurleys, Reidy, Sexton, Hogans etc.

Caisin AD 360
Second son of Cas, and direct ancestor of the MacNamaras, O'Gradys, Mc Clancys, O'Deas, McInerneys, Meehans, etc.

Crimthan (pronounced Criffaun) AD 365
Crimthan was 6th in descent from Oilioll Oluim. He went on to be King of Munster and Ireland after AD 365.

Conal Eachluaith AD 366
King of Munster.

[Between this period and the AD 900's the strength of the south Munster clans, the Eoghanachts, overshadowed that of the Dalcassians. It appears that the Dalcassians consolidated their position in Thomond (North Munster) while at the same time contested their right to the kingship of Munster itself. Records are scant until the Norse caused terror and gained notice with their ferocious raids].

Lorcan AD 900
A Dalcassian King and a direct descendant of Oilioll Oluim.

Cennédig (Kennedy) AD 930
A descendant of Oilioll Oluim and son of Lorcan. Father of Mahon and of Brian Boru who was to become King of the Dalcassians and High King of All Ireland.

Lachtna AD 954
King of Munster. Uncle of Brian Boru.

Mahon AD 964–975
Oldest son of Cennédig (Kennedy). Dalcassian king and Munster king.

Brian Boru (Boroimhe) AD 975–1014
Dubbed 'Brian of the Tributes'. Dalcassian King, King of Munster and High King of All Ireland. Fought the Danes and subsequently broke their power in Ireland. Encouraged the use of surnames (eg Ui Briain ~ O'Brian ~ O'Brien). Most famous Dalcassian and Irish hero of all time.

Taigh AD 1014–1028
Son of Brian Boru. After the death of his father he disputed the Dalcassian and Munster kingships with his brother, Donogh.

Donogh AD 1028–1064
Son of Brian Boru. After the death of his father he disputed the Dalcassian and Munster kingships with his brother, Taigh. He killed Taigh and ruled Munster. Recognised as High King of All Ireland in 1049.

Turlogh AD 1064–1086
Dalcassian and Munster king. He was High King of All Ireland with opposition in the year 1075.

Murtagh More O'Brien AD 1086–1119
Dalcassian, Munster and All Ireland King. He was the last Dalcassian to be Árd Righ na hÉireann (High King of All Ireland).

Conor-na-Catharach AD 1119–1142
Son of Murtagh and brother to Turlogh O'Brien. A Munster King.

Turlogh O'Brien AD 1142–1167
Brother of Conor. Took over the principality of West Thomond. He contested the Munster Kingship. He died in that office in 1167.

[It should be noted that the kingship of the Dalcassians was disputed at this time between **Teigue Gle** Prince of Thomond, and the brother of Turlogh, **Rory O'Brien**, Prince of Thomond; also contesting was **Conor** (son of Donal of Lismore) who was another Prince of Thomond].

Murtagh O'Brien AD 1167–1168

Murtagh was the Eldest son of Turlogh. When he was King of Thomond he was killed by his cousin in 1168.

Donal More O'Brien AD 1168–1194

As the name implies he was one of the most prominent of the O'Brien kings. Brother of Murtagh. Built many abbeys and churches during his reign. Acted most stubbornly against the Norman invaders.

Title vacant (disputed) AD 1194–1201

During this period the Kingship was disputed between:

Murtagh Dall; eldest son of Donal

Conor Roe; brother of Murtagh

Murtagh Finn; another brother.

Donnchad Cairbreach O'Brien AD 1201–1242

King of Thomond. Established new residence for the dynasty at Clonroad in Ennis. Direct ancestor to the kings and earls of Thomond and to the titled families of Inchiquin. He is also credited with having started the construction of Ennis Abbey (now called Ennis Friary) although it was not completed during his lifetime.

Conor O'Brien AD 1242–1267

Son of Donogh. King of Thomond. Ennis Friary (old abbey) was partially completed under his reign and the friars took occupancy. He was known as Conor-na-Suidaine after being killed in the Battle of Suidaine.

Brian Roe O'Brien AD 1267–1277

King of Thomond. Died when drawn between horses in 1277.

Donogh O'Brien AD 1278 (only)

Son of Brian Roe. Ruled only West Thomond (Clare) for a brief period.

Turlogh O'Brien AD 1277–1306

Nephew of Brian Roe. He ruled in East Clare for a short time, and as such was considered King of Thomond. He is buried in the old Friary of Ennis (which in itself was an acknowledgement of his kingship).

Donogh O'Brien AD 1306–1317

King of Thomond. He was a son of Turlogh. He was slain by one of his own kinsmen in 1317.

Dermot O'Brien AD 1311 only.

Grandson of Brian Roe. Became Lord of Thomond when supported by the Norman, de Clare. Didn't reign for long.

Murtagh O'Brien AD 1317–1343

King of Thomond and a brother of Donogh. Recognised as the true heir during this period of upheaval.

Brian Bawn O'Brien AD 1317–1350

Prince of East Thomond (Ormond now known as North Tipperary) until 1343 when he became King of Thomond.

Dermot O'Brien AD 1350–1355

King of Thomond. Reigned without issue.

Mahon Moinmoy O'Brien AD 1355–1367

King of Thomond. A nephew of Dermot O'Brien. Won the seat by violence against his uncle, Dermot.

Turlogh Maol O'Brien AD 1367–1369

Dispossessed by his nephew, Brian.

Brian O'Brien AD 1369–1399

Recognised as King of Thomond. After 1377 he was called Brian Catha-an-Aenagh for having been successful in the battle of Aenagh.

Conor O'Brien AD 1399–1426

King of Thomond and brother of Brian.

Teigue O'Brien AD 1426–1438

King of Thomond. A son of Brian Catha-an-Aenagh.

Mahon Dall O'Brien AD 1438–1446

King of Thomond. A brother of Teigue. Deposed in 1446.

Turlogh O'Brien AD 1446–1459

King of Thomond. A younger brother of Teigue and Mahon. Known as Turlogh Bog (The Soft).

Donogh O'Brien AD 1459–1461

Son of Mahon Dall. King of Thomond.

Teigue (an Chomhaid) O'Brien AD 1461–1466

King of Thomond and Munster. Contender for the Ard Righ (High Kingship). He was the eldest son of Turlogh.

Conor (na Srona) O'Brien AD 1467–1496

So named because of his large nose. He was a brother to Teigue. Not fully recognised as chief of the Dalcassians in the early part of his career. He finished very powerfully as King of Thomond.

Turlogh (Oge) O'Brien AD 1496–1499

Surnamed Gilla Dubh. He died in 1499 after an inconspicuous reign.

Turlogh (Don) O'Brien: AD 1500–1528

King of Thomond. He was involved in many quarrels yet he was recognised for his true nobility.

Conor O'Brien AD 1528–1539

King of Thomond. Eldest son of Turlogh. Last of the direct descendants of Brian Boru to reign as supreme ruler in Thomond.

Murrogh (The Tanist) O'Brien AD 1539–1551

57th and last King of Thomond when he was created 1st Earl of Thomond by the English monarchy on 1 July 1542. He was also recognised as 1st Baron Inchiquin.

Donogh (The Fat) O'Brien AD 1542–1553

Created Baron of Ibricken by the English. Succeeded Murrogh on his death (1551) as Prince of Thomond. By virtue of Henry VIII's patent the title of 2nd Earl of Thomond descended to him.

Donogh O'Brien AD 1550–1559

Disputed the title of Earl of Thomond with Donal and Conor. Restored briefly in Inchiquin.

Teigue O'Brien AD 1550–1559

Disputed the title of Earl of Thomond with Donal and Conor. Restored briefly in Inchiquin.

Sir Donal O'Brien AD 1553–1579

Recognised by his clansmen as true king. Founder of the Ennistymon O'Briens. He died as Tanist of Thomond, thus ending the two thousand year old Brehon Law practice of selecting the Prince of Thomond.

Conor O'Brien AD 1553–1581
Disputed his position as Earl with the English. Surrendered ancient Dalcassian rights to the Crown. Restored as 3rd Earl of Thomond in 1571.

Donogh O'Brien AD 1581–1624
Son of Conor. 4th Earl of Thomond.

Henry O'Brien AD 1624–1639
5th Earl of Thomond.

Barnabus O'Brien AD 1639–1657
6th Earl of Thomond.

Henry O'Brien AD 1657–1691
7th Earl of Thomond. Governor of Clare.

Henry O'Brien AD 1691–1741
8th Earl of Thomond. Last of the line, now discontinued. The family became anglicised when they settled for good in England.

Titles of Inchiquin

Murrogh (the Tanist) O'Brien AD 1539–1551
Murrogh the Tanist was 1st Earl of Thomond and 1st Baron Inchiquin.

Dermot O'Brien AD 1551-1552
2nd Baron Inchiquin.

Murrogh O'Brien AD 1552–1573
3rd Baron Inchiquin.

Murrogh O'Brien AD 1573–1597
4th Baron Inchiquin.

Dermot O'Brien AD 1597–1624
5th Baron Inchiquin.

Murrogh (an Tothaine) O'Brien AD 1624–1674

Called 'Murrogh of the Burnings'. 6th Baron and 1st Earl of Inchiquin. Professional soldier. Governor of Catalonia and Majorca.

William AD 1674–1691

7th Baron Inchiquin. 2nd Earl Inchiquin.

William AD 1691–1719

8th Baron Inchiquin. 3rd Earl Inchiquin.

William AD 1719–1777

9th Baron Inchiquin. 4th Earl Inchiquin.

Murrogh AD 1777–1808

10th Baron Inchiquin. 5th Earl Inchiquin.

William AD 1808–1846

11th Baron Inchiquin. 6th Earl Inchiquin.

Admiral Lord James AD 1846–1855

12th Baron Inchiquin. 7th Earl Inchiquin. Because he had no children all of his titles except Baron of Inchiquin became extinct.

Sir Lucius O'Brien AD 1855–1872

His claim to the title of 13th Baron of Inchiquin was granted by the House of Lords in England in April 1862. It is now the senior branch of the O'Briens. (They are referred to as 'The O'Briens of Thomond').

(Note: With the dying out of titles along with the many splits in the O'Brien family line it becomes a hopelessly futile exercise at this level to state anything other than we are currently left with the last titled O'Brian ie Conor O'Brien as indicated below).

Conor, The O'Brien of Dromoland

18th Baron Inchiquin.

Currently the holder of the last of the English titles and now residing at Dromoland but not in Dromoland Castle.

Appendix 2

Notable persons of the modern era

Bianconi, John O'Connell (1871-1929)

John O'Connell Bianconi lived at Ballylean near Kildysart in south Clare. He was grandson of Charles Bianconi whose road transport system revolutionized 19th century Ireland. O'Connell (on the occasion of his mother's death in 1908) changed his name to Bianconi and consequently inherited large estates in Clare and Tipperary. On his estate he demonstrated his talents in engineering and science by building and utilising many novel pieces of mechanical equipment. Some of the systems which he put into operation included a telephone network, an unusual railway circuit on his farm and an electric generator. It is said that he constructed a steam engine traction system which operated a regular service between Kildysart and Ennis. His farmyard railway was the most famous of his inventions; he used it to transport all his farm produce at harvest time. Another of his transport services included a regular shipping route between Limerick and Kilrush, which also served Kildysart and Labasheeda.

He was Justice of the Peace and High Sheriff for County Clare. He was noted for his generosity and for entertaining guests at gala picnics on his estate. After his death in October 1929 all of his equipment was disposed of by auction for very nominal sums.

Bindon, Samuel Henry (1812-1879)

Samuel Henry Bindon was a highly talented lawyer of the 19th century. Although born in Limerick he represented Ennis in the Irish parliament. He entered Trinity College where he received his BA in 1835. In 1838 he was called to the Irish Bar. Even though he was of landed Cromwellian stock he was an avid champion of the underdog. Bindon's literary output included editing the works of Nicholas French in two volumes in *Duffy's Library of Ireland Series, 1846.* He was also Secretary to the Tenant's League. He demonstrated a strong interest in Irish traditions and he was subsequently a member of the Celtic Society and the Archaeology Society of Ireland. Shortly afterwards he emigrated to Australia where he rose to a position of considerable distinction at the Australian Bar. He went on to become a famous judge and later Cabinet Minister in the administration of that country. He died in Australia in 1879.

Blackwell, James Bartholomew (1765–1825)

Born in Ennis in 1765 James Bartholomew Blackwell was later educated at the Lombardian College in Paris. He was attracted to military service in the army and enlisted in the Esterhazy Regiment of Hussars. At the outbreak of the French Revolution Blackwell was deeply involved in the movement towards political change. It is now believed that he led an assault on the Bastille itself during those heady days of the French Revolution.

He never forgot his homeland and he supported Wolfe Tone and Napper Tandy by sending military expeditions to Ireland in the hope of prizing the English out of the country. The first expedition in 1796 was wrecked in a storm off Bantry Bay; the second expedition in 1798 surrendered to the British Naval forces off the Donegal coast. Blackwell was later captured: for his part in the operation he received two years incarceration in Kilmainham Gaol.

He later returned to France where Napoleon placed him in charge of a Battalion in the Irish Regiment. A man of extraordinary adventure, it seems he took part in the disastrous Russian Campaign and survived to tell the tale. James Blackwell next became military governor of La Petite Pierre in Lorraine. In 1819 he was honoured as Brevet-Officer in the Royal Order of the Legion of Honour. During the second of the two French expeditions to Ireland (while the French fleet was anchored in Bantry Bay) Blackwell secretly made his way to Ennis to visit his friends and family.

Bohan, Revd Fr Harry (1937-)

The Revd Fr Harry Bohan is the son of Michael Bohan and Anne Fitzgerald who ran a pub in Feakle in east Clare. Fr Bohan received his secondary education at the diocesan college of St Flannan in Ennis. From there he went to Maynooth College to study for the priesthood. His third level education was completed at Cardiff University where he took an MA at the University of Wales.

In the 1970's Bohan was manager of the Clare Senior Hurling team when they won two National League titles but failed to go the full distance in the heat of Championship hurling. In 2006 he was recognised for his services to the game of hurling with a special award.

It was in social development that he made a big impact. He set up the Rural Resource Organisation (a movement that encouraged communities across Ireland to participate in determining their own future) and it resulted in the building of 2,500 houses in 120 villages in 13 counties. In 1998 he founded the Céifin Centre for Values-Led Change; its purpose was to carry on the conversation on the direction Ireland is taking in the area of social development.

Fr Harry Bohan has a number of important publications to his name, dealing exclusively with community development: *Swimming Upstream, Community and the Soul of Ireland, The Challenge: Balance Between City and Rural Life* and *Roots in a Changing Society.* He is currently serving as a Catholic priest in Sixmilebridge and is never far from the pulse of rural life.

Brennan, Lt Gen Michael (1896–1986)

One of our latter-day warring Dalcassians, Michael Brennan became famous as a freedom fighter and an outstanding officer in the Irish Army. He was born in Meelick in 1896, the third son of Patrick and Mrs Brennan (nee Clancy). At the age of 16 he was already acting leader of a branch of the Fianna Boys who were operating in Limerick.

As an early member of the volunteers he made a contribution to the events which led to the historic Rising of Easter Week 1916. With his brothers, Paddy and Austin, he organised many of the guerrilla companies which fought in the War of Independence in Clare. Brennan was jailed after the 1916 Rising, but later managed to escape from an English prison. He supported the Sinn Féin candidate in the 1917 East Clare bye-election. Shortly afterwards he was re-captured and subsequently was in and out of jail until 1919. While in prison he supported the hunger strike efforts to regain rights lost after the death of Thomas Ashe. Right up to the truce of 11 July 1921 Michael Brennan was a wanted man.

He organised Flying Columns against the RIC and the Black and Tans. Brennan led the attack on the first police barracks to fall in Clare at Newmarket-on-Fergus. This remarkable soldier led many other daring raids throughout the duration of the 'troubles'. In 1920 Michael Brennan was Chairman of the Sinn Féin monopolised Clare County Council. When the treaty was signed in December 1921 he strongly supported the proposal.

He joined the new Irish Army at its formation and went on to hold a number of distinguished posts. Ultimately he was Chief of General Staff in 1931 – a position he held for a record nine years until he retired from the Army in 1940.

After his military career he worked in the Office of Public Works for some years until his final retirement. Michael Brennan, freedom fighter and soldier, died in the month of October in 1986. As befitting a man who gave such distinguished service to his country he was buried with full military honours in Dean's Grange Cemetery, Dublin.

Burke, John (1978-)

"Hell on earth," was how this man described his last night on Mount Everest before making a final assault to conquer the world's highest peak. Hotelier, John Burke, in fulfilling his life's ambition witnessed the fear of death on the faces of fellow climbers as they encountered the corpses of those who had come to grief in the treacherous jaws of Mount Everest. Burke made his own momentous piece of history when he held the Clare flag aloft on the summit of Mount Everest on Tuesday 16 May 2017 – the first Clare person to do so.

John was inspired to make the climb by such stalwarts as Pat Halvey and Ger McDonnell who had cut pioneering paths in their own endeavours. It's not surprising to learn that his favourite book is *Tom Crean: Unsung Hero* (by Michael Smith). Like his own heroes John Burke credited intense preparation and meticulous planning in overcoming so daunting a challenge. He hopes that his journey to achieve his own particular ambition will help others who seek to establish their individual paths in life. His mantra is one of sticking to the chosen career path and not be daunted – reward will come to those who persevere. In this regard he is particularly indebted to his wife, Aoibhín Garrihy, who provided tremendous support and inspiration.

John Burke received a hero's welcome when he arrived at Shannon Airport on the following Monday where a large crowd of enthusiastic supporters and well-wishers were on hand to greet him and celebrate his assault on the world's greatest mountain. The welcome he received was vindication for the sacrifices made by him and his family. He returned to Spanish Point where he provides much expertise and dedication in running the family-inspired Armada Hotel.

Burton, Sir Frederick William (1816–1900)

Frederick Burton was born in Clifden House, Corofin, in 1816. He was a gifted painter who gained membership to the Royal Irish Academy in 1839. Between the years 1851–58 he went on to pursue advanced studies in Munich, Germany. He became a F.S.A. in 1863 and LLD TCD in 1896. This quite talented Clareman was next appointed Director of the National Gallery of London in 1874. He was renowned for his portraits of many distinguished Irish people of his time. He went into retirement in 1894 and died in London in 1900. His 1864 painting '*Meeting on the Turret Stairs*' was voted Ireland's favourite painting in 2012.

Byrnes, Ollie (1955–)

This unassuming man is a son of Martin and Bridie Byrnes (nee MacMahon). Educated locally at Ennis CBS Primary and Secondary schools (now Rice College), his earliest passion was Irish traditional and folk music which was fostered at home and from listening to the radio.

Ollie worked a variety of jobs, but he was drawn to music. In the mid 1980's he imported LP's from the USA, England and Germany. A significant undertaking came in 1984 when he set up West Coast Radio along with Tony Garland.

As a presenter Ollie aired specialised programmes on Jazz/Blues, American Country, and Irish Traditional (An Bonnán Buí). A notable presentation was the anthology of four one-hour programmes on the Beatles with whom he still holds a great affinity.

By 1987/88 West Coast Radio had become popular and was broadcasting successfully from their Parnell Street studio. When the opportunity arose, WCR applied for an official local radio licence for County Clare. Ollie headed the West Coast Group at the IRTC hearing at Jury's Hotel, Limerick on 9 March 1989. Although West Coast Radio had been successfully broadcasting for some time and had received good national and media reviews the County Clare licence was awarded to an amalgamation of business interests who put Clare FM on the air.

Sidelined by the new station Ollie began writing books on Clare hurling and became so absorbed in the subject that he is now acknowledged as the 'go–to' expert. Between 1996 and 2017 he produced eight books on Clare hurling and one on the success of his neighbourhood soccer team, *Avenue United.*

The hurling titles are; *Against The Wind* – (a seminal publication for its time); also *Blue is the Colour, Around the Square, Saffron and Blue, Clare Hurling Voices, Clare Hurling Captains, Between the Green and the River* and *Heroes Without Laurels.*

Ollie Byrnes as an artistic Ennis man has contributed articles on music to all 32 editions of the North Clare/ South Galway magazine, AdMag. His articles strike a deep level of understanding. He is a regular columnist on sport as well as music to the *Clare County Express, The Clare Champion* and to other publications.

Even today his pulse beats in unison with his two great passions – hurling and music. One feels there are a number of other important works to come from pen of Ollie Byrnes, and even as we write this biography we know that Ollie is busily planning his next publication.

Carroll, William (1817–1889)

William Carroll was a builder and civil contractor who was born in Ennis in 1817. During a cholera outbreak in 1849 he moved his family to Ballybeg, Clarecastle. The house which he built there is still standing and remained in the family's possession until 1976. His other commercial activities included a saw mill and two timber yards, one of which occupied the site of the present entrance to the Dunnes Stores shopping arcade. Carroll built the original 'Post Office' bridge over the River Fergus at Bank Place, Ennis. He also constructed the old metal bridge crossing the Fergus on the Quin Road. It was to remain in situ until 1974 when a concrete structure was erected in its place. Some of the better known civil projects which he was responsible for would include the Franciscan Friary, completed in 1884 and the O'Connell Monument unveiled in 1865.

William Carroll had an entrepreneurial spirit large enough to grace even the most sophisticated society. He was buried in the family vault in Drumcliff Cemetery – a monument which he also built – demonstrating his acute planning as well as his love for the work he did.

Cusack, Michael (1847–1906)

Michael Cusack was born in Carron in the Barony of the Burren in County Clare in the Famine year of 1847. He became a local school teacher and was fluent in Irish from an early age. He developed a great passion for all things Irish to include games, dancing and folklore. He regarded – not just his own district – but all of Ireland his home. He went on to teach school in Corofin, Enniscorthy and Lough Cutra until 1871. Michael Cusack later moved to Dublin where he ran a 'grinding' school at Emmet Street.

From his travels around Ireland he became aware of the declining interest in the Irish games and the old traditions. Cusack showed a distinct interest in rugby and cricket. He became a useful rugby player after making his debut with Cusack's Academy XV and later with the Phoenix Rugby Club. Perhaps it was the organisation of those clubs that inspired him (for inspired he was) to organise the fading Irish games in the same way. After 1882 he became obsessed with the idea of putting the national games on a firm structure. He met P W Nally in Dublin and both expressed great concern at the general disorganised state of Irish athletics. Cusack is credited with reviving Dublin hurling in the 1880's. Michael Cusack died on a Dublin Street in 1906. He had laid the groundwork for hurling and Irish football to become the great games we enjoy today.

Clancy, Willie (1918–1973)

A son of Gilbert Clancy (flute, concertina and pipe player) and Ellen Killeen, Willie Clancy is one of the best traditional musicians of the modern era. From an early age he was steeped in the culture of traditional Irish music. He was born in Miltown Malbay on 24 December 1918 and played his first tin whistle at five years of age. He was greatly influenced by his grandmother who had a keen ear for music. Other influences included his father, Gilbert, and Garrett Barry the celebrated blind piper – Willie would go on to master the pipes himself. Johnny Doran (the 'travelling' piper) was another of his mentors. When Martin Talty caught him playing a tune in his classroom, a friendship was struck up which lasted for a lifetime. Both played concert flutes at every available dance, wake, and wedding – all in the perfection of their craft. Willie won an Oireachtas medal at national level for tin whistle in 1947.

Having trained as a carpenter he was unable to find profitable work locally so he emigrated to London. While in London he continued to play Irish traditional music. He returned to Ireland in 1957 (after a three year stay) to marry Dóirín Healy and resettle in Miltown Malbay. From 1957 until 1972 the summer music sessions in the west Clare town became widely renowned with Willie Clancy as one of the main attractions. Pipe-making, reed-making and all things connected with the musical instrument were explored and advanced by the Clancy style. The *Willie Clancy Summer School* is now an established event in the life of Miltown Malbay. During his lifetime he gave many memorable performances, live, on radio and on television – any of which would have sealed his reputation as a master musician.

Considine, Michael G (1814–1884)

Michael G Considine was a flamboyant Ennis man known for his undying devotion to the Liberator, Daniel O'Connell. Almost singe-handedly he raised the funds for Ennis' best-known landmark the O'Connell monument on the 'Height' of Ennis. His devotion to O'Connell was such that when kissed on the cheek by the Liberator he vowed never to profane the place which the lips of O'Connell had sanctified. He is reputed to never have washed that revered cheek! Considine's persistence resulted in the raising another prominent monument in Ennis – the Manchester Martyrs' Monument called the Maid of Eireann.

As secretary of a workers' union called The United Trades he wielded immense power due mainly to his forceful character and his ability to mobilize people. This self-educated man constantly advanced the lot of the common man in advocating work discipline and abstinence from alcohol.

Ironically Michael G was to die on 22 April 1884 after a long illness at his nephew's residence in Brewery Lane. When he died the trading premises of the town remained shut for the day while delegates from far and wide attended. The funeral procession was headed by the Parnell Fife and Drum Band. The cortege marched with the coffin borne on the shoulders of his fellow tradesmen, followed by the Ennis Mechanics Brass Band. All the trades from town and around paraded with their banners draped in black while the bands played *Dead March in Saul* as they wound their way through the narrow streets of Ennis to deliver Michael G Considine to his grave in the town's oldest building – the Abbey of Ennis.

For a man who was the prime mover in erecting the two most imposing monuments in the town it was unbefitting that his grave remained without a head stone for 40 years. This was rectified in 1924 when a Celtic Cross with plinth was put in place. Fittingly, the inscription is in both Irish and English and is the only monument with a Irish inscription in the Abbey cemetery. Michael G Considine is honoured and remembered in keeping with the man he greatly admired – the Liberator Daniel O'Connell.

Curtis, P J (1944–)

P J Curtis was born in Kilnaboy and in his teen years he went to Ennis CBS for a secondary education. From his many experiences in life he developed his talents as a writer, poet, broadcaster, musician and environmentalist.

Between 1963–65 P J served with the RAF in Borneo during the Malaysian-Indonesian war where he was decorated for chivalry, gallantry, sacrifice and loyalty for his peace-keeping work amongst the Communion countries

After spending many years living and working in England he returned to Ireland in 1974 to take up a position with AnCO in 1975. When one of the greatest of traditional Irish groups – The Bothy Band – was formed, P J became their 'roadie'. His talents as a record producer saw him working with such stalwarts as Freddie White, Stockton's Wing, Mick Hanly and many others.

From his written work, *The Lightning Tree,* it can be seen that P J is a sensitive and captivating writer. His book was described by Nuala O Faoláin as "a poignant elegy for a more beautiful Ireland". He also authored *Notes from the Heart* (a celebration of Irish traditional music).

In pursuit of new inspirations P J divides his time between sunny Spain and the historically-haunting fields of his native Kilnaboy.

Dermody, Thomas (1775–1802)

A renowned writer and romantic poet, Thomas Dermody child prodigy was born in Ennis in 1775. His father ran a school in the town and to offset operating costs he pressed young Dermody into service as a teacher of Latin and Greek.

Dermody's mother and brother died about this time – Thomas's immediate response was to write a commemorative poem in their honour. Shortly afterwards he left for Dublin where he became enchanted with the bookshops and the literary way of life. Unfortunately he was addicted to alcoholic drink from an early age; this marred his literary output and the quality of his life.

One of his better-known accomplishments at that time was a critique he wrote on the contrasting styles of John Milton and William Shakespeare. He published two books of poetry which were put into a collection called *The Harp of Erin.*

Shortly afterwards he left for London against his patron's advice and lived there in desperately trying conditions. He turned to the commercial practice of writing soliciting letters to earn his keep. He joined the army and was sent to Flanders where he gave a good account of himself. On his return to London he reverted to his old ways of living again in inhuman conditions in a broken down hovel; there he died at the very young age of 27 years. He was buried in Lewisham in the city of London where the monument over his grave was restored in 1848 by 'some admirers of his genius' and again in 1886 'by subscription'.

Early, Biddy (1798–1874)

She was baptised Bridget Ellen Connors but always went by her mother's name, Early. Her mother was a noted herbalist who passed on her secrets and potions to her young daughter when she died. Biddy was just 16 years of age at that time. Young Biddy grew to be a striking child of flowing red hair and green-blue eyes. She was said to be constantly conversing with the fairies when she was alone and for this reason the locals were wary of her. After her father died she became a domestic in Carheen but was evicted from it by landlord Sheehy. She put a curse on the landlord – her prophetic ability was enhanced when shortly afterwards he was murdered. While still in her 20's she married a widower named Pat Molloy who was twice her age. The union produced a son called Paddy, but dramatically she was a widow again at 25 years. Next she married her stepson, John Molloy.

By then she had become so famous for her cures and predictions that it was said that Daniel O'Connell once visited her for advice. In 1840 her second husband died from a liver ailment which freed her to marry a young man from Quin named Tom Flannery. They moved to a two-roomed cottage overlooking the lake at Kilbarron. To complement the many potions she already had her son received a special bottle from the fairies after having assisted one of their clans in a midnight hurling match! Her cures and predictions drew large crowds and this was to eventually bring the wrath of the clergy down on her. In 1856 she was charged with practicing witchcraft only to have the charge dismissed for lack of evidence – nobody dared testify against such a conniver.

Biddy married her fourth husband on 27 July 1869 in Limerick. He died from excessive drinking one year later when Biddy was 72 years old. In 1874 she fell ill and was attended by the local priest Fr Connellan in spite of her strange beliefs. It is thought that the priest gained some measure of repentance from her because he threw her magic bottle into Kilbarron lake. Her funeral was attended by 27 priests and yet she was buried in an unmarked grave. A short few years ago RTE were about to screen a TV documentary on her life when the transmitting equipment in nearby Maghera crashed and caused a black-out – it stopped the programme from being aired. Perhaps Biddy Early is still wielding the power!

Fitzgerald, William Vesey (1783–1843)

A landowner and a politician (Conservative) who was born in Ennis. After his education at Oxford he went into local politics. He was MP for Ennis at Westminster from 1808 until 1812; and again from 1813–18. He was further returned for the parliamentary period of 1831–32 and represented County Clare with some distinction during sessions. Fitzgerald became Lord of the Irish Treasury and a Privy Councillor in 1810 and served as Envoy Extraordinary to Sweden from 1820 until 1823. This man was always a popular landlord even though O'Connell defeated him in one electoral contest. However, he was so appreciated that another seat was found for him in Cornwall. Having been elected for Ennis in 1831 he was made President of the Board of Trade where he served from 1841 until 1843.

Hillery, Patrick (1923–2008)

Doctor, politician and President of Ireland best sums up the life story of Patrick K Hillery from Miltown Malbay in County Clare. His father was a popular local doctor and his mother was Ellen McMahon. Patrick was educated at the local national school and Rockwell College. After graduating from Rockwell he went on to study at University College Dublin from which institution he was conferred with an MD in 1947.

After some time in medical practice he was persuaded by Fianna Fail interests to run in the 1951 elections; he was elected TD to Dail Éireann on his first attempt. He served as a Fianna Fail TD until 1973. He was Minister for Education 1959-65; Industry & Commerce 1965-66; Labour 1966-69; External Affairs 1969-73. He was acting as Minister for External Affairs when he conducted negotiations on behalf of Ireland's entry into the EEC in 1973. Hillery then left Irish politics to become Irish Commissioner at the EEC with responsibility for Social Affairs (1973-76).

When President Cearbhall Ó Dálaigh resigned from office, Patrick Hillery became the agreed candidate for all parties, and thus he was elected as President of Ireland in November 1976. While in office he became embroiled in a few political intrigues orchestrated by others from which he extracted himself with considerable aplomb. Having served the maximum two terms he left office in 1990. Patrick Hillery died on 12 April 2008 after a short illness. He received a full state funeral and was buried at St Fintan's Cemetery, Sutton, Dublin.

Holland, John Philip (1841–1914)

John Philip Holland must be credited with the invention of the first underwater powered boat – the submarine. In Liscannor where he was born in 1841 it is said that he got the idea for an underwater boat while wistfully gazing on Liscannor Bay. His father died while he was still quite young, nevertheless young Holland managed to get an education at Ennistymon CBS and later at Limerick CBS. In fact he joined that same congregation in 1858 to train as a teacher – a profession he followed for some years.

He taught in various centres throughout Ireland but he is most associated with the North Monastery in Cork where he taught science and engineering. Even in this position he had some ideas worked out for his 'underwater' boat. When he suffered ill health he was forced to quit the teaching profession and reconsider his career path.

In 1873 at the age of 32 he emigrated to America where he joined his mother and his older brother. Holland spent many years in New Jersey perfecting and building his invention. He was much frustrated by the American Navy who were sceptical about his invention because they found it difficult to use. Finally, the Fenians in America decided to finance him (having been persuaded by Holland that a submarine would be an ideal way to fight the British Navy).

Eventually he went under the surface of the Passaic River in a test boat, *The Fenian Ram*; the dive was of ample duration to convince the Fenians of the project's worth. The US Navy was present when his latest design made its second operational dive on 17 March 1898. In 1900 the US Holland (SS-1) was formally commissioned with a crew of nine. Even the British backed the invention when they launched *The Holland* on 2 October 1901 at Barrow-on-Furness.

John Philip Holland lost control of the John Holland Torpedo Boat Company, which he had founded and is now part of the world renowned Dynamics Corporation of Grotton, Connecticut, USA. Neither Holland, nor any of his family members received due recompense or recognition for Holland's pioneering work on one of the world's great inventions. Holland's vivid imagination of travelling beneath the waves of Liscannor Bay bore remarkable fruit in America. The modern-day submarine has been developed on the principles of the Liscannor man's invention.

Kirby, Pat (1936–)

The unique Irish sport of handball has been mastered to the highest international standard by a truly great Dalcassian sportsman, Pat Kirby. Born in Tuamgraney in east Clare, this remarkable athlete excelled at both hurling and handball from the age of seven. Because there was a handball alley in Tuamgraney Pat learned the rudiments of the game from an early age. His dedication to constant practice throughout his formative years moulded him as a super athlete in both hurling and handball.

In Ireland he won the Worlds Singles Crown in 1970 while representing the USA (after having won their Senior Championship as a prerequisite to qualifying for competition). He then won four successive All Ireland senior softball singles titles (1974–77), and six consecutive 40 x 20 medals (1975–80) while also dominating tournaments in America. He won the Masters Doubles title with Matt Purcell (Kildare) and the Masters Singles in Dublin in 1984. In 1986 he won the World Championship in Canada and also retained the Masters (over 40) Singles and Doubles. And all this at the age of 50 – no wonder they dubbed him 'The Weekend Warrior' in America.

In June of 1986 he captured his sixth US Masters Championship – a feat which prompted the Americans to include him in their Hall of Fame making him the first non-American to be so honoured. Pat Kirby stayed on in America where his talents were both appreciated and rewarded. This unique and talented Clareman must be considered to be one of the greatest sportsman to grace any sporting code anywhere in the world.

Laffan, Sir Robert Michael (1821-1882)

Born on 21 September 1821 in Skehana in the Banner County, Robert Laffan went to France at an early age where he was educated at the French College of Point Levoy and later at the Royal Military College at Woolwich from which he gazetted a second lieutenant in the Royal Engineers in 1837.

He saw service in South Africa where he was employed in frontier service. He also served in Mauritius, Malta and Ceylon. Sir Robert became a respected authority on military engineering and consequently he was sent to examine and report on the development of the Suez Canal; he was present for its official opening in 1869. He is further credited with laying out the barracks and manoeuvring plains at Aldershot Military Academy (which was renamed 'Laffan's Plain' in his honour).

After having served as a commander in Gibraltar he went on to become Commander-in-Chief of the Bermudas, where he was promoted to the rank of Brigadier-General. It was while there that he received a knighthood and was duly recognised as Governor of Bermuda. He died there in 1882. Robert Laffan was buried in Bermuda with full military honours after having lain in state for two days.

Loughnane, Gerard (1953–)

Although an outstanding hurler in his own right Loughnane's fame rests in his inspiring leadership as manager of the Clare Senior Hurling team. Born in Feakle in 1953 he attended the local school there before going on to St Flannan's College for his secondary education. At that famed Ennis hurling nursery Loughnane perfected the craft of hurling and perhaps subconsciously imbibed the winning organisational skills so associated with the college – even though they did not win a Harty Cup final during his tenure there.

He first played with the Clare minor hurlers as a 17 year old in 1970. His minor and U-21 days with Clare saw no provincial titles but he was ready for the Senior team when he lined out in the 1972-73 National League team. He became a regular on the Clare Senior team and won two National Hurling League medals in 1977 and 1978 – overcoming the much-vaunted Kilkenny in the final. Beating Kilkenny in the League Clare could manage but the winning of a Munster title seemed to be a psychological barrier that was too far beyond them. Loughnane's personal achievements were noteworthy. Although he secured an All Star and the distinction of representing his province on seven consecutive occasions, he retired as a hurler in 1987 with the bad memory of contesting five Munster Finals without anything to show for them.

By the time he became Manager of the Clare Senior Hurling team in 1994 Loughnane was more than ready to bring down Clare's arch rivals in Munster. Introducing an ever-higher standard of training, Clare marched through Munster victorious in 1995. The psychological barrier was shattered! Biddy Early's curse was debunked for the myth it was. So Loughnane at the head of his Dalcassian hurlers marched on Dublin to defeat a valiant Offaly team in the All-Ireland Hurling Final of 1995. Clare under Loughnane repeated the success in 1997.

Like Brian Boru of old, Ger Loughnane had roused his fellow clansmen to a most notable victory in Dublin. When Clare failed to annexe the Munster Final of 1999 either Loughnane's magic touch had evaporated or the team was ready for change. Ger Loughnane, the teacher who had many successes in his personal life, became a sports journalist and a TV pundit specialising in the game of hurling. In this regard he is also a well-respected authority. His skill in analysing games places him to the fore in the world of hurling punditry.

MacConMara, Donnachadh Ruadh (1715–1810)

Donnachadh Ruadh was a poet and raconteur who was born in Cratloe in 1715. He spent some years in the Irish College in Rome where he studied for the priesthood.

When he realised that he was unsuitable for the religious life he returned to Ireland and lived in Waterford for a time. He hovered between Protestantism and Catholicism and was once dismissed from a teaching post.

While in Waterford he became famous as a poet and a singer of poetic songs in many of the seamen's taverns in that city. He also developed prowess in the writing of Irish poetry. Some of his better-known compositions include, *The Adventures of a Luckless fellow* and *As I was Walking One Evening Fair.* Irish scholars would be in disagreement as to the quality of his work perhaps suggesting that he was careless and more concerned with popularising his compositions. He did though produce some epic poems, and he was one of the few classical lyrists during the impoverished years prior to the famine.

MacCurtin, Andrew (? –1749)

Andrew MacCurtin came from a long line of poets, and he remained a strict disciplinarian in the traditional Irish method of rhyming. Born at Moyglass, Kilmurry Ibrickan, he quickly succeeded to the hereditary title of Ollamh to the O'Briens of Thomond. This alone places him in a high position of prestige in the historical line of traditional Irish poets who preserved the old techniques of rhyming. It was a singular achievement.

Many of his manuscripts are preserved in Trinity College, the Royal Irish Academy, the British Museum, whilst some others are held in private collections. Eugene O'Curry considered MacCurtin to be one of the best Irish scholars of his day. He sold much of his property to finance his travels and his learning. Eventually, he opened a poetry school in his native parish in order to earn a living (having deserted his patrons, the O'Briens, in a fit of pique). When he died in 1749 he was buried in an unmarked grave in the church of Kilfarboy.

McDonald, Patrick Joseph (1878 – 1954)

Although born in Doonbeg as Patrick McDonnell, through some clerical confusion he was always known as "Pat" McDonald after he emigrated to the USA. Once there he joined the New York City Police Department and posed an impressive figure at 6' - 2½" and weighing in at 120 kg. He would have been a standout figure around Times Square where he operated as a traffic cop for a number of years.

He became a prominent member of the Irish-American Athletic Club for whom he competed in many track and field events. McDonald was part of a loose group of athletes who were known as the "Irish Whales".

In 1912 he represented the USA in the shot put competition at the Summer Olympics in Stockholm, Sweden. At the same games he also came second in the novel 'two-handed shot put" which was its only appearance on the Olympic programme. The competition involved the shot putter throwing with each hand and then both throws added together to get the final result. The object of the exercise was to test the overall strength and dexterity of the competitor; however Pat McDonald finished second behind teammate Ralph Rose who ironically was to be placed second to him in the 'single' shot competition.

McDonald's athletic career was somewhat restricted during the course of WW 1 but when Pat returned to Olympic competition in the 1920 Summer Games held in Antwerp, Belgium, he won the gold medal in the 56 lb shot put throw; it was the second and final time that this competition was included in the Olympic programme.

Patrick Joseph McDonald (McDonnell) died in 1954 at 75 years of age and his body was interred at the Gate of Heaven Cemetery in Hawthorne, New York. "Pat" was inducted into the USA's National Track and Field Hall of Fame in 2012 and will forever remain a legend of Olympic sport.

MacLysaght, Edward (1887–1986)
Mac Giolla Iasachta, Éamon

Although reputedly born at sea, Flax Bourton near Bristol is registered as the birthplace of Edward MacLysaght. However, he always claimed County Clare as his spiritual home and he was to demonstrate his affinity with the county all through his long life. Born to a Cork father and a Lincolnshire mother the young Edward MacLysaght attended prestigious universities like Rugby and Oxford.

After having suffered an injury while playing rugby he went to Lahinch in County Clare for six months to recuperate. There he came across some of his paternal namesakes, an occurrence which prompted him to engage in the study of Irish surnames. He also gained good proficiency in speaking the Irish language.

His love for Clare was further strengthened when his father purchased a 600 acre farm in Raheen mainly for the young MacLysaght to engage in pioneer farming. He installed electric light generating equipment on the farm some 40 years before rural electrification came to Ireland. Edward's cultural involvements had reached their zenith by the time he met and married Mabel Pattison in 1913.

About that time he founded the Nua-Ghaeltacht in Raheen. Edward MacLysaght became deeply involved in the Irish independence movement. It is not known if he was actually a member of the IRA, but he did become quite active in the struggle for independence as a supporter and financier. He was imprisoned when he returned to England to publicize the atrocities of the Black-and-Tan war taking place in Ireland.

Edward MacLysaght was elected to Seanad Éireann in 1922. His appointment as inspector for the Irish Manuscripts Commission was probably what set him on a course of onomastics in which he left a distinguishing mark. He served as Chief Herald of Ireland between 1943 and 1954 and also as Keeper of Manuscripts of Ireland from 1948 to 1954.

Some of his better-known works include, *Irish Life in the Seventeenth Century (1939), The Surnames of Ireland, Irish Families: Their Names, Arms and Origins, Supplement to Irish Families* and *More Irish Families incorporating Supplement to Irish Families.*

Edward MacLysaght died on 4 March 1986 and he was interred in St. Cronan's Church, Tuamgraney, in County Clare.

MacMahon, Maire Rua (1615- 1686)

Maire Rua (Red Mary) MacMahon was born in 1615 or 1616 to Torlach Rua MacMahon Lord of Clonderlaw and to Mary O'Brien youngest daughter of the 3rd Earl of Thomond. That lineage puts her squarely amongst the nobility of Thomond (County Clare). Her place of birth remains unknown.

She was still in her teens when a match was made between her and Daniel Neylon from Dysert O'Dea. They were married until the death of Neylon in 1639, which resulted in Maire Rua gaining control of a 4,000 acre estate. Shortly after Neylon's death Maire Rua married a kinsman, Conor O'Brien of Leamaneh whose estate was contiguous to her own. They had eight children in the marriage, five of whom lived to adulthood, although we know very little of their progress thereafter.

When the Cromwellian's raided in Clare they sought out Conor – a man whom they feared – and grievously injured him. He was brought mortally wounded to Leamaneh Castle where Maire Rua tended him through the night until he died. Instead of raging against the Cromwellians who had murdered her husband she drove 'a coach and six horses' to Bunratty where she confronted Ireton and the Cromwellians. She offered to marry any of the officers to prove her loyalty to the Parliamentarians (it was actually a ploy to retain her estates). The offer was accepted by Coronet John Cooper; they were married and it proved to be a mutually successful arrangement.

Maire Rua eluded many other attempts at discrediting her and her position. Towards the end of her life she resided at Dromoland Castle to where her son, Donogh, had moved the family seat. He was brought up as a Protestant and at the time he was considered to be 'the richest commoner Ireland'. Some claim that Maire Rua is buried at Coad church with her daughters; others believe that she was buried beside her beloved husband, Conor O'Brien, in the Franciscan Friary (old Abbey) of Ennis as stipulated in her last will and testament. However, no grave or record has been found to corroborate either version.

MacMahon, Tony (1939–)

Tony MacMahon was born in The Turnpike area of Ennis to musical parents, P J MacMahon and Kitty Murphy, both of whom hailed from an area of Kilmaley that was steeped in traditional music. The young Tony was soon captivated with all things traditional. By his late teens he was accomplished enough in accordion playing to compete in the All-Ireland Fleadh of 1956 in Ennis. He became absorbed in the Irish language and was a fluent Irish speaker from an early age. However, it was the button accordion which captivated him most in life.

While at teacher training college in Dublin Tony was struck by the music of Sonny Brogan. Other musicians to influence him were Seamus Ennis, Willie Clancy, Johnny and Felix Doran and the accordion players Paddy O'Brien and particularly Joe Cooley. After he qualified as a teacher he taught at Rice College (then Ennis CBS) for a couple of years. In his spare time he travelled to Morocco and Spain with his brother Dermot where they busked on accordion and bodhrán. His American adventure with piper and singer Seamus Ennis instilled in him a love for slow airs, a genre which he went on to master to a high degree. MacMahon extracted much from the haunting Irish airs on the button accordion using the 'press and draw' technique of his mentor, Joe Cooley.

His main career was with RTE as a presenter of traditional music on TV. Some of his radio programmes like *The Long Note, The Pure Drop* and *Aisling Geal* were classics of their kind. He was celebrated for making the TV series called *The Green Linnet* in which both he and banjoist Barney McKenna drove through Europe in a green Citroën 2 CV van and stopped to play traditional music at many exotic locations along the way.

MacMahon's strong views on the performing and exploitation of traditional music often saw him at loggerheads with other enthusiasts. In 2014 he was afflicted with tremors in his hands which was diagnosed as Parkinson's disease. The diagnosis was later found to be incorrect, suggesting that it may have been something of a more mundane nature such as repetitive strain injury. Tony MacMahon currently lives in retirement in Dublin.

MacNamara, John 'Fireball' (1790–1836) MacConmara, Seán Buidhe

From one of the great warring clans of Clare came John MacNamara who was dubbed 'Fireball' early on in life due to his propensity for fighting duels. Many of them ended fatally for his opponents. He was born in Clare towards the end of the 18th century of a Moyreisk father (Colonel Francis MacNamara) who was MP for County Clare in 1790.

Fireball spent much of his time at sport and leisure from which many a legend sprung up around his outrageous activities. Michael Hogan, Bard of Thomond, wrote two poems in his honour, *The Grave of Sean Buidhe MacNamara* and *Fireball MacNamara's Address to his Pistols*.

MacNamara claimed to have been wounded in the Battle of Vinegar Hill in Wexford. It is known that he fought at least 40 duels and acted as second in many others. He gave a particular name to his pistols – 'Bás gan Sagart' (death without a priest in attendance). He was the last of the Moyreisk MacNamaras and one of the few remaining 'fire-eating' Irish chieftains. Because of his wild actions his entire family estate was squandered during his lifetime.

Fireball MacNamara is buried in Quin Abbey where even his admiring poet, Michael Hogan, the Bard of Thomond, recognised his life of folly when he wrote in part, 'Where are the honours you have won?' His memory is perpetuated by a Celtic Cross in the Lady Chapel of Quin's Franciscan Abbey and bears the following inscription: *Erected by Clan MacNamara to the memory of Sean Buidhe'Fireball' MacNamara, Chief of Clan and a 1798 patriot.* With the death of Fireball MacNamara went one of the last outrageous Dalcassians in the old spirit of living a wild life.

Meany, Stephen Joseph (1822/5–1888)

Born in Newhall, about three miles from Ennis Meany received an early education in that district. Although he published some verse and pamphlets he was primarily famous as a journalist and newspaper editor of some ability. In the beginning he reported with the *Limerick Chronicle*; shortly afterwards he went to Dublin to work for the *Daily Freeman* in a similar capacity. It was not long before he was running two newspapers, *The Irish Tribune* and *The Irish Felon,* both publications were outspoken against the English administration in Ireland. His views soon got him into hot water with the authorities; he was detained in Carrigfergus Castle for one year by the Crown administrators. On his release he resumed his journalism as editor of the *Limerick and Clare Examiner* which was a local paper offering a strong Nationalist opinion and political information for the people of Clare and Limerick.

Perhaps feeling the heat from his fiery journalism he then abruptly left for America. He became editor of a number of publications there but he settled in Toledo City where he made many friends, including the famous General Sherman. On a subsequent visit to England he was arrested and imprisoned by the authorities. He served two years of a 15 year sentence in Mountjoy Prison. He was released in dramatic fashion due to pressure from the American Government. Joseph Meany returned to America and he quickly set about editing the *Evening Democrat* in Waterbury, Connecticut which is where he died in 1888. His body was returned to Ennis for interment.

Merriman, Brian (1747–1805)

Merriman was born in County Clare in or around the year 1747. Brian who was a wild youth fond of amusement could play the fiddle well. He left his birth place while still quite young; although its exact location is uncertain it has been given variously as Ennis, Ennistymon, Cranny and Clondegad. In recent times he is most associated with Feakle where he taught school for 20 years. He married a local woman; two girls were born of the marriage. His reason for being in Feakle could have been that he inherited his father's farm there.

He is best known for his famous poem, *Cuirt an Mhean Oiche* (The Midnight Court) which is considered to be one of the great classic compositions of the 18th century. It has been translated into English by many translators with varying degrees of satisfaction. The poem has a sequence whereby Aoibheall, Queen of the Sidh at Craig Liath, Killaloe, considers the plight of young women who lack husbands. An ancient surviving copy of the poem was found in a house in the old Bohereen area of Ennis and was presented to the Clare County Library. An older version of the poem is reputed to exceed 2,000 lines; a copy/version in the British Museum is known to have 1024 lines. It first appeared in manuscript form circa 1780 with a number of printed editions having come out under mysterious circumstances in the 1850's.

A critic wrote of him, 'he was content to write the everyday speech of County Clare, a marvellously vigorous and expressive speech of which he had a royal command.' Merriman's poetic works are studied and recited each year in the Merriman Summer School held at various locations throughout the county.

Brian Merriman, one of the last great Irish scholars and poets, moved to Limerick later in life where he taught mathematics. He died in Limerick on 27 July 1805. In Feakle churchyard there is a plaque honouring his memory although the grave itself is not marked and has not been located. *Cuirt an Mhean Oiche* is Merriman's greatest legacy.

Mulready RA, William (1786–1863)

Mulready was a noted painter who was born in Ennis in 1786. His works included landscapes, rural and homely scenes in which he displayed an unusual talent in presenting detail and in capturing the essence of the quieter scenes of his day. Such was his talent that he was elected to the Royal Academy School at the young age of 30 which was an outstanding achievement. His output was low, most likely due to his meticulous attention to detail; he often produced a number of sketches before committing himself to canvas.

The Queen of England purchased some of his work for the Royal Collection at an exhibition which was held in Gore House, London, in 1853. Again in 1972 a major exhibition of his drawings was staged in the Victoria and Albert Museum where some of his best works were seen. The bi-centenary of his birth was commemorated with an exhibition in the de Valera Library in Ennis in 1986.

William Mulready died at his home in Bayswater London in July 1863. His body is buried in Kensal Green where there is an impressive memorial marking his final resting place.

O'Brien, Catherine Amelia. (1881–1963)

Catherine Amelia O'Brien was a highly talented artist who designed stained glass windows. She was born at Durra House near Spancilhill. Her father was Pierce O'Brien, a man of property as well as a Justice of the Peace for County Clare. Amelia's work includes a memorial in stained glass to her parents, which may be seen in St. Columba's Parish Church, on Bindon Street in Ennis. She extended her skills to the craft of *opus sectile* (inserting stained glass into concrete frames); an example of this part of her work may be seen in the Franciscan Friary of Athlone.

She advanced her skills by further study under A E Child and William Orpen and by working in the Tower Glass Studios where she produced work for home and abroad. Further examples of her creations can be seen in the Church of Ireland, Kiloughter, Co Cavan, eg *The Sower.*

The Church of Ireland in Harold's Cross has on display *The Good Samaritan* and there are two windows showcasing her talents in the Church of Ireland in Gorey, Co Wexford. She and her colleagues in the 'Studio' raised the art of working in stained glass to a new level. One of the commissions she was working on when she died was a window for Áras an Uachtaráin in the Phoenix Park, Dublin. It was completed by her companions in the Studio. To commemorate her death and her life's work her brother Pierce O'Brien commissioned a window from Patrick Pollen for the St Lawrence O'Toole Chapel of Christ Church in Dublin. Amelia's dedication to her art was uncompromising.

O'Brien, Charlotte Grace (1845–1909)

Although primarily known as an author Charlotte also took an active part in politics and social work. She was born in Cahirmoyle on the Clare/Limerick border in 1845. She was a daughter of the famous Smith O'Brien who spent much of her childhood abroad with her father. When she returned to Ireland she became involved in the plight of emigrants, urging better accommodation and helping in whatever way she could. She initiated a beneficiary scheme for the peasantry which had some success. Her writings consisted of lyrical poems and a particularly clever novel called *Light and Shade* which she wrote in 1878. She was a staunch advocate of the Irish League. When she died in 1909 her life and work was commemorated in the memoir that Stephen Glynn wrote of her life.

O'Brien, Edna (1930–)

Edna O'Brien is easily Clare's most famous living writer. She was born in Tuamgraney and brought up in a devoutly Catholic family. Referring to her attendance at the local Sisters of Mercy Catholic schools she reputedly said, 'they contributed to a suffocating childhood'. The schools were strict institutions run on boarding school rules where harsh punishment would have been meted out.

She was awarded a licence to operate as a pharmacist in 1950. Shortly afterwards she married Carlo Gébler and moved to London. They had two sons, Carlo who was also to become a writer, and Sasha who studied and practiced architecture. Her marriage was dissolved in 1998.

She burst onto the literary scene in 1960 with a 'shocking' (for that time) story called *Country Girls*. It was the first part of a trilogy; *Lonely Girls* was published in 1962, and *Girls in their Married Bliss* came out in 1964. The books were promptly banned in the then devoutly Catholic State of Ireland mainly because of the frank and intimate portrayal of some characters in her books.

Since then Edna has written many successful novels and volumes of short stories, some of which were adapted for film and television. In another twist she turned to writing plays and had some success there. According to Scottish novelist, Andrew O'Hagan, Edna O'Brien's place in literature is assured because of the way she influenced the course of Irish fiction writing. A proliferation of Irish female writers has followed in her literary wake.

O'Brien, Frances Marcella (1840–1883)

She was born at Peafield near Ennis on 24 June 1840. Her parents were William O'Brien, a farmer, and his wife Marcella (née Burke-Browne) of Newgrove, County Clare. Her mother, Marcella, died at 30 years of age. William, her father emigrated with the older children, leaving Attie (as Frances Marcella became affectionately known) behind in Newgrove with her grandmother. Attie was always delicate as a child when she suffered from asthma; perhaps it was because of this that she took a deep interest in books.

At a comparatively young age she developed into a highly accomplished poet and novelist. She regularly contributed stories to the *Irish Monthly* and poems to many other periodicals, all of which were of a high standard. O'Brien's journals reveal she was self-deprecating about her writing, and that she mainly wrote to stave off boredom and to earn money. She had four novels serialised in the *Irish Monthly* and the *Weekly Freeman*, which went on to be published as books, three of them after her death.

She travelled to Dublin in March of 1873 but the rigours of the journey adversely effected her. Her untimely death occurred in Dublin on 5 April 1883 and it undoubtedly robbed us of many more quality works. She is buried in the old churchyard of Kildysart in the village she knew quite well.

O'Brien, Mathew (1814–1855)

Son of Mathew O'Brien, a medical doctor who had a good practice in Ennis, the younger Mathew became an astronomer and a mathematician. He studied at Cambridge where he received his MA in 1841. Notably he was awarded the Moderatorship of Mathematics in 1843. His next appointment made him Professor of Natural Philosophy and Astronomy at King's College, London, in 1844. He authored many mathematical works including *Differential Calculus* (1842), *Plane Co-ordinate Geometry* (1844) and a *Treatise on Mathematical Geography*

(1852). As well as the above he published many pamphlets on a variety of mathematical subjects. He was sent to the Channel Islands for health reasons but regrettably he died there on 23 August 1855.

O'Brien, William Smith (1803–1864)

Smith O'Brien was a noted 'Young Irelander' who was born at Dromoland in 1803. He went on to receive a first class education at both Harrow and Cambridge. On returning to Clare he was elected MP for Ennis in 1828 whereupon he became a strong advocate of support schemes for the poor as well as payment for the Catholic clergy.

He joined the Repeal Association in 1843; he also helped found the Irish Confederation in 1847. When he urged the formation of a 'National Guard' in 1848 he fought the authorities. At his trial the jury failed to agree and on his release he began to 'raise the country'. A reward was offered for his arrest but this met with little support from the populous at large.

An attack by him on widow McCormack's house at Boulah Common brought the wrath of the police on him once again. Another arrest followed and he was brought to Clonmel for trial. The jury found him guilty of high treason with the sentence of death attached; it was later commuted to penal servitude for life. Smith O'Brien was transported to Tasmania but gained his freedom in 1854; he was then unconditionally pardoned in 1856. He then returned to Ireland and never engaged in politics again. This highly original rebel died in Bangor, Wales, in 1864.

O'Cahan, Eugene (1600–1650 approx.)

Born of noble parents in the beginning of the 17th century Eugene O'Cahan went on to become a Franciscan priest. At 16 years he entered the Order of St Francis and later went to Rome where he was ordained in 1622. While abroad his brilliance in theology enabled him to defend public theses in the years between 1635–39. During that particular period he also taught philosophy at Boretta in northern Italy.

He returned to Ireland in 1641. In 1644 he opened a public school at Quin. Such was the reputation of the school that it contained up to 800 students from all over Ireland, including 19 of the O'Broudin family (distinguished Thomond historians). Eugene O'Cahan was Guardian of Ennis Friary from 1644–47; in his last year there he also acted as Lector. He was transferred to County Limerick in 1648. While travelling on a mission through north Cork he was captured by the Puritans who immediately strangled him without mercy. His case has been put to Rome for recognition as a martyr.

O'Connell, Maura (1958–)
Uí Chonaill, Máire

Maura is principally known as a folk singer who hit the headlines with a number of distinctive Irish songs. Although born in Ennis she received a secondary education in Spanish Point between 1971-74 where she was prominent in the school choir. Her family was a musical one with mother delighting in parlour songs while dad sang the traditional ballads during their family sessions.

Maura's musical career took off when she was still a teenager; she sang in America with the traditionally-based Irish group, *Dé Dannan.* A year later she became something of a national phenomenon with *Star Spangled Molly,* which was the band's landmark album. Her first solo album came out in 1983 but it was not universally received.

She did achieve a Grammy nomination for her 1989 album, *Helpless Heart.* There were a number of modest successes along the way before she greatly impacted the music scene with such milestone numbers as *Living in These Troubled Times,* and *A Woman's Heart* – all of which featured on her 1993 album. Her heartfelt renditions of *Trouble in the Fields* as well as the haunting *Western Highway* were epic releases.

After sampling the American bluegrass music for a time Maura returned to traditional ways, working with such artists as Van Morrison, Eric Clapton, Mary Black, Paul Brady, Dolly Parton and particularly the local group Stockton's Wing.

She recorded a prestigious 12 albums between 1983 and 2009: *Maura O'Connell* (1983); *Western Highway* (1987); *Just in Time* (1988); *Always* (1989); *A Real Life Story* (1990); *Stories* (1995); *Wandering Home* (1997); *Walls and Windows* (2001); *Don't I Know* (2004); *The View From Here; The Very Best Of* (2006) and *Naked With Friends* (2009).

Maura O'Connell continued performing and recording beautiful songs in the USA where she has lived for most of her professional life.

O'Connell, Peter (1775–1826)

Peter O'Connell was a renowned scholar who was born at Carne (Moneypoint) in 1775. He organised a school there for the study of Irish Literature. O'Connell collected much material locally for his great Irish-English dictionary. When he was unable to obtain patronage to keep up his studies he was forced to sell his manuscripts in Tralee for a few paltry shillings. The manuscripts were subsequently retrieved by Eugene O'Curry; they are now stored in the British Museum. Some sources claim that Peter O'Connell was the best scholar in the country over a century ago. He is buried in the same grave as the Coleen Bawn, which is in Burrane Cemetery in south Clare.

O Comhraidhe, Eoin (1794–1862)
O'Curry, Eugene

One of the most remarkable literary geniuses to come out of County Clare must surely be the Doonaha man, Eugene O'Curry. He was steeped in Irish folklore from birth. His father, 'Eoin of the Prayers' – was a competent singer and a great storyteller.

When Eugene's father died in 1865, he realised what an amount of music and oral literature died with him. His father sang long-forgotten Fenian Lays from a boat in the Shannon to strollers rambling on the banks. Eoin was also a Gaelic scholar who had a number of ancient manuscripts in the house; he was able to teach Eugene much about the history and grammar of the Irish language.

Eugene's career began as a teacher in 'cottage schools' from which he went on to open a hedge school. He learned English by listening to visitors in Kilkee. He gained such a level of competence that a translation of his work was printed in the 'Oxford Book of Irish Verse'. After the Battle of Waterloo in 1815 and moving into the famine era, work and money became scarce for Eugene. It forced him to take a position as a warder in the Limerick Lunatic Asylum in 1824.

Having made the acquaintance and gained the respect of John O'Donovan, O'Curry secured employment from 1835 to 1842 in the topographical and historical section of the Irish Ordnance Survey. There he worked under George Petrie, the outstanding antiquarian.

It is estimated that he read and studied over 30,000 pages of manuscripts during his tenure at the Ordnance Survey. It was invaluable work for both the State and for O'Curry himself who greatly enhanced his knowledge of the ancient Irish language in the process.

O'Curry's finest work was in the translation of the Brehon Laws, in which both he and O'Donovan excelled, even though O'Curry's contribution is not widely acknowledged. In fact the triumvirate of Petrie, O'Donovan and O'Curry did not immediately receive the credit or recognition for the immense work they did on behalf of the country's folklore and history.

Eugene O'Curry translated such works as *The Tain Bó* and uncovered the long lost *Triparite Life of Saint Patrick.* Some of his important lectures published in book form are valued beyond price, *The Manners and Customs of the Irish People* and *Manuscript Materials of Ancient Irish History*.

When Eugene O'Curry died suddenly on 30 July 1862 he was virtually unappreciated. He is buried in Glasnevin Cemetery in Dublin.

O'Donnell, Art (1890–1973)

Art O'Donnell, a republican, a teacher and a staff member of the Clare County Council who was born to Simon and Mary O'Donnell and into a family of 15 in Tullycrine in the west of Clare in 1890.

He was sworn into the Irish Republican Brotherhood by his cousin Con Colbert (who would be executed by the British for his part in the 1916 Rising). The young O'Donnell went to St Patrick's College in Drumcondra, Dublin, to train as a teacher. In Dublin he became further steeped in IRB activity and cemented his convictions after contact with high profile republicans there.

On returning to Clare he continued to promote the IRB cause by distributing leaflets, doing talks and forming republican groups. He secured a teaching post in Low Island near Killadysert. O'Donnell became Vice Commandant of the West Clare Brigade of the Irish Volunteers with Eamonn Fennell as Commandant.

When Eoin O'Neill's counter-command to cancel the 1916 Rising was published it threw the volunteers into some confusion; many IRB men were subsequently rounded up by the authorities. Most were incarcerated in Frognoch, Wales, including Art O'Donnell. While interned O'Donnell wrote a valuable manuscript on IRB activities now on view on the Clare County Library website.

After his release in 1916 Art O'Donnell was made commandant of the 7th Clare Battalion of the Irish Volunteers. Again it cost him a jail term of two years in Mountjoy and Dundalk jails. When WW 1 ended in November 1918 Art and his fellow prisoners were released; however he was arrested again in 1920 and incarcerated in Ballykinlar Camp, Belfast. His final release came in 1921.

Art O'Donnell, who lived for most of his life at Steele's Terrace, Ennis, worked as a staff member of the Clare County Council; above all he was a patriot of high ideals and extraordinary tenacity.

O'Gorman Mahon, The (1800–1891)

This gentleman's correct name was James Patrick Mahon. He adopted the title 'The O'Gorman Mahon' to incorporate his mother's maiden name – and woe betide the man who failed to respect it. Born at 40 Mill Street (now Parnell Street), Ennis, he came into much property at an early age – it was left to him by his father who was a successful merchant in the town and had participated in the 1798 rebellion. James received his BA from Trinity College Dublin in 1822 and an MA in law in 1832. He married Christina O'Brien from Dublin (she was an heiress whose dowry afforded him to live an idle life). The O'Gorman Mahon claimed to have fought 13 duels and was injured in some.

The O'Gorman Mahon played a major role in supporting the Liberator, Daniel O'Connell, in the Clare bye-election of 1828. O'Connell's success helped get the Catholic Relief Act of 1829 which was instrumental in the finalising of Catholic Emancipation. A rift developed between O'Connell and the O'Gorman Mahon which unfortunately never healed.

Before he went abroad he was called to the Bar in 1834. On his return he was elected MP for Ennis in the 1847 general election, having unseated O'Connell and then quarrelled with him. He lost the seat in 1852 when he was seen as being opposed to the Young Irelanders.

The O'Gorman Mahon led a cavalier life fighting on both hemispheres under many flags. When he again returned he was re-elected MP for Ennis in 1879. After many in-out successes in Ennis he was finally persuaded by Parnell to run as a candidate in the 1887 Carlow bye-election, which he won for the Liberals at the age of 87 years. As the oldest MP in the House of Commons he died at his home in South Kensington while still serving in Parliament. This dare-devil Clare man was as well known in Berlin, Paris and London as he was in Ireland.

O'Gorman, Thomas (1725–1809)

Known as 'The Chevalier' because he was created Chevalier by Louis XV of France. In addition he married the sister of Chevalier D'Eon and received large vineyards as his dowry. The royalty in France greatly appreciated O'Gorman's standing as a military man.

Thomas O'Gorman was born at Kilmihil sometime around 1725. His imposing stature of 6 feet 5 inches made him an outstanding presence as a soldier in the Irish Brigade. King Louis was quite impressed by O'Gorman's commanding presence – the main reason for him being made Chavalier. O'Gorman started a wine trade between France and Ireland and it quickly flourished. He visited Ireland many times during his wine trade business. He became interested in Irish genealogy and pretty soon he was making a good profit from importing family pedigrees to the continent. He procured pedigrees for many descendants of the 'Wild Geese'. One such family history which he compiled was that of Count O'Reilly, General-in-Chief of the Spanish Army.

With the advent of the French Revolution, The Chevalier's property was confiscated and he was obliged to return to Dublin where he lived for many years in poverty. Unable to recover his former position in spite of him having three sons in His Majesty's Army, he finally returned to Clare to spend his last days at Dromellihy. He died on 18 November 1809; he was buried in the historic churchyard of Kilmacduane.

O'Looney, Brian (1828–1901)

Brian O'Looney was another of those distinguished Irish scholars who operated under trying conditions. He was born in the parish of Inagh where he attended the local hedge school under bardic tutor Seamus MacCruitin – an experience which instilled in him a love for manuscripts and all things historically Irish.

Being quite patriotic he became involved in an insurrection staged by William Smith O'Brien at Ballingarry, Co Tipperary. This little rising was more symbolic than anything else but it did get him into hot water with the authorities. He escaped to Limerick city and from there he obtained a passage on a ship sailing for America. It was some years later before he returned to Ireland – and only then after the Ballingarry incident had been largely forgotten.

He renewed his acquaintance with Smith O'Brien who was residing in Brussels at that time. Smith O'Brien introduced him to the work of cataloguing Irish papers. This led to his appointment (in succession to the renowned Eugene O'Curry) as Professor of Irish Language, Literature and of Celtic Archaeology at the Catholic University in Dublin. Later on he founded the society for the Preservation of the Irish Language.

O'Looney is best known for his translations of the Clare poets such as Ó Cormin, MacCruitin and Ó hUiginn. He also completed an extensive study on the importance of ancient ruins on Mount Callan. As a result of his findings, traditional worship at the Mount Callan site was later transferred to St Muchan's holy well, Ennistymon. Brian O'Looney died in Killiney, Co Dublin, in 1901.

O'Regan, Brendan (1917–2008)

Brendan O'Regan has been described as one of Ireland's most noted peace ambassadors and initiator of commercial and industrial projects. Hailing from Sixmilebridge he went for early training in the hotel business. His family were at that time owners of the Old Ground Hotel in Ennis. As a young man he resided in France, Switzerland and Germany while he studied hotel management. His first appointment was as manager of the Falls Hotel in Ennistymon in County Clare.

At the age of 25 he was appointed first comptroller of the international airport for flying boats at Foynes, Co Limerick. When the flying base was switched to Rineanna, Co Clare, in 1945, O'Regan then took control there. He set up the now famous duty free shop at the airport in 1947, which was the first of its kind anywhere in the world. Brendan became the first chief executive of SFADCo and in 1958 he was appointed Chairman of Bord Failte (Irish Tourist Board).

International recognition came his way in 1977 when he was elected to the Travel Hall of Fame in Madrid. After his retirement from public life he turned his attentions to the problems of Northern Ireland and once again he came up with a novel 'O'Regan' solution – the setting up of the North-South co-operative movement. The objective of the movement was to break down the barriers of hatred between the communities with the idea that it could pave the way for lasting peace. Ultimately, it was successful – although it may not have been immediately obvious to all.

O'Regan's contribution was instrumental in achieving the peace goal. He was awarded a CBE in 1993 for his contribution to peace. In February 2007 the Clare Museum staged an exhibition which was opened by Taoiseach Bertie Ahern to mark Brendan's achievements – it was an unheard of honour for the time. President Mary McAleese said that Brendan O'Regan was a true visionary and that he left a legacy that permeated all levels of social, economic and cultural life in Ireland. He was married to Rita Barrow and they had two sons and three daughters. Brendan O'Regan died in 2008 at 90 years of age.

Patterson, Johnny (1840–1889)

Johnny Patterson was a famous circus clown and songwriter who was born in his father's roadside forge-house in Kilbarron near Feakle. His father was a nailer-gunsmith who sent his son to Ennis as an apprentice nailer serving under his uncle Mark. Seemingly, nail making wasn't to young Johnny's liking; instead he was driven by his love of music to join the British Army as a drummer at the age of 14 years. One of the earliest songs Johnny wrote was about his youthful days in Ennis, entitled, *The Stone Outside Dan Murphy's Door*. It is a popular number even today. While in the army Johnny mastered both piccolo and drums.

After three years he bought himself out of the regiment and joined John Swallow's circus. Even though he became a famous as a clown in the circus he did not neglect his music. During this period we find him writing *The Roving Irish Boy* and *The Dingle Puck Goat*. He married another circus performer, Selena Hickey, in Liverpool in 1869. Shortly afterwards one of his best known works appeared, *The Garden Where The Praties Grow*. Johnny moved on to a number of other circuses and became a national success by the age of 35 years. His fame reached America and he was enticed him to go there to perform in one of their most famous touring shows.

During his voyage to America he wrote the song, *Goodbye Johnny Dear*. In America he was billed as 'The Rambler from Clare'. He performed successfully in that country until his return to Ireland when he was 45 years of age. In 1885 he went to live in Belfast and in 1887 he joined Keely and Patterson when they put their own circus on the road.

A songbook was published in America containing many of Johnny Patterson's best-know songs. During this period he wrote *The Auld Turf Fire*. While performing in Tralee a section of the audience mistook his symbolic wearing of the Harp and the Crown. As a result he was attacked, punched and kicked and suffered serious injury. Tragically, he did not recover but died of his wounds a few days later on 31 May 1889.

Johnny Patterson is buried in the grave of a friend in the New Cemetery in Tralee. His last song, *Do Your Best for One Another* was never published.

Shannon, Sharon (1968–)

A Celtic and folk musician of great natural talent who can play accordion, flute, tin whistle and melodeon with equal aplomb, Sharon Shannon is a most highly regarded musician on the world stage. Born in Ruan in County Clare, it wasn't long (at eight years) before she was playing with the local band, *Disirt Tola*. At 14 years she was touring the United States with the same band. In her formative years she was an accomplished show jumper, but she gave it up to concentrate on her music and began studying with Karen Tweed (accordion) and Frank Custy (fiddle).

Early on she worked with *The Waterboys*, contributing to their album, *Room to Room,* and gained experienced touring with them. Her own debut album, *Sharon Shannon*, is the best selling album of traditional Irish music on the market. Due to her solo work with accordion and the amount of air time she gained on radio and television, her debut album sales skyrocketed. Her second album, *Out The Gap,* (1994), was produced by Denis Blackbeard Bovell, and it whiffed of a pronounced reggae atmosphere. Sharon also did a number of compilation albums, one of which, *Common Ground: Voices of Modern Irish Music,* (1996), featured one of her classic tracks, *Cavan Potholes.*

Sharon Shannon has played with many distinguished musicians, which includes Nigel Kennedy, Jackson Browne, Dónal Lunny, Moya Brennan, Kirsty MacColl, Christy Moore, Sinéad O'Connor, Liam O'Maonlai, Mundy and John Prine amongst others. She recorded *The Galway Girl* with Steve Earle, which was released simultaneously in Earle's album, *Transcendental Blues,* and in her own album, *Sharon and Friends The Diamond Mountain Sessions*. Both albums were released in the year 2000. In 2006 she came out with *The Sharon Shannon Collection 1990-2005*. In all she has released 16 quality albums between 1991 and 2017. Surely there is much more to come from this highly gifted virtuoso of traditional music. Sharon currently lives in Galway.

Smithson, Harriet Constance (1800–1854)

Harriet Smithson was a theatre actress who was born in Ennis in 1800. She went to school in Waterford but at an early age she had to drop out and work as an actress to support her father who was ill.

She gained much experience touring all over the country. At the age of 15 she played Lady Teazle in Sheridan's *School for Scandal.* Harriet went on to perform in Drury Lane in London where her strong Irish accent proved to be something of a hindrance with British audiences (even though she was an accomplished actress at the time).

Macready's Company invited her to tour France with them; it was an offer she was glad to accept. Her Paris performances were an instant hit because her Irish brogue went unnoticed there. Harriet Smithson met Hector Berlioz in Paris where they married in the British Embassy in 1833. They lived in poverty, mainly because her fame was fading, and Berlioz was yet to establish himself. Although they separated in 1840, Berlioz supported her to the end particularly for the last four years of her life when Harriet was paralysed. She eventually died in Montmartre, Paris on the 3rd day of March in 1854.

Steele, Thomas (1788–1848)

Thomas Steele was born at Derrymore House in east Clare on 3 November 1788. He belonged to an old Somerset family which had settled in Ireland in the 17th century. Steele was affectionately referred to as 'Honest Tom Steele' because he was a carefree and likeable man. He went on to take a BA degree at Trinity College and an MA at Cambridge in 1820. In a short time he was qualified as a member of the Institute of Civil Engineers. He inherited the family estate at Cullane and while there he developed a compulsive interest in restoring the castle of Craggaunowen and turned it into a summer house. Steele fought at Cadiz in Spain against the Spanish King Ferdinand. He mortgaged his entire estate in Ireland to raise £10,000 to fund the rebel army.

On his return to Ireland he joined with O'Connell in the massive struggle for Catholic Emancipation – even though he was a Protestant. Working with the O'Gorman Mahon they protected the Liberator (O'Connell) from his personal enemies. His position as a Protestant landlord made him particularly valuable to O'Connell and it was believed that he contributed more than any other individual to the return of O'Connell on 5 July 1828.

He was named 'The Head Pacificator' by O'Connell because of his ability to quell faction fights. Whatever little money he had left he squandered it on wild schemes until he was forced to go to London to work on engineering projects to earn a living. Tom was so distraught by poverty and remorse over the loss of his friend O'Connell (who died in 1847) that he jumped off Waterloo Bridge into the Thames. Even though he was rescued he died a few days later on 15 June 1848. He is buried in Glasnevin Cemetery, Dublin, beside his beloved chieftain, The Liberator himself.

Smyth, Jimmy (1931–2013)

This hurling prodigy was born to a Ruan schoolteacher, Mary Kate Considine from Clooney and a Garda sergeant Jim Smyth from County Monaghan.

Soon after Jimmy Smyth entered St Flannan's secondary school in Ennis it was obvious that he was destined for hurling greatness. He played five years (1945-49) on the school's Harty Cup team, winning three Harty Cup medals (1945-47) and three Croke Cup medals (All Irelands 1945-47). He played on the Clare Minor Hurling teams for an unprecedented five years (1945–49). It was no surprise when he burst onto the Clare senior hurling team at the tender age of 17 years. He made his debut at the beginning of the 1948-49 National Hurling League campaign.

Although he played in an estimated 158 matches for Clare at adult level and scored 150 goals and 332 points, Smyth's reward was scanty. All he had to show from inter-county hurling with Clare at adult level was a meagre one Oireachtas medal, a Thomond Feis medal, one Munster Junior Championship (1949) and two runner up medals from Munster Finals. In one amazing display in a championship match against Limerick in Ennis, he scored 6–4 to blast the Limerick team off the Park. When he later recalled the day Smyth remembered nothing of the scoring.

Jimmy's most rewarding achievements were with his home hurling club of Ruan. During Smyth's playing career, Ruan were always a force to be reckoned with and this was in an era when Eire Óg, St Joseph's, Newmarket-on-Fergus and Whitegate were at their zeniths. Nevertheless, Ruan and Jimmy Smyth landed five Club County Championships between 1948 and 1962.

Smyth did enjoy additional distinction and success when he played for his province, Munster, on a staggering 23 occasions. Such was his hurling ability, the Munster selectors could place him at centre-field, centre-forward, full-forward or corner-forward to facilitate the selection of less-accomplished players struggling to find a spot.

Although sometimes assigned a limiting role with the province Smyth always played with great creditability for Munster; he was rewarded by winning eight Railway Cup medals with them. In 2000 he was named on the Munster hurling team of the Millennium.

After retirement from hurling Jimmy studied philosophy at Trinity College, Dublin, where he was awarded a Bachelor of Arts degree in 1993. He gained a Master of Arts thesis at Limerick studying the songs, poems and recitations of Irish times in Munster. Subsequently, he published two books on songs and recitations, *Ballads of the Banner,* (1998); and *In Praise of Heroes,* (2007).

Jimmy's brothers Gerard, Michael and Kevin all hurled with him for Ruan. Jimmy Smyth hurled with Clare when they were in the doldrums which must have restricted his achievements. In the true spirit of sportsmanship he played out a long sporting career simply hurling his best in each and every match. Even today, Jimmy Smyth is regarded as one of game's greatest players.

Smythe, Tim (1905–1982)

Tim Smythe was born near Feakle on 12 April 1905 and grew up in nearby O'Callaghan's Mills. His athletic career was launched in 1925 when he came 2nd in a half mile event and 3rd in a bicycle race.

Throughout the 1920's Tim won many races and thereby demonstrated his unique capacity in events ranging from one to five miles in distance. He hit the headlines with 2nd and 3rd positions at the 1929 All-Ireland Junior and Senior Championships – successes which led to him qualifying for the International Cross Country meeting in Paris.

More accolades followed in '29 when Smythe annexed a number of Munster Championships along with the All-Ireland Individual Championship in 1930 ensuring his selection for the team competition at the prestigious Lemington Spa event in England. The climax of Smythe's career came with a first in the World Cross Country Championship at Baldoyle on 28 March 1931. Thereafter, Tim Smythe continued competing and winning events in athletics until 1949 by which time he had secured ten All-Ireland Championship titles.

Smythe's successes continued in politics after he retired from running in 1949; he often topped the polls in local elections and seemed to be the man for all occasions. His interests extended to Irish games – he helped two Ennis teams, Faughs (football) and Eire Óg (hurling), to win Clare County Championships. Tim kept himself active by hunting with the Old Mill Street Harriers until well into his twilight years.

He was married to Maura Duggan from Ennis and they had three sons and five daughters all of whom followed their own particular sporting pursuits. This extraordinary runner died at his Cahercalla residence in Ennis and was interred at Drumcliff Cemetery. The Fairgreen of Ennis was officially named Tim Smythe Park and Playground in his honour.

Westropp, T J (1860–1922)

Although born in Patrickswell in County Limerick there is much justification for including him in a County Clare list of notable personalities especially when his volume of work on Clare's antiquities is considered. Westropp's love of things Irish as well as his archaeological achievements set him apart as a man of remarkable talent. Although he was descended from landed gentry, Westropp the man was a natural part of Irish culture who contributed much to establishing a rich base by recording the existence of field monuments.

Thomas Johnson Westropp graduated with an MA from Trinity College in 1882. The field work on Irish monuments and antiquities completed by Westropp remain unmatched for quantity and quality. His draughtsmanship alone in capturing monuments and historical artefacts at a time when photography was not readily available to record such works is an invaluable legacy for present-day historians and archaeologists.

The depth, variety and breadth of Westropp's scholarly output is staggering when one considers the conditions he worked in, as well as the time span available to him to carry out such work in the field. Some notable contributions worth mentioning include:

The Ancient Forts of Ireland; Archaeology of the Burren; Folklore of Clare; The Antiquarian Houses of County Clare; Prehistoric Stone Forts of Central Clare; The Churches of County Clare; The Earthworks and Castle of Bunratty, Co Clare.

His work is a staple of the prestigious *Journal of the North Munster Archaeological Society*. Another outstanding work by Westropp is the *County Clare Folk-Tales and Myths* which is available in Clare's County Library. Westropp's *Archaeology of the Burren* is so rich in detail on forts, dolmen and place names that it is considered an essential tool for anyone contemplating a study of those antiquities. There is also his fine dissertation on the old Abbey (Friary) of Ennis, complemented with accurate sketches of the many ornamental sculptures which he found lost amongst the ruins (not widely known about or catalogued until his intervention).

Although T J Westropp came from outside the county's boundaries he made County Clare his very own preserve in the field of antiquities. He also endowed the county with a range of riches it was somewhat unaware of and became all the better for knowing. T J Westropp would grace an anthology of any county – it would have been churlish of us not to include him in a subject area that was so dear to him and of great value to the people of County Clare.

Wood, Keith (1972–)

This renowned Irish international rugby player was born in Killaloe in 1972. He is a son of Gordon Wood who was capped 29 times for Ireland as a prop. As a Rugby Union player Keith played for Garryowen, Munster, Harlequins, Ireland and the British and Irish Lions. In all he played with great distinction and often with even greater originality.

Playing in the field position of hooker, Keith soon established himself as a forceful competitor who made the most inspirational if unlikely plays for a hooker. His endeavours earned for him the title of 'The Raging Potato', possibly inspired by his oval bald head. His sometimes lack of accuracy from line throws was more than compensated for by his mobility, his try scoring capability, not to mention his fine leadership qualities.

Wood made his international debut against Australia in 1994. He was subsequently capped 58 times for Ireland. Keith achieved one of the great accolades of the game when he was selected to play for the 1997 and 2001 Lions teams. In 2001 he was the inaugural winner of the IRB World Player of the Year award and went into the Rugby Hall of Fame in 2005. He followed that by being inducted into the IRB Hall of Fame in 2014.

He was a standout player in most games that he played in, including the Pool contests of the 1999 World Cup when he touched down for four tries against the USA. He reportedly went on one Lions tour and according to the tour doctor, James Robson, 'with chest injuries that would have sidelined lesser men, and he played through the pain trying to defeat the world champions'. He currently holds a world record of 15 full international test tries scored by a hooker.

After retiring from the playing field he continued in rugby by appearing as a pundit on the BBC for over 20 years. He also worked as a journalist for *The Daily Telegraph* as well as contributing on a freelance basis to many more sporting publications. Right up to the present day he is doing punditry for *Sky Sport's* coverage of the Lions Tour 2017 to New Zealand.

Keith Wood was and is and always will be a giant of the game of rugby.

Appendix 3

An Index of Clare's ancient Gaelic family names

A-B

(O) Aherne: Gaelic origin. Clare, Munster.
Bane: Gaelic origin. Clare and Galway.
(O) Baskin: Gaelic origin. Clare.
(O) Beakey; O Beice: Gaelic origin. Clare.
Blood (Ui Blod): Gaelic origin. Clare.
(O) Bolan(d): Norse/Gaelic or'n. Clare, Sligo.
(Mac) Brady: Gaelic origin. From O Grady.
(O) Brady: Gaelic origin. Clare & others.
(Mac) Bran: Gaelic origin, Clare primarily.
O Brien: Gaelic origin, Clare & others.
(Mac) Brody: Gaelic origin. Clare & others.

C

(Mac) Cahan: Gaelic origin. Clare primarily.
O Cahan: Gaelic origin. Ulster and Munster.
(O) Cahill: Gaelic origin. Galway to Clare.
(O) Cahir: Gaelic origin. Clare primarily.
(O) Callinan: Gaelic. Clare, Cork, Galway.
(Mac) Cannalty: Gaelic origin. Clare.
(Mac) Canny: Gaelic origin. Clare, Limerick.
(O) Carmody: Gaelic origin. Clare, Kerry.
(Mac) Carrig(y): Gaelic. Clare, Limerick.
(Mac) Clancy: Gaelic origin. Clare, Leitrim.
(O) Clohessy: Gaelic origin. Clare, Limerick.
(Mac) Clune: Gaelic origin. Clare primarily.
(Mac) Conheady: Gaelic origin. Clare.
O Connerty: Gaelic origin. Primarily Clare.
(O) Connoo, Cunnoe: Gaelic. Clare & others.
O Connor: Gaelic origin. North Clare sept.
(Mac) Connulty: Clare version of MacNulty.
(O) Conole: Gaelic origin. Sligo; west Clare.
(O) Conroy: Gaelic origin, Clare and Galway.
(Mac) Considine: Gaelic origin. Clare mainly.
Cooley: Gaelic origin. Clare and Galway.
(O) Cooney: Gaelic origin. Clare & others.
Crowe (MacEnchroe): Gaelic origin, Clare. [See MacEnchroe below].
(Mac) Conheady: Gaelic origin. Clare.
O Connor: Gaelic origin. Sept in Clare.
(O) Conole: Gaelic origin. Sligo & Clare.
(Mac) Conroy: Gaelic origin. Clare, Galway.
(Mac) Considine: Gaelic origin. Clare.
(Mac) Conway: Gaelic origin. Clare.
(O) Corridon: Gaelic origin. South Clare.
(O) Corry: Gaelic origin. Clare & others.
Creagh: Gaelic origin. Clare. Some in Cork.
(O) Crotty: Gaelic or'n. Clare, Cork, and Waterford.
(O) Culligan: Gaelic origin. Clare primarily.
(O) Cullinan(e): Gaelic or'n. Clare, Munster.
(Mac) Culliney: Gaelic origin. Clare. Mayo.
(O) Cunneen: Gaelic origin. Clare & others.
O Curry: Gaelic origin. Clare, Cavan.
MacCurtin: Gaelic origin. Clare, Munster.
Custy: [See (Mac) Hosty later].

D-E

(O) Daffy: Gaelic origin. A Clare name.
(O) Daly: Gaelic origin. Clare, Cork, and Westmeath.
(O) Davoren: Gaelic origin. Clare & Tipp.
O Dea: Gaelic origin. Mostly Clare.
(O) Deegan: Gaelic origin. Clare, Galway, and Laois.
(O) Degidan: Gaelic origin. Clare primarily.
(O) Dilgan: Gaelic origin. Clare primarily.
(O) Dilleen: Gaelic origin. Clare and Galway.
(O) Dinan: Gaelic origin. Tipperary, Clare, Limerick and Cork.
(Mac) Donegan: Gaelic origin. Clare.
MacDonnell: Gaelic origin. Clare and Ulster.
O Donnell: Gaelic origin. Clare, Donegal.
(O) Doohan: Gaelic origin. Clare.
Drew (O'Dree): Gaelic origin. Clare.
(O) Durack: Gaelic origin. East Clare.
Dwane: Gaelic origin. Clare and Limerick.
(Mac) Enchroe: Gaelic origin. Clare.

F-G

(O) Falvey: Gaelic origin. Kerry, Cork, Clare.
Fawl, Faul: Gaelic origin. Clare association.
Fanning (O'Fannin): Gaelic org. Limerick, Clare.
(O) Fennell: Gaelic origin. Some in Clare.
(Mac) Finucane: Gaelic origin. Clare.
(O) Frawley: Gaelic origin. Clare, Limerick.
(O) Galvin: Gaelic origin. Clare, Kerry.
(Mac) Gallery: Gaelic origin. Clare primarily.
(Mac) Gillereagh: Gaelic origin. Clare.
(Mac) Gorman: Gaelic origin. Clare & others.
O Gorman: Gaelic origin. Clare primarily.
(Mac) Glynn: Gaelic origin. Some in Clare.
O Grady: Gaelic origin. Clare and Limerick.
MacGrath: Gaelic origin. Some in Clare.
(Mac) Green(e): Gaelic origin, Clare, Cork,
(O) Griffy: Gaelic origin. Clare and Munster.
(O) Griffin: [As above].
(O) Guinnane (Ginnane): Gaelic origin. A variant of **O Cunneen:** Gaelic origin. Clare.

H

O Halloran: Gaelic origin. Clare & others.
(O) Halpin: Gaelic origin. Clare. Limerick etc.
(O) Hannon: Gaelic origin. Clare. Limerick.
(O) Hanrahan: Gaelic origin. Clare. Limerick.
(O) Harkin: Gaelic or'n. West of Ire, Clare

(O) Hassett: Gaelic origin. Clare and others.
(O) Haugh: Gaelic origin. Clare mainly.
(O) Hey (Hayes): Gaelic org. Clare & others.
(O) Hederman: Gaelic origin. Clare and Lim.
(O) Heffernan: Gaelic origin. Clare and Lim.
O Hehir: Gaelic origin. Clare and Limerick.
(O) Hickey: Gaelic origin. Clare, Tipperary.
Hillery: Norman and Gaelic origin. Clare.
(O) Hogan: Gaelic origin. Clare, Tipperary.
(O) Horan (Haran): Gaelic origin. Clare and Munster generally.
(O) Honan: Gaelic origin. Clare, Munster.
(O) Honeen (Green(e): Gaelic origin. Clare, Cork.
(Mac) Hosty (Custy): Gaelic origin. Clare etc.
(O) Howard: Norse/Gaelic origin. Clare.
(O) Howley: Gaelic origin. Cork, Gal, Clare.
(O) Hure: [As for Howard].
(O) Hurley (O Herlihy): Gaelic origin. Clare, Limerick, Cork and others.

I-K

MacInerney: Gaelic origin. Clare primarily.
(Mac) Keane: O Kane: O Cahan & others: Gaelic origin, Clare and throughout Ulster.
(O) Kearney: Gaelic origin. Clare & Munster.
(O) Kelleher: Gaelic origin. Clare. Cork etc.
(O) Kennedy: Gaelic origin. Clare, Tipperary.
(O) Kenny: Gaelic origin. Clare & others.
(O) Kett: Gaelic origin. Clare.
(Mac)Kilcooley: Gaelic org. Clare.
(O) Killeen: Gaelic origin. Mayo, Gal, Clare.
(Mac) Killoughrey: Gaelic origin. Clare.

L

(O) Lahiff(e): Gaelic origin. Clare & Galway.
(O) Lernihan: Gaelic origin. County Clare.
(O) Liddy: Gaelic origin. A Clare name.
(O) Logue: Gaelic origin. Clare, Galway.
(O) Looney: Gaelic origin. Clare and Munster.
(O) Loughlin: Gaelic origin. Primarily Clare.
(O) Loughnane: Gaelic origin. Clare. Meath.
(Mac) Lysaght: Gaelic origin. Clare primarily.

M

MacMahon: Gaelic origin. Strong in Clare.
(O) Malone: (O) Mulloon: Gaelic origin. Clare and others.
(O) Mangan: Gaelic origin. Clare & others.
(O) Markham: Gaelic origin. East Clare.
Marlborough: Gaelic origin. Clare primarily.
(O) Meere: Gaelic origin. Clare primarily.
(O) Meehan: Gaelic origin. Clare and others.
(O) Melody: Gaelic origin. Clare and Galway.
(O) Mescall: Gaelic origin. Clare and Munster.
(O) Minogue: Gaelic origin. Clare exclusively.
(O) Mohan: Gaelic origin. Clare and others.
(O) Molon(e)y: Gaelic origin. Clare, Limerick and Tipperary.
(O) Moron(e)y: Gaelic origin. Clare primarily.
(O) Moylan: Gaelic origin. Clare and Munster.
(O) Moynihan: Gaelic origin. Mun. & Clare.
(O) Muldoon: Gaelic org. From Malone (in Clare).
(O) Mullahan: Gaelic origin. Clare primarily.
(O) Mullins: Gaelic origin. Clare primarily.
(O) Mulqueen: Gaelic origin. Clare mainly.
(O) Mulvey: Gaelic origin. Clare and Leitrim.
(O) Mulvihil: Gaelic origin. County Clare.
(O) Murrihy: Gaelic origin. Clare primarily.

N-P

MacNamara: Gaelic origin. Clare primarily.
(Mac) Naughton: Gaelic origin. Clare, others.
(O) Nealon: Gaelic origin. Clare, a variant of (O) Neylan.
(O) Neilan: [As above]
(O) Neenan: Gaelic origin. Clare primarily.
(Mac) Nestor: Gaelic origin. Clare primarily.
(O) Neylan: Gaelic origin. Clare primarily.
(O) Nihil: Gaelic origin. Clare primarily.
(Mac) Normoyle: Gaelic origin. Clare mostly.
(O) Purcell (Purtill): Gaelic origin: Clare etc.

Q-R

(O) Queally: Gaelic origin. Clare and others.
(O) Quilligan: Gaelic origin. Clare and others.
(O) Quinlevan (Quinlan): Gaelic origin. Clare, Tipperary and now mostly Munster.
(O) Quinn: Gaelic origin. Strong in Clare.
(O) Reddan: Gaelic origin. Clare origin.
O Regan: Gaelic origin. Clare and others.
(O) Reidy: Gaelic origin. Clare and Munster.
(O) Roughan: Gaelic origin. Clare & others.
(Mac) Rynne: Gaelic origin, Clare primarily.

S-T

(O) Scanlan: Gaelic origin. Clare & others.
(O) Shalloo: (O) Shelley: Gaelic origin. Clare.
(O) Shanahan (Shannon): Gaelic origin. Some in Clare. Many others elsewhere.
(O) Shannon: (Derived from Shanahan).
(O) Shanny: [Possible variation of above]
(Mac) Sheedy: Gaelic origin. Clare primarily.
(O) Skerrett: Gaelic origin. Clare, Gal. or'n.
(O) Slattery: Gaelic origin. Clare mainly.
Synan: Gaelic origin. Clare and Cork.
(O) Talty: Gaelic origin. Clare essentially.
MacTigue: Gaelic origin. Clare and others.
(O) Tubridy: Gaelic origin. Primarily Clare.
(O) Tuohy: Gaelic origin. Galway and Clare.
(O) Tyne: Gaelic origin. Clare primarily.

Appendix 4

Gaelic games

Gaelic football

By the inaugural year of the GAA Clare club football teams stood ready to do battle. Newmarket-on-Fergus won the County Championship in the first two years of 1887 and 1888. In that era the successful clubs were mostly centred around mid Clare, which included the districts of Ennis, Labasheeda, Clarecastle and Doora. Later when the west Clare clubs became established and better organised the engine of Clare football swung to the western half of the county.

Clare won their first Munster Senior Football Championship when they defeated Cork by 5–4 to 0–1 in 1917. Either Clare were great, or Cork were poor – perhaps a bit of both. Prior to that initial victory they had lost finals in 1912 and 1915 to Kerry and in 1916 to Cork. In the 1917 campaign they beat Galway in the All-Ireland semi-final but then went down to a strong and experienced Wexford outfit who had won the title in the two previous years. In fact Wexford made it four in-a-row in 1918. As regards the number of appearances in finals, this was probably Clare's best period. The Cork and Kerry monopoly of Munster championships shut Clare out of meaningful competition in the province for many years. Clare football was slow to progress and we note a lack of adventure judging from the miserably low score-lines in club games within the county.

The Clare football team did eventually make an impression in the National Football League by putting together a string of victories in the '76 campaign. In a playoff against Monaghan in Croke Park in March, Clare were denied by the craftier northerners who 'swamped' Croke Park with an overwhelming number of vociferous supporters. It was on 19 July 1992 that a John Maughan-trained Clare team finally struck gold. At the Gaelic Grounds in Limerick they shocked Kerry with a 2–10 to 0–12 scoreline, the goals being scored by Colm Clancy and Martin Daly. Then on 23 August Clare took on Dublin in the All-Ireland semi-final – this time with the aid of tumultuous supporters who rattled the rafters of the stands when the team took the field. Although they were pipped by a more experienced Dublin side the 1992 Clare footballers warmed the hearts of all who witnessed their displays. Seamus Clancy was awarded an 'All-Star' for his performances during the year. Recently, Clare footballers have climbed back from division four to division two under the stewardship of Colm Collins as a new-found confidence and skill level has come to the fore.

54. ***Clare Senior Football Munster Champions 1992***

Seated from left to right: *Martin Flynn, Noel Roche, Padraig Conway, Francis McInerney (team captain), Ciaran O Mahoney, Ciaran O Neill, Frank Griffin.*
Standing from left to right: *Seamus Clancy, Colm Clancy, Tom Morrissey, James Hanrahan, Aidan Moloney, J J Rouine, Gerry Kelly, Gerry Killeen.*

(Photo Brooks Studio)

— — — —

Hurling

One of the first inter-county hurling matches involving County Clare and the hurlers of County Galway took place at Turloughmore, County Galway in 1759. This was a very loose and traditional affair, not at all resembling the codified games we enjoy today. In the olden days the number of players on teams was quite large, often with more than 20 participating in each.

The first championship games under the auspices of the GAA took place in 1887. When Clare won the Dr Croke Cup in 1896/97 the side was essentially a Tulla Club selection.

In 1913 the number of players on teams was reduced from 17 down to 15. In the following year a very well prepared Clare side won the All-Ireland title (Great Southern Railway Cup) for the first time. Captained by Amby Power, Clare defeated Leix (Laois) in the 1914 final at Croke Park.

Clare did not emerge again as a strong force until the 1927–32 era. Cork, the then dominant team, lost Munster Championship games to Clare in 1930 and 1932. Clare made a rare appearance in the All-Ireland Final (MacCarthy Cup) in 1932. They lost that particular match to Kilkenny by a scoreline of 3–3 to 2–3.

Clare's next appearance in a Munster Final was in 1938 when they lost to Waterford by a single goal. They entered the doldrums for a period and did not feature again until 1946 when they won a National League title. The county remained strong for a time, even running Waterford (who were the Munster Champions in 1948) and then Tipperary in 1950 very close in championship games. By 1953 the side had flowered but a crushing defeat to Limerick in 1955 devastated both players and supporters.

A young talented team displayed promise from 1964 to 1969 without winning anything until 1977 and 1978 when a Fr Harry Bohan managed-side achieved success in the National League. Narrow Munster Final defeats to Cork followed in those years – with the '78 loss of 0–13 to 0–11 being particularly galling. Oireachtas Cup victories came in 1982 and 1983 but optimism for the main prize was lacking. After a humiliating defeat in the Munster Championship of 1993 against Tipperary, Clare rebounded to make the most dramatic breakthrough under Ger Loughnane in 1995 and take Munster and All-Ireland titles.

An even better win followed in 1997 when similar honours were captured, with the added satisfaction of defeating the 'big three' of Cork, Kilkenny and Tipperary (twice)! This truly great senior side were winners again in Munster, but were denied All-Ireland honours in '98 in very controversial circumstances against Offaly. The 1995–2000 teams had been managed by Ger Loughnane who proved to be both inspirational and a master tactician. The 1997 senior victory was further sweetened by the remarkable All-Ireland win of the Clare minor hurlers under manager Kevin Kennedy.

The 2002 team managed by Cyril Lyons reached the Championship final but lost to a good Kilkenny side. By 2005 Anthony Daly was in charge, only to see his team lose by a single point against a Cork team that made a dramatic fight back to turn the game around 0–16 to 0–15. In 2009 Clare won the U–21 for the first time since the grade was introduced in 1964.

Even better things were to come with the three-in-a-row success of 2012–14, including a 2–17 to 2–11 victory over Kilkenny in the U–21 final of 2012.

55. ***Clare All-Ireland Senior Hurling Champions 1914 (The Mould-Breakers)***

Front row left to right: *Brendan Considine, James 'Sham' Spellissy.*

Second row left to right: *Jim Guerin, Pat 'Fowler' McInerney, Willie 'Dodger' Considine, Amby Power (captain), Martin 'Handsome' Moloney, Edward 'Ned' Grace, John 'Jack' Shalloo, James Hehir (trainer).*

Third row left to right: *Dr H McDonagh (Feakle), Tom McGrath, John Fox, Rob Doherty, Michael Flanagan, Jim 'Bawn' Clancy, Joe Power, Stephen Clune (secretary of the training committee),*

Extreme back left to right: *Dr T FitzGerald (Newmarket), J P McGuire (Lisdoonvarna), P E Kenneally (Ennis), William Hoey Kearney Redmond (MP for East Clare), John Rodgers, Rev Canon O'Kennedy (St Flannan's College), Paddy McDermott, Rev J M McCreedy (Crusheen), Batt Culligan (Kilrush), Patrick 'Bucky' Moloney, John Jones.*

(NB: For easier identification, the three reserves in the final – John Rodgers (Tulla), Paddy McDermott (Whitegate) and Patrick 'Bucky' Moloney (Killanena) – are all togged in the darker jerseys).

Note: The above is the complete caption from the ***Clare County Express,*** *'Let's Wear the Sash Again', by Seamas O'Reilly*

In 2013 came the stuff of dreams when a golden crop of young Clare hurlers overcame a gallant Cork team by 5–16 to 3–16 in a replay. Arguably it was one of the finest hurling matches ever played. The double (U–21 and Seniors) of 2013 was celebrated by 30,000 enthusiastic supporters crammed into Tim Smythe Park in Ennis to greet the teams on the following balmy evening of great joy. The team manager, Davy Fitzgerald, copper-fastened the All-Ireland by taking the National Hurling League in 2016. Certainly a good run of success by any standards.

However, individual hurlers will always strive to fulfil their own particular targets in the game and in so doing emulate or even better the successes of those who went before them. Clare now have much to live up to in the hurling world and so it is that Clare hurling fans await with bated breath what the new joint managers, Donal Moloney and Gerry O'Connor, will bring to Clare's ever-appealing hurling table.

The heady days of 1995 and 1997 may be gone forever – we do not know - but there is no doubt that the Clare hurlers of today have convincingly proven that they are every bit as determined and as skilful as their immediate predecessors..

56. ***Clare Senior Hurling Champions 1995***

Back Row left to right: *Brian Lohan, Michael O'Halloran, Frank Lohan, Conor Clancy, David Fitzgerald, Sean McMahon, Ger O'Loughlin.*

Seated left to right: *Liam Doyle, P J O'Connell, Ollie Baker, Anthony Daly (captain), James O'Connor, Fergal Hegarty, Fergus Touhy, Stephen McNamara.*

57. ***Clare, 1997 All-Ireland Senior Hurling Champions***
(Picture of the semi-final team v Kilkenny, which Clare won by 1–17 to 1–13).
Back row left to right: *Brian Lohan, Michael O'Halloran, Conor Clancy, David Fitzgerald, Frank Lohan, Sean MacMahon, Fergus Touhy, Gerard O'Loughlin.*
Front row left to right; *Liam Doyle, P.J. O'Connell, Ollie Baker, Anthony Daly (captain), James O'Connor, Stephen MacNamara, Fergal Hegarty.*
(Niall Gilligan started for Clare against Tipperary in the All-Ireland final at Croke Park)

58. ***Clare Senior Hurling Team, All-Ireland Champions 2013***
(Replay panel shown when they beat Cork by 5–16 to 3–16 in Croke Park).
Back row left to right: *Jonathan Clancy, Shane O'Donnell, Peter Duggan, Fergal Lynch, Cian Dillon, Conor Ryan, Darach Honan, Tony Kelly, Conor McGrath, John Conlon, Nicky O'Connell, Aron Cunningham, Cathal McInerney, Patrick Donnellan (captain), Liam Markham, Donal Touhy, Paul Flanagan, Derek Fahy.*
Front row left to right: *Conor Cooney, Brendan Bugler, Paudge Collins, Colin Ryan, Colm Galvin, Patrick Kelly, Domhnall O'Donovan, Patrick O'Connor, David McInerney, Cathal O'Connell , Seadna Morey.*

Appendix 5

Clare County Council Coat of Arms

59. (Courtesy of Clare County Council)

Clare County Council's Coat of Arms signifies six symbols relevant to County Clare. The saffron and blue colours are the sporting colours of the county. This heraldic design reflects the topography, history and achievements of County Clare. The shield design conveys both the flat and craggy aspects of Clare's landscape. Illustrated are six compartments on the shield, representing the six ancient areas of Clare (Thomond) in olden times: Dal gCais, Clanculein, Ui Caisin, Corcomruadh, Corcobaiscinn and Ui Bracain.

Symbols on the shield

Top Left: Rose motif, from the old diocese of Kilfenora, represents the Burren area of County Clare.
Top Centre: Kilnaboy tau cross represents the rich heritage of antiquity of County Clare.
Top Right: Ancient Irish Crown represents the old Kingdom of Thomond (mostly the County of Clare).
Lower Left: The circle of fire represents the electricity-producing installations of Ardnacrusha and Moneypoint.
Lower Centre: The pile reversed flueried suggest aircraft lift off at Shannon. The barry wavy effect at base point represents the Shannon river which is a prominent boundary to the county.
Lower Right: The stag's head commemorates the many Clare families whose shields and crests bear this motif.

[The winning motto for the Coat of Arms, 'Dílis d'ar nOideacht' (True to our Heritage), was the suggestion of Miss Rebecca Maher of Ennis in County Clare when she responded to Clare County Council's request for appropriate slogans].

Appendix 6 - General Index

Bibliography

Brennan, Michael. *The War in Clare.* Four Courts Press & Academic Press, 1980, Dublin.

Browne, Kevin J. *Éamon de Valera and the Banner County.* Glendale Press, 1982, Dublin.

Byrnes, Ollie. *Against the Wind: Memories of Clare Hurling.* Ollie Byrnes, 1997, Ennis.

Conlan, Patrick, OFM. *The Franciscans in Ennis.* Franciscan Community, 1984, Athlone.

Dinan, Brian. *Clare and its People.* The Mercier Press, 1987, Cork.

Duffy, Seán. *Brian Boru and the Battle of Clontarf.* Gill & Macmillan, 2013, 2014, Dublin.

Dutton, Hely. *Statistical Survey of County Clare (1808).* The Royal Dublin Society, 1808, Dublin.

Dwyer, Rev Canon. *The Diocese of Killaloe from the Reformation to the close of the Eighteenth Century.* Hodges, Foster & Figgis, 1878, Dublin.

Eluère, Christiane. (Translated by Daphne Briggs). *The Celts First Masters of Europe.* Thames and Hudson Ltd, 1993, London and New York.

Faucett, William. *County Clare Pamphlets.* R Y Moffat & Co, 1867, Dublin.

Feehan, J M. *The Secret Places of the Burren.* Royal Carbery Books, 1987, Cork.

Filip, Jan. *Celtic Civilization and its Heritage.* Academia, 1977, Prague.

Frost, James. *The History and Topography of the County of Clare.* Sealy, Bryers & Walker, 1893, Dublin. (Reissued by The Mercier Press, 1973, Cork & Dublin).

Gleeson, Demot F. *A History of the Diocese of Killaloe, Part II–IV, The Middle Ages.* M H Gill & Sons, 1962, Dublin.

Grogan, Dr Eoin. *The Late Bronze Age Hillfort of Mooghaun South.* The Discovery Programme Limited. Cahill Printers, 1999, Dublin.

Gwynn, Aubrey. *A History of the Diocese of Killaloe, Part I.* M H Gill & Sons, 1962, Dublin.

Harris, Nathaniel. *Heritage of Ireland – A History of Ireland and its People.* Bounty Books, 2015, London.

Herbert, Robert. *Worthies of Thomond,* (Five Volumes collected and edited). Limerick Leader, 1944, Limerick.

Hubert, Henri. *The History of the Celtic People.* Bracken Books, 1993, London.

Herity, Michael & George Egan. *Ireland in Prehistory.* Routledge & Keegan Paul Ltd, 1989, London & New York.

Houlihan, Michael. *The Holy Wells of County Clare.* Printed by Walsh Colour Print, Castleisland, 2015, County Kerry.

Jebb, Mathew & Colm Crowley. *Secrets of the Irish Landscape.* Cork University Press, 2013, Cork.

Lenihan, E. *In the Tracks of the West Clare Railway.* The Mercier Press, 1990, Cork.

Lenihan, E. *Long Ago by Shannonside.* The Mercier Press, 1982, Cork.

MacCraith, Sean MacRuaidhrí. *Caithréim Thoirdealbhaigh: The Triumphs of Turlough,* 1459. Translated by Standish O'Grady, Irish Texts Society, 1929, London.

MacNamara, N C. *The Story of an Irish Sept.* J M Dent & Co, 1896, London.

MacManus, Seamus. *The Story of the Irish Race.* The Devin–Adair Company, 1921–1992 editions, 1992, Old Greenwich, Connecticut.

McGuane, James T. *Kilrush from Olden Times.* Clodóirí Lurgan, Inverin, 1984, Galway.

O'Brien, Honourable Donough. *History of the O'Briens from Brian Boroimhe, AD 1000–1945.* Batsford, 1949, London.

O'Brien, Ivor. *O'Brien of Thomond – The O'Briens in Irish History 1500– 1865.* Phillimore & Co Ltd, 1986, Sussex.

O'Connell, Daniel. *A memoir on Ireland Native and Saxon.* James Duffy and Co, 1884, Dublin.

O'Connell, Gerald. *A Signposted Walking Tour of Ennis Town.* Midwestern Regional Tourism Organisation Ltd, 1970, Ennis.

Ó Dalaigh, Brian. *Irish Historical Town Atlas No 25.* Royal Irish Academy, 2012, Dublin.

O'Donoghue, John. *Historical Memoir of The O'Briens.* Hodge, Smith & Co, 1860, Dublin.

O'Donovan, John. *Annála Ríoghachta Ėireann.* Ed. (1856). Annals of the Kingdom of Ireland by the Four Masters (in Irish and English) (2nd ed). 7 Volumes. Royal Irish Academy, 1856, Dublin.

O'Kelly, M G. *Early Ireland – An Introduction to Irish Prehistory.* Cambridge University Press, 1989, London & New York.

Ó Murchadha, Ciarán. *Sable Wings Over The Land.* Claspress, 1998, Ennis, Co Clare.

Ó Murchadha, Ciarán. *The Great Famine, Ireland's Agony 1845–1852.* Continuum International Publishing Group, 2011, London & New York.

Ó Ruairc, Pádraig Óg. *Blood on the Banner.* Mercier Press, 2009, Cork.

Power, Joe. *An Ennis Miscellany.* Ennis 750 Ltd. An Ennis Miscellany edited by Joe Power, 1990, Ennis.

Power, Joe. *History of Clare Abbey and Killone.* J Power, 1987, Clarecastle.

Roche, Richard. *The Norman Invasion of Ireland.* Anvil Books, 1970, Dublin.

Ryan, Meda. *Biddy Early: The Wise Woman of Clare.* Mercier Press, 1984, Cork.

Spellissy, Seán (author) and **O'Brien, John** (photographer). *Clare - County of Contrast.* S Spellissy & J O'Brien, 1987, Ennis, Co Clare.

Ua Cróinín, Risteárd and **Breen, Martin.** [Many articles on Clare's castles]. *The Other Clare, vol 5 & others, 2000-2019,* Co Clare.

Weir, Hugh. *Houses of Clare.* Ballinakella Press, 1986, Whitegate, Co Clare.

Weir, Hugh. *O'Brien People and Places.* Ballinakella Press, 1983, Whitegate, Co Clare.

Woodham-Smith, Cecil. *The Great Hunger: Ireland 1845–1849.* Hamish Hamilton, 1962, London.

Wheeler, James Scott. *Cromwell in Ireland.* Gill & Macmillan Ltd, 1999, Dublin.

White, Very Revd P. *History of Clare and the Dalcassian Clans.* M H Gill & Sons. 1893, Dublin. (Reissued by The Mercier Press, 1973, Cork & Dublin).

Ancient manuscripts

1. Annals of the Four Masters. [When it was compiled it was entitled *Annála Ríoghachta Éireann (Annals of the Kingdom of Ireland*].
This is the most important of all the annals. Chief compiler was *Mícheál Ó Cléirigh (Michael O'Clery),* between 1632–36. He was ably assisted by three other monks, namely: *Fearfasa Ó Maol Chonaire, Cú Choigcriche Ó Cléirigh* and *Peregrinus Ó Duibhgennain.*
2. Annals of Inisfallen. Contains over 2,500 entries for the period between AD 433–1450. First compilation work began about 1215 by the monks of Inisfallen, Lower Lake, Killarney. It is housed in the Bodleian Library in Oxford.

Newspapers & journals

Clare Champion; Clare County Express; Clare People; Clare Journal; Clare Yearbook; The Other Clare; The Dalcassian; North Munster Antiquarian Journal.

Bibliography in Local Studies Centre, Ennis Library

Ainsworth, John. *The Inchiquin Manuscripts.* Irish Manuscript Commission, 1960, Dublin.
Apjohn, James. *The Spas of Lisdoonvarna in County Clare 1856.* Hodge, Smith & Co, 1856, Dublin.
de Valera and Ó Nualláin. *Survey of Megalithic Tombs of Ireland, Vol. I, Co. Clare.* Stationary Office, 1961, Dublin.
Dinan, Brian. *The Megaliths of Clare.* Dissertation for Diploma in Local Studies at University College Cork, 1998, Ennis.
Brash, Richard R. *Inishcealtra Island in County Clare 1886.* An article in the Gentleman's Magazine & Historical Review, 1866, London.
Flynn, Maurice J. *A Bibliography of Clare History and Antiquities.* Bound Typescript, 1967.
Mason, William Shaw. *Mason's Parochial Survey.* Three Volumes, 1814-1819, Dublin.
O'Donovan, John. *Ordnance Survey Letters.* Vol I & II, 1839. Vol III, 1841. Edited by Rev M O'Flannagan, 1928, Bray.
Scott, J B. *Property in County Clare 1856.* Hodge, Smith & Co, 1856, Dublin.
Westropp, Thomas J. *The Forts of Limerick and Clare.* Journal RSAI, 1908, Dublin.
Westropp, Thomas J. *History of Ennis Abbey.* Journal RSAI, Vol XIX, 1889, Dublin.

Other publications by Brian Dinan

History

1. ***Clare and its People–A Concise History***. Written by Brian Dinan and originally published by the Mercier Press in 1987. It is a slimmed down version of this Second Edition. In it you will find the same basic story of the complete history of County Clare. It is compiled of 140 page with 37 illustrations displayed throughout; it is a very readable publication in illustrated soft cover format. The print edition has since run out and will not be renewed.

2. A Terrace of Houses–A Passion of People. The story of St Flannan's Terrace in Ennis. Hundreds of photos and stories about the past lives of residents since the building of St Flannan's Terrace in 1912 right up to present times. Many original photos not seen before were unearthed and offered for publication by past and present residents. In A4 size it contains 92 pages of stories, reports, records, maps and plans to include 244 illustrations, compiled, written and edited by Brian Dinan. Published in 2013 in association with *Clare Roots Society*. Original print edition still available from *Clare Roots Society.*

Fiction

3. *Jousting with the Devil and Other Stories.* Away from the world of history Brian Dinan indulges in the fascinating world of the short story. After being published many times in *Ireland's Own*, and winning a number of literary prizes, he decided to bring out his own collection of short stories based on his *Ireland's Own* successes. Amongst the 25 short stories in *Jousting with the Devil and Other Stories* are 14 stories which first appeared in *Ireland's Own*. Of the remaining 11, ten are published in this collection for the first time – the exception being 'Mulholland's Day'.

In *Jousting with the Devil and Other Stories* the reader is treated to a play that resulted in the scorching of a cantankerous cat, young love, the disappointment of a homecoming, a prophetic crow, sweet dancers and, as might be expected, a joust with the devil himself. If that is not entertainment enough, the reader can turn to equally lovable characters in 'Fandango Flynn and the Tailors'. The collection is rounded off with a touch of poignancy in the final story, 'Goodbye Dromleen'. More information at: https://amazon.com/jousting with the devil and other stories

60.

Clare and its People

a concise history

Presented by Brian Dinan and Elisabeth Dinan
to the President of Ireland, Dr Patrick Hillery,
(The first Clare person to hold the office)
at Áras an Uachtaróin, Dublin,
on 26 November 1987.

Printed in Great Britain
by Amazon

34685032R00112